Ancient China: Towns

112 Chinese Towns

Ancient China: Towns

Explore a world of ancient Chinese towns

Xigu Town 黄龙溪古镇

【 Shuangliu County, Sichuan Province 】

Magnificent wharf, traditional old streets, tranquil tea houses

Lying beside a river and with its back against a hill, this small town features serene stone lanes, old dwellings and temples, exquisite carvings and authentic flavours.

Attractions: Old Streets, Old Theatre Stage, Government Offices, Tea House

Wu Town 乌镇

【 Tongxiang County, Zhejiang Province 】

Classical waterside village

Located beside Jinghang Canal, Wu Town is the poster child of south China towns. With crystal waters cutting through the town, and residences built on water, Wu Town is considered a living museum of ancient East China culture. Hangzhou chrysanthemum, blue print and Sanbai wine are among traditional local produce.

Attractions: Water Residences, Maodun Residences, Hongyuantai Dye House

Xitang Old Town 西塘古镇

【 Jiashan County, Zhejiang Province 】

Authentic waterside village, deep lanes and stone bridges

From a distance, with its white walls, black-tiled roofs and reflections on the lake, Xitang Town looks just like a painting .. What really makes Xitang stand out is that it has maintained its status as a waterside town for over a thousand years.

Attractions: Shipi Lane, Huanxiu Bridge, Zunwen Hall, Ni Family Residence

Tongli Town 同里古镇

【 Wujiang County, Jiangsu Province 】

Garden waterside village, enormous mansions, boats and bridges

Tongli Town is like a landscape painting that uses water to harmoniously balance the man-made roads, dwellings and gardens, creating a leisurely, serene and homely atmosphere.

Attractions: Tuisi Garden, Two Halls and Three Bridges, Chuanxin Lane, Nanyuan Tea House

Laitan Old Town 涞滩古镇

【 Lin County, Shanxi Province 】

Military town on old mountaintop

Laitan Town sits atop Peak Jiu and is the only well-preserved military–style defense complex in the Chongqing area. Wenchang Palace Opera Tower from the Qing Dynasty is a delight and Erfo Temple features the largest stone carving statues in all of China.

Attractions: Laitanweng city , Erfo Temole, Wenchang Palace

Qikou Town 碛口古镇

【Huang He port, cave dwellings, traditional commerce】

Huang He port, cave dwellings, traditional commerce

The unique sceneries of Datongqi gives Qikou Town the reputation of the "No. 1 Town on the Yellow River". Ancient streets, rough caves and the roaring Yellow River offer visitors a unique experience.

Attractions: Datongqi, Black Dragon Temple, Caves, Xiwan Village

⑧

Chikan Town 赤坎古镇

【Shengping County, Guangdong Province】

Great watchtowers

Built during the Qing Dynasty, Chikan Town is famous for its watchtowers and its links to populations of Chinese overeas. With flowing water, rainbow-like bridges, exquisite arcades and unique European-style streets, Chikan Town is a must-visit.

Attractions: Arcades, Canadian Village, Yinglong Pavilion

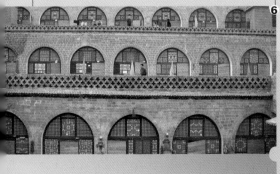

6

7

⑨

Zhuxian Town 朱仙镇

【Kaifeng County, Henan Province】

Central port; where General Yuefei defeated King Jin

Zhuxian Town is one of the four most famous towns from the Ming and Qing Dynasties. With Dongjing Transportation River running through the town, this typical southern waterside village features many temples, one of which is Yuefei Temple, one of the four largest Yuefei temples in China.

Attractions: Yuefei Temple, Mosque, Chinese New Year Picture Museum

Huangyao Town 黄姚古镇

【Shaooing County, Guangxi Province】

Dreamy landscape, Nine Palaces and Eight Trigrams

Huangyao is a dreamy town with many caves, pavilions, temples, ancestral halls, old trees and plaques. Hidden in the old banyan trees are residences laid out in the "Nine Palaces and Eight Trigrams" design and connected by green stones.

Attractions: Stone-paved Roads, Xinxing Street, Wenming Pavilion, Ancient Banyan Trees

Heshun Town 和顺古镇

【Tengchong County, Yunnan Province】

Plateau waterside village with rich architecture and overseas Chinese connections

This beautiful town in south Yunnan Province enjoys the reputation of being a "Shangri-La Encircled by Volcanoes ". The architecture is rich in variety, subtle and modest with European, Western and Northern overtones.

Attractions: Heshun Library, Laundry Pavilion, Original Residence of Ai Siqi (Philosophy teacher of Chairman Mao)

⑩

Location of Ancient Chinese Towns

· Urumqi

· Lukeqin

XINJIANG UYGUR AUTONOMOUS REGION

GANSU

Xining

QINGHAI

TIBET

· Sajia   · Lhasa

· Changzhu

Xinchar

SICH

Lijiang

Panz

Shaxi

Baoshan   · Dali

· Heshun   Heijing·   Ku

YUNNA

· Nayun

Ⓐ PROVINCES   Ⓐ Nearest Cities   Ⓐ Towns

A Jiangnan Towns
P001-077

B Bashu Towns
P078-127

C Northern Towns
P128-163

D Central Plains Towns
P164-191

E Lingnan Towns
P192-221

F Borderland Towns
P222-241

Ancient China

Over the last few years, the aggressive roll-out of a high-speed rail network has transformed travel in China. Ancient China: Towns is a guide to a largely unknown world of 112 Chinese towns that have remained largely unchanged for generations.

History

Many of the towns in this book are of a startling antiquity. Zhaohua Town in northern Sichuan was founded during the Spring and Autumn Period more than 2,300 years ago. Guxing Town near present-day Zhengzhou was built in the Warring States Period(B.C. 475 – B.C. 221). Many of the towns bore witness to ancient migrations. Almost all are home to ancestral temples and halls, many of which were built by merchants and government officials who returned home after making their fortunes away from their hometowns.

Location was the key determinant of destiny for most of the places in this book. Many of the towns, such as Zhuxian in Henan, grew to fame as transportation hubs and market towns. Heshun Town on the old Silk Road was a cultural crossroads for people from all over the world.

Other towns were associated with a particular craft or trade. Town in Sichuan was built on the back of the salt industry, which began in the Qin dynasty. Other towns were famous for different reasons. In the Tang and Song dynasties, Yacheng Town on Hainan Island was home to a multitude of people in exile.

Many of the towns are associated with great moments in Chinese history or legend. One story that crops up a lot is the legend of the Three Kingdoms, one of the four great classics of Chinese literature. The story tells the tale of how the three rival states of Shu-Han, Wei, and Wu battled for supremacy at the end of the Han Dynasty. Characters such as Zhu Geliang (a legendary military strategist) and Lord Guan, a fierce general who gave his name to myriad temples, have enormous resonance in Chinese culture.

Town Architecture

Given the vastness of China, there is unsurprisingly a commensurate variety of architecture. Grand courtyards, overlapping ridges, high eaves, river ports, bamboo-like stone rails and water pavilions are all components of a typical Yangtze River town such as Zhouzhuang south of Suzhou. The Hakka homes of Luodai Town in Sichuan are simple but elegant constructions with single quadrangle courtyards and two principal halls. Ancient towns of southern Guangdong Province often combine architectural and cultural elements from both China and the west. Unique architecture

in the region's towns includes arcade towers, which are suited to the hot, rainy climate of southern China.

Religion and Culture

Since ancient times, the Chinese have placed a heavy emphasis on Confucian education and literature. As a result, the imperial examination system of feudal China, which lasted from the Sui Dynasty (589-618) to its abolition in 1905, had a huge influence on the culture of China's ancient villages. The achievements of those native sons who succeeded in the examinations have been memorialised in monuments and inscriptions.

The towns are also physical embodiments of China's religious system, which merges Buddhism, Daoism, Confucianism, and a pantheon of other ancient philosophies, religions, and local gods.

Arts and Festivals

The towns were also incubators of ancient culture such as martial arts and Chinese opera. Shawan Town is known as the "Guangdong's town of music". During the late Qing Dynasty and the early Republic of China Period, Shawan gave birth to many famous Cantonese opera and pop singers. Guangfu Town near Suzhou is well-known as a bewitching waterside town, and as the birthplace of the martial art Tai Chi

(太极拳, shadowboxing).

Most villages also continue to hold traditional ceremonies on holidays. The Dragon Lantern Burning (烧火龙) of Huanglongxi Village in Sichuan, held during the Chinese New Year (in late January or early February) dates back to the Southern Song Dynasty and has a history of more than 800 years. Meanwhile, the Open-Door Festival (开门节) of Nayun Town in Yunnan is a traditional Dai festival marking the end of the three-month rainy season. During the festival restrictions on interactions between young men and women are relaxed and boys and girls can date.

Getting There

The development of high-speed rail has made it possible for tourists to explore a once remote world of ancient Chinese towns in a dramatically shorter period of time. While many of the towns in this book are quite easy to find, visiting some the more remote or isolated locations may require a little extra effort. To make the towns easier to locate, each chapter provides directions (public transport where possible) to the town from its nearest major city or tourist hub. Develop your own travel plan with care – it will be well worth it.

Off the Beaten Path in China

Getting beyond the PRC's shiny facade is something many visitors never achieve. The cities of the "booming" eastern seaboard brim with gargantuan malls and luxury hotels. The state-of-the-art transport infrastructure – newly laid metro lines and high-speed trains – is second to none and there are enough English speakers on hand to make getting where you're going a simple affair.

Because of China's vastness, many sightseers opt for guided tours that conveniently hop from Beijing's Great Wall to Xi'an's Terracotta Warriors to the colonial Bund in Shanghai. Meanwhile, backpackers head for the retreats of the south, like Guilin and Dali, spending a few enchanted weeks in the blissful locales.

But of course there's much more to the most populous nation on Earth than burnished cities and globally recognizable sites. Within China you'll discover the oldest and most fascinating culture on the planet.

Veering off the beaten path can be challenging but also incredibly rewarding. For the seasoned traveller there's perhaps no better place to test your travel legs than around China's provincial cities or in the small towns and villages. Vast swathes of the country remain rural, offering fantastic hiking opportunities. In isolated areas you may encounter one of the China's 55 ethnic minority groups. Many still wear traditional clothing, speak their own languages and live altogether mysterious lives, cut off from the Han majority by China's immense and rugged geography.

Small towns and remote villages often hide historic treasures, largely unknown to

the outside world. These can be challenging to reach, as Daoist, Buddhist, and Confucian temples were traditionally built as out-of-town retreats. But after your crowded, often bumpy bus leaves the suburbs and you come upon a colourful, isolated monument – perhaps dating back over a thousand years – all your efforts will be rewarded.

Provincial cities are currently playing catch-up, as they attempt to reach the same level of development as the coastal metropolises. While this might mean a lot of building work, many third-tier cities still offer a glance into China's recent past with roads cluttered with bicycles and lined by block-style Soviet architecture. Second-tier cities are already sampling their portion of the "boom" with malls and car culture making inroads. They are also often cleaner, friendlier, and easier to navigate on foot than the economic giants.

There are, of course, certain considerations you'll need to make before venturing further afield. Hygiene usually sits at the top of people's concerns. If you leave international enclaves expect the quality of latrines to go down rapidly. Always carry tissue paper with you and avoid loose-fitting clothes that might dangle and get wet. As you head to smaller towns, toilets often don't have doors whilst in rural areas expect an outhouse at best.

Take care with the food you eat as well. While China is one of the world's great culinary destinations, it's best to waver on the side of caution in small towns, as an upset stomach can offset a journey considerably. Always size-up the restaurant. You can even be nosey and poke your head in the kitchen – the Chinese never seem to mind. If you're really daunted, most second tier-cities have both Western and Chinese-chain restaurants that maintain a higher standard of cleanliness. In the countryside try to wash food first and don't set out without necessary stomach medication, as rural hospitals still lack many modern amenities.

Language is perhaps the primary reason why travellers avoid China in favour of destinations like India or Southeast Asia. This is a great shame, but it does pose one advantage, namely, it filters out the fainthearted, leaving more unique experiences for those courageous enough to brave the confusion.

In fact, basic Mandarin is not as difficult as it seems and there is an alphabetized system – pinyin – to help you get started. It pays to learn a few basic phrases. In rural areas many elders only speak the local dialect, but literacy is nominally high for a developing country (around 95%) so just point to the phrases in your guidebook and you should get what you want. Remember, the Chinese are world-renowned businesspeople and lowly restaurateurs will try their very best understand you. After all, they want your cash!

That said, normal standards of caution are required, especially in small-town China. Hotel prices listed are often not the actual price, so be wary and inquire first. If taxi drivers don't run the meter, agree on a price beforehand. When buying a ticket for an attraction or museum, make sure the sight is open: more than a few disappointed travellers have bought an entrance ticket to an exhibition only to find a pile of rubble and sign that reads "undergoing renovation".

In small towns you can almost always question prices but don't go overboard. The last thing you want to do is offend the locals for a few measly kuai. In fact, you might discover yourself living rather cheaply as the Chinese are incredibly generous. The novelty of having a wandering foreigner join a group's dinner table will provoke hosts to order local delicacies and as much Tsingtao beer as you can sink in an evening.

Most precautions you need to make before heading out into the Chinese hinterland are commonsensical and apply just about everywhere. So once you've made your checklist, all you need to do is follow the timeless Confucian adage, "A journey of a thousand miles begins with one step". Get out there and see the vastness of a country that's home to 20% of the earth's population. Witness the great changes currently sweeping the PRC. Take yourself to places that are literally off the map to discover a way of life untouched by modernization. Make friends and dine on spicy, delicious, and sometimes utterly bizarre fare. For once you've tasted what this continent-sized nation has to offer, you'll undoubtedly be hungry for more.

– Tom Bird, Shenzhen-based writer

Formation of Ancient Towns

Ancient towns in China were founded primarily for trade purposes, whereas ancient cities placed more emphasis on political and military functions. The development of the ancient towns in this book was driven by various forces, including: government (Cicheng Town, Wangye Town), temples (Shangqing Town, Sajia Town), rich and powerful families (Anren Town, Longmen Town), military (Huiyuan Town, Shaohua Town) and revolutionary (Huangqiao Town, Gutian Town). China's ancient towns can be grouped into several types:

Waterside Towns

This kind of town is found beside water, especially in areas with an abundance in rivers and lakes (such as Wu Town). Their many wooden boats and stone bridges give them a photogenic and artistic quality. Due to dense population and limited space, lanes in such towns are usually very narrow. Rainy weather in these regions also means there are usually many corridoors and covered bridges. The residences feature lofts on water and "tianjing" courtyards . The lofts have stairs connecting to a back door which opens to the river, making it convenient for washing clothes and parking boats.

Landscape Towns

This type of town is usually situated be This type of town is usually situated beside hills and often at big bends in the river, so there are ports and long bridges but no criss-crossing river systems inside the towns. As rivers are vital communication lines, the streets in such towns are particularly prosperous, with many guild halls and a developed handicraft industry and trade infrastructure.

Mountain Towns

This kind of town is located in mountain areas, embraced by forests and water, though most are just tiny streams (a typical example is Fusheng Ancient Town). Such towns usually became prosperous because of their temples, courier stations, imperial mausoleums, barracks or factories. The residences and streets are built upon steep hills, meaning some streets can have up to 18 twists and 300 stairs.

Fortress Towns

This kind of town was usually built to take advantage of dangerous terrain or was situated at the frontier (for instance, Nianziguan Town). Town defenses include tall city walls and gates with grand gate towers and barbicans. The streets are typically well-planned and grid-like, with some built on steep mountains.

Architectural Styles

The architectural style of ancient Chinese towns can be roughly divided into two categories: private buildings (like residences and private gardens) and public buildings (like ancestral halls, temples, colleges, opera towers, guild halls and bridges).

Private Buildings

The main type of residence is the "siheyuan" (a square courtyard surrounded by rooms on four sides) – the luxurious ones have more doors. In mountain areas where buildings could not be expanded, structures would be built vertically or extended into the hills (for example diaojiaolous and extension of the residence to the natural landscape. cave dwellings). Private gardens are an and focus more on bringing balance

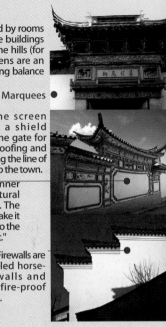

Marquees ●

正房 The main room is the most important room in a residence, and usually sits in the north and faces the south. As the living space of the family, it is usually large, with three or five bays and an ancestral hall in the middle.

照壁 The screen wall is a shield inside the gate for wind proofing and obscuring the line of sight into the town.

天井 The "tianjing" is an inner courtyard which allows natural light to flow into the building. The roofs on all four sides slope in to make it easier to capture the rain, giving rise to the saying, "Four waters gather at one point."

厢房 Wing rooms are rooms on either side of the main room, are the living quarters for families.

大门 The main gate is the most frequently used passageway. The gates usually include a massive marquee, inscribed plaque, exquisite wooden doors and stone carvings.

封火墙 Firewalls are also called horse-head walls and servea fire-proof function.

Public Buildings

Green stone streets: the streets in old Chinese towns are usually paved with big green stones and have water channels on both sides. Residences and stores line opposite sides of the street. The following structures are commonly found in ancient Chinese towns.

文昌阁 Wenchang Pavilion, also called Wenchanglou or Wenfeng Tower, is a piece of feng shui architecture located near the entrance of a town to worshiping the "God of Learning".

寺庙 Temples are typically small and are either Buddhist or Taoist, though there are also churches. Yuwang Palace, Guandi Temple, Dragon King Temple and Guanyin Hall are the most commonly seen.

祠堂 Ancestral halls or family temples are used to worship a family's ancestors, but is also used for family conferences, celebrations and teaching. In ancient towns they are usually tall and magnificent.

戏台 The theatre stages are the main location for entertainment in many towns and usually includes a public square before the stage.

桥 Bridges serve as traffic aids. Most towns feature several varieties and styles, and they have become an indispensible part of ancient town scenery.

会馆 Guild halls were built by travelling merchants to provide mutual assistance. Most of them are luxurious and each has its own unique style.

Residential college

Cultural Significance

TThe differences between ancient towns from different parts of China are not only reflected in their appearances, but also in their respective cultures. The richness of these varying cultures is where the true fascination of China's ancient towns lies.

Feng shui philosophy   Ancient town layouts placed great emphasis on feng shui, using various investigative methods and techniques to find the right balance between man and nature. For instance, in waterside towns, harmony was often sought through the arrangement of the streets and lanes. . Where there was a lack of positive feng shui, ancient towns used pagodas, pools and trees to bridge the shortfall.

Clan system   Many ancient towns were developed by one or several clans. Clan ancestral halls in ancient towns are where culture is accumulated; female clan halls, as rare as they are, demonstrate the diversity of this culture. Grand archways and luxurious compounds are considered symbols of a clan's honour.

Commercial culture   Whether it is a wharf or a dry dock, ancient towns served important trade functions. The old streets of the villages were the centre of trade and commerce; guild hall were the gathering place for merchants. Dye houses, kilns, cellars and mines were also the crucial business hubs.

Street culture   Trade and production dictated the lives of ancient town residents, who have over the years developed their own unique street culture.

Architectural and artistic culture   Ancient towns were often able to persist because of their ability to produce culturally valuable things. In the towns of this book, arts such as colorful paintings are showcased; wood, stone and brick carvings are also well represented. China's memorial archways, combined with sculptures, paintings, couplets, feudal morality and folk customs, were an undeniably profound symbol of Chinese culture for centuries.

Folk customs   Traditional customs have been passed down well in many ancient towns. Weddings, funerals, sacrifices and taboos, as well as folktales, mythologies and literary quotations, may vary according to the specific part of the country where the town is situated.

Food culture   FFood is an essential part of the identity of many Chinese towns. Different climates and produce have a significant impact on the cuisine of a particular town, and even the cooking methods are said to reflect the residents' wisdom and way of life.

CONTENTS

A
P1—77

South
of the
Yangtze
River

CONTENTS

B Bashu

P78—127 Towns

C Northern Towns

P128—163

D Central Plains Towns

P164—191

E Lingnan Towns
P192—221

F Borderland Towns
P222—241

江 南 古 镇
South of the Yangtze River(Jiangnan)

Rivers, bridges and temples

Tongli Town 同里镇
Little Eastern Venice

Tongli is a peaceful ancient town surrounded by five lakes. The town's delicate gardens and its bridges arching over meandering streams have earned Tongli the nickname "Little Eastern Venice".

Tongli Town, Wujiang District, Suzhou City, Jiangsu Province
江苏省吴江市同里镇
Nearest city: Shanghai or Suzhou
From Shanghai
Shanghai is served by Pudong International Airport and Hongqiao Shanghai Airport. Shanghai Station is the city's main rail terminus, with services to around 70 cities in China. Trains to Hangzhou leave from the South Station.
Several bus routes reach Tongli Town from Shanghai Long-distance Bus Terminal Station (上海长途汽车站) a 20-minute taxi ride from the Shanghai Bund. The journey takes about 2 hours.

From Suzhou
Downtown Suzhou is a 50-minute drive from Southern Jiangsu Shuofang International Airport. High-speed trains from Shanghai and Nanjing stop at Suzhou Station or Suzhou South Station.
There are regular buses from Suzhou Railway Station (苏州火车站) to Tongli Town. They take about 30 minutes.

An ancient waterside town in the Taihu Lake (太湖) resort area, Tongli used to be called "Rich Land" (富土). During the early years of the Tang Dynasty, the name was changed to "Copper Village" (铜里, Tongli) because "Rich Land" sounded too extravagant. In the Song Dynasty, the name was changed

Tongli Ancient Town

Tongli Water Alley

simple elegance make it classic. The garden is divided into three parts — the western house, centre courtyard, and eastern garden. The external rooms are used for accommodating guests and the owner and his family live in the Wan Xiang Building (畹荔楼). The Great View Pavilion (揽胜阁) sits in the centre courtyard. In the eastern garden are corridors, a bridge, and other scenic spots.

The three bridges on the cross-shaped river in the town's center are called Peace (太平

again to the current Tongli (同里), a homonym for Copper Village but with different Chinese characters.

Self-reflection Garden (退思园) is Tongli's most loved garden. It displays the best features of a Qing Dynasty garden — its small size and

Water Signs

Many of the place names in Tongli contain the Chinese character for water. The "Nine Miles of Clear Sky" (九里晴澜), "Fragrant Breeze from the Lotus Pool" (莲浦香风) and the "Fisherman's Flute in the Waterside Village" (水村渔笛) are just a few of the sites that contain the water radical in part of their Chinese name.

桥), Luck (吉利桥) and Chang Qing Bridge (长庆桥) and are the most famous of the town's many bridges. There are meticulously carved arch stone structures lying across the clear water and hidden in the green woods. According to local tradition, when a townsperson gets married, the bride's sedan must pass by all three bridges while onlookers wish the couple luck, peace, and tranquility.

Tongli Town is home to the grand Jiayin Hall (嘉荫堂), Chongben Hall (崇本堂), and Shide Hall (世德堂), as well as the former residence of poet and revolutionary Chen Qubing (陈去病故居). Jiayin Hall is famed for the exquisite carvings on its doors, windows, and beams. The main building, Gauze Cap Hall (纱帽厅), is tall and spacious, with five beams that double as artwork. There are eight openwork carvings on the head of the beams, featuring scenes from operas. The carving "Three Heroes Combating Lu Bu" depicts a classic scene from the Ming Dynasty epic Romance of the Three Kingdoms where Liu Bei, Guan Yu and Zhang Fei fight against the general Li Bu. More wood carvings can be found in the Yanqing Building (衍庆楼).

If you have some time, the South Garden Tea House (南园茶社) is a good place to sit with a cup of tea and listen to folk music. Chicken head (芡实) is one of the local culinary specialties. Stocking-sole pastry (袜底酥) is another popular snack. It is crisp and tastes sweet and salty. The seasonal snack adzuki bean cake (赤豆糕) is another local hit.

Tongli Zheng Fu Hall

Self-reflection Garden

Night view of Tongli

Zhouzhuang Town 周庄镇

A Classic Chinese Water Town

Zhouzhuang Town, located to the southeast of Suzhou, is built along a river and connected by bridges. Grand courtyards, overlapping ridges, high eaves, river ports, bamboo-like stone rails and water pavilions all make Zhouzhuang a typical Yangtze River town.

Zhouzhuang Town, Kunshan City , Jiangsu Province
江苏省昆山市周庄镇
Nearest city: Shanghai or Suzhou
From Shanghai
Shanghai is served by Pudong International Airport and Hongqiao Shanghai Airport. Shanghai Station is the city's main rail terminus, with services to around 70 cities in China. Trains to Hangzhou leave from the South Station. Several buses run each day from Shanghai Long-distance Bus Terminal Station (上海长途汽车), a 20-minute taxi ride from the Shanghai Bund, to Zhouzhuang Town. The journey takes about 1.5 hours.

From Suzhou
Downtown Suzhou is a 50-minute drive from Southern Jiangsu Shuofang International Airport. High-speed trains from Shanghai and Nanjing stop at Suzhou Station or Suzhou South Station. Buses run to Zhouzhuang Town from Suzhou North Bus Station (苏州汽车北), a 13-minute taxi ride from Suzhou Railway Station. The journey takes about 1 hour and costs RMB18.
A Zhouzhuang Town one-day sightseeing round-trip ticket costs RMB 100 (or RMB80 at night), and is valid from 08:00-16:00. The ticket covers access to 16 scenic spots. Boat trips cost RMB 80.

Zhouzhuang Town is mentioned in the Spring and Autumn Annals (covering the period 722-481 BC) as the "Shaking City" (摇城) and was later called Zhenfengli (贞丰里). During the Northern Song Dynasty period, a man named Zhoudi Gonglang donated 13 hectares of farmland to the Buddhist Quanfu Temple (全福寺), and thus the area was renamed Zhouzhuang in his honour. Toward the end of the Ming Dynasty, Shen You, father of the legendary merchant Shen Wansan, set up Zhouzhuang as a trading centre for grain, silk, and handicrafts, turning Zhouzhuang into a bustling market town.

Zhouzhuang is now a quiet town with quaint architecture. Despite a history of more than 900 years, much of the town's original style has been preserved. More than 60% of the dwellings are in Ming and Qing dynasty style, and the small (0.47 square-kilometre) town features 100 classical

Zhouzhuang Marble Boat

Kunqu Opera

On Zhouzhuang's ancient stage (古戏台), visitors can watch free performances of Kunqu opera, one of the oldest forms of Chinese opera. Kunqu opera evolved from Kun Mountain songs and dominated Chinese theatre from the 16th to the 18th century. There are daily performances in Zhouzhuang of condensed versions of Kunqu classics.

courtyards and more than 60 brick gateways. The most representative of these dwellings are Shen Hall (沈厅) and Zhang Hall (张厅). The 14 unique ancient bridges make the town even more picturesque.

The Double Bridges (双桥) of Zhouzhuang are prime examples of Yangtze River bridge architecture, and a major tourist draw. The bridges are perpendicular, and one has a square opening while the other's is round, together forming a shape like an ancient key. Locals also call the bridges Key Bridge (钥匙桥).

The grounds of Quanfu Temple sit along the water, including ponds, pavilions and halls. The Buddhist-inspired architecture and art is magnificent and the gardens are scenic.

Since ancient times there have been

Zhouzhuang is a peaceful waterside town

Zhouzhuang Double Bridges

numerous drinking establishments in the town, and the streets are heady with the aroma of wine. If you'd like to sample a glass of Zhouzhuang's famed Wansan Yellow Wine (万三黄酒), you can step into the bars on Culture Street (文化街) and Zhenfeng Street (贞丰街).

Another popular sight in the town, perhaps appreciated all the more after a few drinks, is the Weird Pavilion (怪楼). Here visitors are invited to experience a number of illusions and magic tricks.

The Baixian River (白蚬江) to the west of Zhouzhuang is a paradise for fishermen. Here you will encounter bamboo fish cages and the loud cries of fish hawks being released. At dusk, fishermen sing and play musical instruments, dry their nets, and have a few drinks. According to a local drinking song, "The bund of the Baixian River is where fishermen dry their nets in the sun. Fishing and drinking, singing drunk, they seem to forget all the troubles on earth".

A one-day sightseeing ticket is 100 yuan, from 8am to 4pm, and includes 16 scenic spots. The price falls to 80 yuan for a night visit. A boat tour costs 80 yuan.

Luzhi Town 甪直镇

The Hall of Five Lakes

The still water, old bridges, delicate landscapes, and scattered historical sites all make Luzhi Town a special destination.

Luzhi Town, Wuzhong District, Suzhou City, Jiangsu Province
江苏省苏州市吴中区甪直镇
Nearest city: Suzhou
Downtown Suzhou is a 50-minute drive from Southern Jiangsu Shuofang International Airport. High-speed trains from Shanghai and Nanjing stop at Suzhou Station or Suzhou South Station.
From Suzhou Train Station, take a No. 18, No. 52 or No. 518 bus and get off at Luzhi Bus Station.

Luzhi was originally called Puli (甫里), named after Puli Pond (甫里塘) on the west side of town. In the eastern part of town there was once a dock with six main areas that met in the shape of the character Lu (甪), and eventually Puli was changed to Luzhi. According to a folk tale, the ancient unicorn Luduan (甪端) settled in Luzhi because he thought the town had good geographic omens. Thanks to Luduan's stay, Luzhi has supposedly suffered no wars, no chaos and no droughts or floods throughout its history.

Crisscrossed by numerous rivers, Luzhi is also known as "the hall of five lakes" (五湖之厅). These are Cheng Lake (澄湖), Myriad Lake (万千湖), Golden Pheasant Lake (金鸡湖), Dushu Lake (独墅湖), and Yangcheng Lake (阳澄湖).

Built in the year 503, Luzhi's Baosheng Temple (保圣寺) has nine clay figurines of Buddhist Arhat sculpted by Yang Hui (杨惠), a famous Tang Dynasty sculptor. The figurines are well-preserved. Zhao Mengfu (赵孟頫), a Yuan Dynasty

A watery lane in Luzhi

calligraphist, created an antithetical couplet to admire the temple. highlights at the Baosheng Temple include Duckfighting Pond (斗鸭池), Fresh Breeze Pavilion (清风亭) and unearthed cultural relics at the Museum of Cheng Lake (澄湖出土文物馆).

Within an area of 1 square kilometre, Luzhi has 41 stone arched bridges from the Song, Yuan, Ming, and Qing dynasties. The bridges have various styles and include bridges with multiple apertures, small bridges, spacious arched bridges, narrow bridges with flat tops, double bridges, and twin bridges. Bridges and streets are generally connected.

Old ginkgo trees are one of the ancient symbols of Luzhi. Today there are seven ginkgos in the town, and the oldest is 1,300 years old.

The lanes, and the ancient buildings that sit along the town's granite-paved lanes, were mostly built in the Ming and Qing dynasties. The Shen Mansion (沈宅), Xiao Mansion (萧宅), and Wang Tao Memorial (王涛纪念馆), with their grey bricks and tilted ridges, are good representations of the town's architecture. There are 58 lanes in the town, with the longest being more than 150 metres long.

In addition to Ye Shengtao, the old town was home to several other literary figures. Lu Guimeng (陆龟蒙), a Tang Dynasty writer, and Gao Qi (高启), a poet in the Ming Dynasty, both lived in and wrote about the town. Wang Tao (王韬), a late Qing Dyansty reformer, political activist and the first newspaper publisher, was also born in Luzhi. The town has many cultural sites associated with celebrities from ancient times, like the White Lotus temple (白莲花寺), the grave of the Sun Princess (孙妃墓), and the palace of King Wu (吴王宫).

In recent years, the local government has done a lot of work to fix up and preserve the old town. Many of the mansions and historical sites, including the Shen Mansion and the Xiao Mansion, have been restored.

Puli pig's foot and Puli duck are the most famous dishes in Luzhi. Luzhi radish is made using a salt-and-can method from the Qing Dynasty.

Stores beside the river in Luzhi

Mudu Town 木渎镇

A Serene Garden Town

Mudu is located to the west of Suzhou near the bank of Taihu Lake and at the centre of a group of mountains famous in the Wu Dynasty, including Lingyan Mountain, earning the town the nickname "Treasure Bowl".

Mudu Town, Wuzhong District, Suzhou City, Jiangsu Province
江苏省吴中区木渎镇
Nearest city: Shanghai or Suzhou
From Shanghai
Shanghai is served by Pudong International Airport and Hongqiao Shanghai Airport. Shanghai Station is the city's main rail terminus, with services to around 70 cities in China. Trains to Hangzhou leave from the South Station.
Shanghai Tourist Distribution Centre (上海旅游集散中心), a 16-minute taxi ride from the Shanghai Bund, has a special line bus that heads to Mudu Town. The journey takes about 90 minutes.

From Suzhou
Downtown Suzhou is a 50-minute drive from Southern Jiangsu Shuofang International Airport. High-speed trains from Shanghai and Nanjing stop at Suzhou Station or Suzhou South Station.
From Suzhou Railway Station, take the No. 38 bus then get off at Mudu Station (27 stops).

Mudu is a garden town whose history is inextricably linked to Suzhou. It is said that in the late Spring and Autumn period, the Wu Dynasty emperor once tried to please Hsi Shih — said to be the most beautiful woman in ancient China — by ordering that Guanwa Palace (馆娃宫) be built on top of the spectacular Lingyan Mountain (灵岩山) and Gusu Platform (姑苏台) be built on Purple Stone Mountain (紫岩山). The construction took five years and the vast quantities of wood transported by river for the project blocked up the ditch at the bottom of the mountains, thus, the town was named Mudu. "Mu" (木) means woods and "du" (渎) means ditch.

During the Ming and Qing dynasties, Mudu became the most prosperous commercial port west of Suzhou. The town is filled with ancient buildings, courtyards, and foot bridges. The town's Xu River (胥江), which was constructed in the Wu dynasty, was the first artificial river in China. Another river, Fragrant Brook (香溪),supposedly earned its name after the

Hsi Shih Bridge

Ancient stone tracks, soft flowing waters

beautiful Hsi Shih once washed and dressed here.

Only 10 private gardens have been preserved in Mudu, though there were once more than 30. The gardens have a similar appeal to those of Suzhou; they are delicate, remote, and deep, and retain their own character surrounded by a mountainous wildness.

The most famous private garden in Mudu — the Yan Family Garden (严家花园) — is located beside the Wang Family Bridge (王家桥) on Shantang Street (山塘街). The garden is the former residence of Shen Deqian, the teacher of the Qianlong Emperor during the Qing Dynasty. Fragment Brook flows in front of the door of the garden, and the back of the garden is Lingyan Mountain. The garden is made up of four small sites representing the beauty of spring, summer, autumn, and winter.

Hong Yin Mountain House (虹饮山房) lies about 200 metres east of the Yan Family Garden (严家花园) and is a powerful-looking building. Inside the Age-old Pine Tree Garden (古松园), a building has been carefully carved with delicate patterns. Meanwhile Bangyan Mansion (榜眼楼 ; "Bangyan" indicates a second-place score in the imperial examinations) is the former residence of the politician Feng Guifen, who was also a pioneer of the Self-strengthening Movement of the late Qing Dynasty (洋务运动 ; 1864-1894.

Many Wu-era cultural activities have been preserved in the village. During the Lantern Festival, there are horse-riding performances and gong and drum playing. On July 7 there is the Qixi Qiqiao Festival, when girls wear new clothes and pray to Zhi Nu, an ancient weaver. For the Moon Festival, people venture to Ramadan Palace and ascend Lingyan Mountain to view the moon.

Playing with the Moon

Lingyan Mountain (灵岩山) has been known for its beauty since the Wu Dynasty. It is said that during the Spring and Autumn Period, the beautiful Hsi Shih loved the moon and since emperor Fu Chai wanted to win her favor, he built Playing Moon Pond (玩月池) on the mountain. Meanwhile Lingyan Mountain Temple (灵岩山寺) is a famous garden on the southeast side of the mountain. Beside the temple is the high Lingyan Tower (灵岩塔).

Yan Family Garden

Jinxi Town 锦溪镇

A Folk Museum Town

Jinxi Town offers a selection of buildings, street houses, pavilions and villas built along the river bank. Water bonds the splendid scenery of the town and there are stone bridges everywhere.

Jinxi Town, Kunshan District, Suzhou City, Jiangsu Province
江苏省昆山市锦溪镇
Nearest city: Suzhou
Downtown Suzhou is a 50-minute drive from Southern Jiangsu Shuofang International Airport. High-speed trains from Shanghai and Nanjing stop at Suzhou Station or Suzhou South Station.
From Suzhou Railway Station there are tourist lines heading directly to Jinxi Town. A ticket costs RMB 13 and the trip takes 1 hour. Alternatively, you can take a minibus from Suzhou North Bus Station (苏州汽车北站, a 15-minute taxi ride from Suzhou Railway Station) to the town. The journey takes about 40 minutes and costs RMB6.

Jinxi (Splendid River) Town is located southwest of Kunshan City, facing Blue Mountain Lake(淀山湖) in the east, Sterile Lake (澄湖) in the west, Five-Guard Lake (五保湖) in the south, Crystal Lake (矾清湖) and White Lotus Lake (白莲湖) in the north. As early as 5000 years ago, ancestors of the town farmed and fished here. In the early Southern Song Dynasty, Imperial Consort Chen Fei of Emperor Xiaozong (1619-1659) died from disease in Jinxi Town. The Emperor honored this Town as" Chen Tomb." The town resumed the name of Jinxi in October 1992.

A couplet on Peace Bridge (Taiping Bridge太平桥) describe the unique "water" environment of this ancient town:"Eastern greeting; golden surges away from Blue Mountain Lake, western meeting; peaceful jade waves in Clear Lake". The supposedly dragon-shaped water system of the ancient town passes through from south to north. The dragon mouth is the south end of the Shi River, while the

Splendid River Town enjoys a setting of "Five Lakes and Three Pools "

Jinxi water lanes

water tomb of Imperial Consort Chen in the Five-Guard Lake is supposedly like a pearl within the dragon mouth.

Most of the ancient bridges in the town boast inscriptions and columns with exquisite patterns. Village Peace Bridge(里和桥) is the oldest large-span ancient bridge, and was considered one of the Ming Dynasty "Eight Sights (明代锦溪八景)." North Bodhisattva Bridge (北观音桥) is a single-hole stone arch bridge.. There are also many other well-protected complete ancient bridges.

The town's unique "bricks and tiles culture" dates back to Ming Dynasty days. Jinxi Bricks and Tiles Museum is said to be the foremost such museum in China..

Jinxi was a gathering point for arty types of many dynasties. The Wenchang Pavilion (文昌古阁) stands in the south town by the Five-Guard Lake bank(五保湖畔) and has traditionally been a place for poets to hang out

Jinxi has many colourful folk traditions. They include Dragon and Lion Dances, the ritual of"beating-the-stick" (打连厢), Boat Racing, and distinctive folk songs. The Si Xian Xuan Juan (丝弦宣卷) is considered unique to Jinxi.

"Sock Croissant"

Well known Jinxi delicacies include the "sock croissant", which was a favoured royal snack at the time of Emperor Xiao Zong (1619–1659). The shape is like the bottom of a sock, with the "croissant" comprising layers of extremely thin pastries, crispy and salty-sweet.

Ancient lotus bridge of the Splendid River Town

Shaxi Town 苏州沙溪镇

An Ancient Tourist Resort

Shaxi had already developed into a village more than 1,300 years ago, during the Tang and Song dynasties.

Shaxi Town ,Taicang District, Suzhou city, Jiangsu Province
江苏省苏州太仓市沙溪镇。
Nearest city: Shanghai
Shanghai is served by Pudong International Airport and Hongqiao Shanghai Airport. Shanghai Station is the city's main rail terminus, with services to around 70 cities in China. Trains to Hangzhou leave from the South Station.
Buses leave from Shanghai Tourist Distribution Centre (上海旅游集散中心), a 16-minute taxi ride from the Shanghai Bund) to Shaxi town. The journey takes about 1 hour.

Shaxi Town prospered throughout the Hongzhi Period of the Ming Dynasty. As its urban landscape took shape, the town became a popular scenic travel destination, famed for its "Eight Sights". Prosperity gave rise to the ancient mansions and famed residences along the Qipu River (戚浦河), which stone bridges cross with elegant and classic simplicity.

"The Best Ancient Alley in the Land," reads a plaque inviting travellers to roam through the town's Ancient Street, which extends for three straight kilometres. Long-established shops line the street. Along the street, yellow flags wave in the wind and bridges peek through the alleys.

The most striking structure that lines the Ancient Street is the Gongs' Carved-Pattern Hall (龚氏雕花厅), ornamented with carved pillars and painted rafters. The hall's supporting beams are decorated with cloud patterns, and are finely engraved with graceful and delicate intertwining flower veins. The second floor is home to a "Horseback Riding Building" (走马楼), where a traveller can conceivably visit each room on horseback, unobstructed by obstacles.

The Qipu River, roughly 3 to 5 metres across, runs parallel to the Ancient Street and through Shaxi.. Three ancient bridges straddle the river: the Xin Bridge (新桥), An Bridge (庵桥) and Yixin Bridge (义新桥), all single-arch stone bridges from the Ming and Qing dynasties. An Bridge (庵桥), originally built using wood in the Song Dynasty, was rebuilt with stone during Kangxi Period of the Qing Dynasty. One-third of An Bridge is embedded into the north shore, where it becomes part of the residential area.

Perhaps the most characteristic feature of Shaxi Town is the well-preserved group of waterside buildings along the Qipu. Each riverside home features a shanty and a small stone bridge for the family living in it. Almost half of each

home hangs above the river, supported by stone pillars. The clever design means people can live at a safe distance from the water, and allows boats to anchor under the homes.

At the east end of the Ancient Street lies Olive Island (橄榄岛), named for its oval shape. This island was once connected to the town by three ancient bridges.

Also in Shaxi is the "Delightful Shade Garden" (乐荫园), a quiet and soothing place with calm pools and scattered bamboo where Qu Xiaozhen, a hermit from late Song Dynasty, used to read and study while relaxing in the shade. Stone stools adorn the garden, providing an elegant contrast with the main hall that stands alone near the pools.

Since ancient times, people have come to burn incense and pray to the Buddha in Shaxi, especially at the town's "Temple Blessing for All Beings", "Long-Life Temple", and YanzhenTaoist Temple.

Present and past of the ancient town

The Ancient Street

Lord of the Dance

Famous Shaxi residents include Chinese modern dance pioneer Wu Xiaobang, whose former home on West Town Street (西市街) is a two-story European style building constructed in the early Republic of China period, and known by townsfolk as "the White Chamber" (小白楼) for its colour. The observatory set on its roof offers a panoramic view of the whole town.

Huangqiao Town 黄桥镇

The Song Dynasty Town of Heroes

The ancient town of Huangqiao — or "yellow bridge" offers visitors well-preserved Ming and Qing dynasty streets, 24 ancient alleys, temples, antique bridges and residences of famous historical figures. Huangqiao is also widely known for its role as an old revolutionary base.

Huangqiao Town , Taixing, Changshu City, Jiangsu Province
江苏省常熟市泰兴黄桥镇
Nearest city: Suzhou
Downtown Suzhou is a 50-minute drive from Southern Jiangsu Shuofang International Airport. High-speed trains from Shanghai and Nanjing stop at Suzhou Station or Suzhou South Station.
Take a taxi from Suzhou's Southern Shoufang International Airport (苏南硕放国际机场) to Changshu South Bus Station (常熟长途汽车南站), which will take about 45 minutes. From the bus station many buses depart for Huangqiao Town (30 minutes).

First built in the Northern Song Dynasty, the history of Huangqiao dates back nearly 1,000 years. There are over 2,000 buildings remaining from the Ming and Qing dynasties, as well as a handful from the Song. In addition to the ancient alleys, the ancient water transportation hub Huangqiao features three ancient temples, seven ancestral halls and myriad stone inscriptions and wooden tablets from the Tang, Song, Ming, and Qing dynasties. Among the famous people associated with the city is Niu Gao, known as a legendary soldier under the command of Yue Fei (a famous Song Dynasty general) and a hero in the wars against the Jin Dynasty. The Ming Dynasty Emperor Yongle also wrote in praise of the virtues of the town's people.

Huangqiao's Ancestral Hall of the He Family (何氏宗祠) is known as the top ancestral hall north of Yangtze River. The large hall remains well-preserved, and its main room is grand and stately.

The Battle of Huangqiao in the autumn of 1940 was a significant victory for the Red Army. The Communists fought off the Nationalist Kuomintang and established an anti-Japanese base in the town, a legacy that has left no shortage of revolutionary sites. The Memorial Hall for the New Fourth Army's Battle of Huangqiao (官方译文) is one of the nation's most famous revolutionary tourism spots, and is located in the Ding Family Garden (丁家花园) at No. 10 Mi Alley (米巷). The garden itself, meanwhile, has a modern design. There are carved beams, painted rafters, upward eaves, and winding corridors and paths. Other "red tourism" sites are scattered around the town.

The 1,000-year old Fu Hui Temple (福慧寺), the Military Hiding Place of Niu Gao (牛皋藏兵洞), and the Horse Pond (洗马池) are also well-known and interesting sites.

Filial Son

Another of the town's famous sons is Gu Xin, born in the Song Dynasty, who is known for his reputation as a filial son. As legend has it, when Gu Xin's mother was ill, he took care of her day and night. When she went blind, Gu cried every day until she made a miraculous recovery. After hearing about his filial piety, Emperor Cheng Zu of the Ming Dynasty wrote two poems and a preface to praise him. A later generation built Filial Son Gu's Pavilion (顾孝子亭) in honour of him. The monument is now preserved in Huangqiao Park.

After 500 years, the He Family Ancestral Hall is still standing.

Shajiabang Town 沙家浜镇

Green Park & Red Town

Shajiabang, a town with 500 years of history, is poetic regardless of the weather, and is also known for its "red history".

Shajiabang Town, Changshu City, Suzhou City, Jiangsu Province
江苏省常熟市沙家浜镇
Nearest city: Suzhou
Downtown Suzhou is a 50-minute drive from Southern Jiangsu Shuofang International Airport. High-speed trains from Shanghai and Nanjing stop at Suzhou Station or Suzhou South Station.
Take a taxi from Suzhou's Southern Shoufang International Airport (苏南硕放国际机场) to Changshu South Bus Station (常熟长途汽车南站), which takes about 45 minutes. From the bus station, many buses depart for ShajiabangTown (45 minutes).

With a picturesque lakeside location, Shajiabang boasts elements typical of regions south of the Yangtze River: rice paddies, fishing, farming, and local operas. A growing number of Chinese tourists have been brought to the town by the construction of facilities such as a Spring Teahouse (春来茶馆) and Shajiabang Memorial Hall.

Shajiabang's natural attractions include the region's largest Reed Maze (芦苇迷宫), which occupies about 1,000 acres. Standing in the peaceful place — with thatched cottages accompanied by the sound of water and birds taking flight — it is hard to imagine the revolutionary battles that once took place there. Late autumn is a good time to visit the town. During this season, the reed flowers are in bloom and the reeds that grow on both sides of the maze

Reeds in Shajiabang

18

Ancient China: Towns

stand taller than most people. Their light red colour creates a moving tableau as they dance in the breeze, a "great reed sea". On the south side of the maze are remote tracks home to rare animal species.

In the district of Hong Shi Village (红石村), surrounded by a sea of green reeds and the debris of willow trees, one can experience Shajiabang as it was in the 1940s. The corridor that runs beside Hidden Lake (隐湖) is roughly 175 meters long, and was built as a memorial for the 175th group of the No. 20 corps in the Jinan Military Regiment (also known as the Shajiabing Regiment).

Shajiabang is a land of abundance characterised by blossoming reed flowers, fragrant rice and lines of willow trees. An open market is set on the water — sculls filled with different daily needs including vegetables, fish, and crabs line up on the "water street". Shoppers make their way around the market on their own sculls. The unique "market on water" is an unforgettable site.

The steamed crabs of Yangcheng Lake are also recommended for visitors. In the Shajiabang region, lakes are densely covered, the water is clean, and water weeds thrive. This means that the mud on the bottom of the lake is hard and tough, making it the perfect home for crabs. Every September, pregnant female crabs and

A quiet spot

Red Opera

Shajiabang's revolutionary history has inspired several modern classic operas. The story "Fire in Reed Waves" by Cui Zuofu tells the story of Shajiabang's guerrilla warfare. In 1964, the tale was renamed "Shajiabang" for a Peking opera adaptation. A scene from the play Zhi Dou ("Fighting Smart") is still popular at many festivals.

their roe are abundant, making autumn the perfect time to get a taste.

The Shajiabang lakeside is a pleasant place to relax and enjoy pastimes such as fishing and playing cards. Famous teas and high-quality coffee are available, as well as local speciality foods. In mid-autumn, the steamed crabs of Yang Cheng Lake can be tasted, and a popular option is for travellers to catch and cook crabs themselves.

Ancient architecture of Shajiabang

Anfeng Town 安丰镇

The Salt Town

The ancient town of Anfeng, first recorded in the history books in 713, the first year of the Tang Dynasty, is associated with a multitude of historical figures, from Ming Dynasty philosopher Wang Gen (1483-1541), to Red Army commander Chen Yi (1901-1972).

Anfeng Town, Dongtai District, Yancheng City , Jiangsu Province
江苏省盐城市东台市安丰镇
Nearest city: Nanjing
Direct flight connections to cities across China serve Nanjing Lukou International Airport. High-speed trains arrive at the Nanjing Railway Station and regular trains at Nanjing South Station.
Take a high-speed train from Nanjing Railway Station to Yancheng Railway Station (four hours). Walk 10 minutes, or take a taxi, to Yancheng Bus Station (盐城汽车客运站). From there, regular scheduled buses to Haian County will wll pass Anfeng Town(1 hour). Alternatively, from Nanjing take a train to Dongtai Station (four hours), and then transfer to Dongtai City Bus Station (东台汽车站, a 10-minute walk. From there frequent buses leave for Anfeng Town for 5 yuan.

Anfeng's first name was Dongtao, which in Chinese suggests "going east to find gold". In its early years, the town, near the sea, was often hit by tidal waves, making life hard for residents. The people built a dam to stop the rushing water in the fifth year of the Tian Sheng emperor of the Northern Song Dynasty, and under the command of local official Fan Zhongyan, the town was renamed Anfeng. The character "An" signifies peace and contentment, while "Feng" means abundant and plentiful.

In the Ming and Qing dynasties, Anfeng grew rich on the back of its salt industry. At its peak the number of salt workers reached 48,000, and Anfeng was one of "the top 10 markets in Huainan area". Salt merchants gathered from across the country. The Chuanchang River (串场河) was busy with the traffic of salt sellers.

In the Ming and Qing dynasties there were more than 100 century-old stores that hung gold-lettered signboards, such as Wanyingmao Sauce Shop, Zhuxingji Cloth Shop, Yanxiasheng Grocery, Penglai Village Teahouse, and Happy Garden Restaurant. There were also many portable stalls of sellers who carried their goods and peddled on the streets or in the narrow lanes.

One special place in Anfeng is the Qipan Teahouse (7片茶社), a popular gathering spot for listening to storytellers. A piece called "Dongtao Story" is told over the course of several months or even half a year, and the daily audience still numbers in the hundreds.

The Family Bao Building (鲍氏大楼) located at No. 1 Wangjia Lane was built by the ancestor of a local Xiucai (one who passed the imperial examination at the county level in ancient China). It is surrounded by high walls on all four sides. In the walls of the upper and lower wings west of the second entrance are hidden doors linked to the drawing room. There are 18 rooms with three entrances; everything is ornately decorated, especially the brick carvings and wooden decoration the Hui architectural style.

The Clan Hall of the Wu Family

Salt of the Earth

One of Anfeng's famous sons was poet Wu Jiaji, who wrote a four-line poem for the salt workers: "Inside the small thatched cottage, workers refine salt beside the fire in June. Walking outside the cottage is the only cool moment". Wu's contrast between the "fire" of the salt refinery and the cool outdoors evokes salt workers' difficult lives.

The Clan Hall of the Wu Family (吴氏宗祠) located at No. 8 Nanshi Street, was built in memory of the patriotic poet Wu Jiaji, from the late Ming and early Qing. The protected site has a brick-wood structure and two entrances, and covers an area of 120 square meters.

Mituo Temple (弥陀寺), originally named North Pole Hall (北极殿), was built in the second year of the Wanli Emperor in the Ming Dynasty (1575 CE). Its reputation spread far and wide at that time, attracting many eminent monks. The temple was burnt down during the Sino-Japanese War, however, and the Mituo Temple that stands today is a reconstruction.

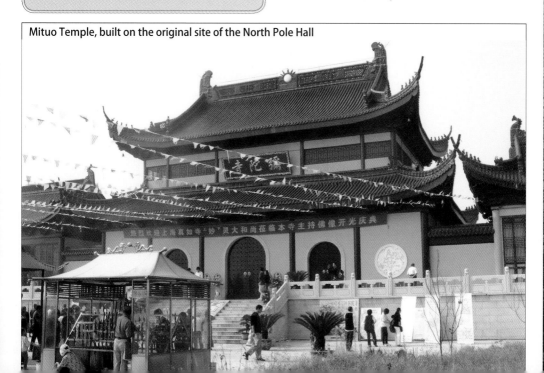

Mituo Temple, built on the original site of the North Pole Hall

Chunxi Town 淳溪镇

A World of Alleys

The people of Chunxi Town, originally known as Gaochun Town, have diligently cultivated the area's land here since the Shang Dynasty.

Chunci Town, Nanchun County, Nanjing City, Jiangsu Province
江苏省南京市高淳县淳溪镇
Nearest city: Nanjing
Direct flight connections to cities across China serve Nanjing Lukou International Airport. High-speed trains arrive at the Nanjing Railway Station and regular trains at Nanjing South Station.
From Nanjing Zhonghuamen Bus Station (南京中华门汽车站, a 35-minute taxi ride from the airport), transfer to a bus to Gaochun Long-distance bus Station(高淳长途汽车站). After arrival, a No. 3 bus will reach Chunxi Old Street.

The land occupied by Chuni Town was turned into a formal commercial market during the Song Dynasty. In 1491, Gaochun County (高淳县) was set up and the name of town's name was changed to Chunxi; it became the county's capital.

Chunxi Old Street (淳溪老街) is the most well-preserved ancient street from the Ming and Qing dynasties. Because it is shaped like a straight line, similar to the Chinese character for "one" (一), it is also called One Street (一字街).

Most buildings on Chunxi Old Street (淳溪老街) are half-timbered, and were constructed in the Ming and Qing dynasties. Paved with blue stones, the street has stores and

Chunxi Old Street is known as the best old street in the town

Chunxi scenery

houses with false fronts, a typical feature of Huizhou (徽州) construction. Shops on both sides face the street, while water lies behind them. Sundries come from and go to the Guanxi River (官溪河) on back alleys.

Chunxi has a variety of cultural relics, which range from Baosheng Pagoda (保圣寺塔), the Paintings of Daoist Gods Exhibition Hall (道教神像画展览馆), and the Yang Mansion (杨宅). Revolutionary relics — the headquarters of the first unit of the New Fourth Army (新四军) in Sino-Japanese war.

Chunxi is a wonderland of water. Highlights are the vast Danyan Lake (丹阳湖) in the west, Shijiu Lake (石臼湖) in the north, and Gucheng Lake (固城湖) in the central-south. In 541 BC, the king of Wu Country (吴国), Yu Ji (余祭), built the city of Gucheng to the north of the lake, which gave the latter its name. The water is a striking blue, and its beauty is complemented by the surrounding mountains.

Gaochun, or Chunxi, is also associated with Romance of the Three Kingdoms, one of China's most famous literary works. In the Three Kingdoms Period, as battling states contended for rule, Wu Zixu (伍子胥, a Wu official) set fire to Gucheng. Also during the period, Zhou Yu (周瑜, an esteemed military strategist) trained his navy in the city.

Poets and painters of all ages have long admired the amazing scenery of Chunxi. There are many other historical associations. Song Dynasty official Cai Jing (蔡京) pioneered in Chunxi a method of building dams in lakes to reclaim cultivated land. The innovation brought the prosperity of One Street. In the Ming Dynasty, statesman Liu Ji built the East Dam, but lost 100,000 fields and many of the treasures of Gaochun sank to the bottom of the lake.

Since the Song period, a series of temples were built on One Street and its surrounding neighbourhood. On festival days, the street teemed with processions making sacrifices to the gods; these events were called "Bodhisattva's coming"

Crabs

It is said that, from Gucheng Lake (固城湖) and Shijiu Lake (石臼湖), people can "earn gold in the morning and silver in the evening", a reference to the edible riches held in their waters. These include crabs, soft-shelled turtles, and shrimp. Pearls have also been farmed in the lakes. The Gaochun Crab festival, held every September, is the best chance for people to try out its special crab dishes and is also the perfect time to admire the chrysanthemums.

Yudong Town 余东镇

Phoenix Town

Yudong is another town whose historical legacy has been shaped by the salt trade. Its 1,000-metre stone old street is ancient and elegant, is lined with shops that have hundreds of years of history.

Yudong Town, Haimen City, Jiangsu Province
江苏省海门市余东镇
Nearest city: Nanjing
Direct flight connections to cities across China serve Nanjing Lukou International Airport. High-speed trains arrive at the Nanjing Railway Station and regular trains at Nanjing South Station.
Take a high-speed train from Nanjing Railway Station to Nantong Railway Station (南通站) (about three hours). Then take a taxi to Nantong Yongxing Bus Terminal Station (南通永兴汽车客运站, 10 minutes) and a bus to Haimen City Bus Terminal Station (海门汽车总站, 40 minutes). From Haimen City Bus Terminal Station, the shuttle bus to Yudong Town takes another 40 minutes. The entrance fee for Faguang Temple is 10 yuan.

Yudong (余东), also known as Phoenix Town (凤城), got its start in the Tang Dynasty. The town grew during the Northern Song Dynasty, and reached its peak during the Ming and Qing dynasties thanks to trade coming from the widespread practice of boiling salt out of seawater. Yudong Town faces the golden waterway of the Yangtze River.

Yudong's salt canal was dug during the Tang Dynasty, and was later used as a moat to defend the town against the Japanese during the Sino-Japanese War.

Built beginning in the 4th year of the Qianlong Emperor of the Qing Dynasty (1739), Guarding Peace Bridge (保安桥) is the best existing ancient stone bridge in the area. The

Faguang Temple

The Money and Grain House

二狼山). The temple's buildings, such as the Wenchang Pavilion (文昌阁) and Hibiscus Pool (芙蓉池), reflect the architectural styles of various periods and provide a picture of the harmonious coexistence of Confucianism, Buddhism and Taoism.

The most characteristic folk art in Yudong is Haimen folk dance, which includes the "Wealth God Dance" (跳财神) and "Feed Dance" (放施食).

emperor's name is still recognizable, inscribed in the stone of the pier.

The Great Gate of Cheng Family (程氏大门堂) is another landmark. Its eaves are lined with carved bricks and diamond-shaped decorations. Inside the larger diamond ornaments are beautiful lime-carved (灰雕) images of people and animals.

Yudong Money and Grain House (钱粮房) was an organization that collected the rice or silver-money levied as rent, and was managed by the Liu, Jiang (江), He and Jiang (姜) families, a task that was passed down from generation to generation.

Guolimao Silver House (郭利茂银楼) was built by Anhui merchant Guolimao in the Jiaqing years (1796-1820) of the Qing Dynasty. The house is typical of Anhui-style architecture used for commerce or manufacturing, and is a landmark in Yudong. The main business during the Jiaqing era was to process the silver jewellery, for which it was known in the east Nantong area.

At the centre of the ancient town is the Octagon Pavilion (八角亭), which features a golden phoenix that appears ready to take off and fly south.

The Light of Rule Temple (法光寺), formerly known as the East Mountain Temple (东岳庙), is located on the town's East Street. It is the only existing Ming Dynasty temple in Haimen, and is also called Second Wolf Mountain (地

Octagon Pavilion

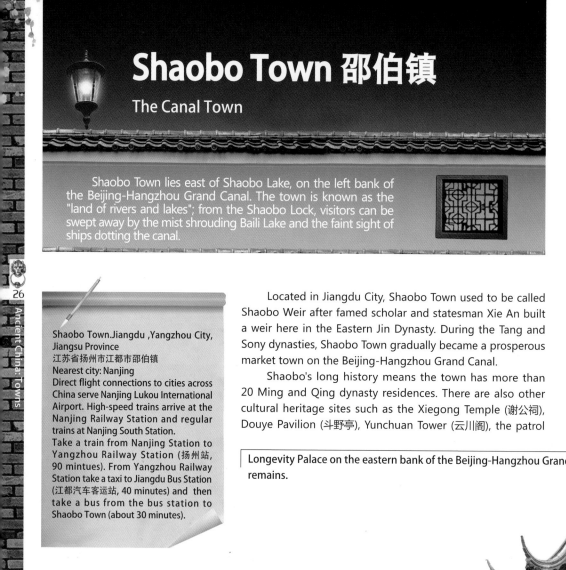

Shaobo Town 邵伯镇

The Canal Town

Shaobo Town lies east of Shaobo Lake, on the left bank of the Beijing-Hangzhou Grand Canal. The town is known as the "land of rivers and lakes"; from the Shaobo Lock, visitors can be swept away by the mist shrouding Baili Lake and the faint sight of ships dotting the canal.

Shaobo Town.Jiangdu ,Yangzhou City, Jiangsu Province
江苏省扬州市江都市邵伯镇
Nearest city: Nanjing
Direct flight connections to cities across China serve Nanjing Lukou International Airport. High-speed trains arrive at the Nanjing Railway Station and regular trains at Nanjing South Station.
Take a train from Nanjing Station to Yangzhou Railway Station (扬州站, 90 mintues). From Yangzhou Railway Station take a taxi to Jiangdu Bus Station (江都汽车客运站, 40 minutes) and then take a bus from the bus station to Shaobo Town (about 30 minutes).

Located in Jiangdu City, Shaobo Town used to be called Shaobo Weir after famed scholar and statesman Xie An built a weir here in the Eastern Jin Dynasty. During the Tang and Sony dynasties, Shaobo Town gradually became a prosperous market town on the Beijing-Hangzhou Grand Canal.

Shaobo's long history means the town has more than 20 Ming and Qing dynasty residences. There are also other cultural heritage sites such as the Xiegong Temple (谢公祠), Douye Pavilion (斗野亭), Yunchuan Tower (云川阁), the patrol

Longevity Palace on the eastern bank of the Beijing-Hangzhou Gran remains.

and inspection office (巡检司), Shaobo stage (邵伯驿) and an inscription of "big dock" (大马头) personally written by Emperor Qianlong (1735-1796). The town also holds less obvious witnesses of time, like an ancient road from the Eastern Jin Dynasty, and a 300-year-old iron ox to protect the town from floods. A 1.5-kilometre stone slab street (明清条石街) built in the Ming

Shaobo Lock

and Qing is well-preserved, a rarity in central Jiangsu.

Longevity Palace (万寿宫), located on the eastern bank of the Beijing-Hangzhou Grand Canal, was built in the Qianlong period of the Qing Dynasty. It is a pity that the palace itself is no longer standing and only an iron ox in the Douye Pavilion (斗野亭) remains - the ox was used to protect people from the floods. However

you can stand outside the Longevity Palace and look towards the west to enjoy beautiful scenes of Shaobo Lake (邵伯湖).

Walking out of Douye Pavilion (斗野亭), on the overpass of the Shaobo Lock (邵伯船闸), you will find a busy scene of ships coming and going below. Shaobo Lake (邵伯湖), also known as Tang Lake (棠湖) is particularly beautiful after the ships' sails have been lowered for the day.

After leaving Shaobo Lake, the street in front of you is the thriving Gourmet Street (美食街). Every summer, people flock here to eat lobster and other fine foods. The lobsters (邵伯龙虾) are known for their size and tender meat.

Meanwhile around the Mid-Autumn Festival in September you can see women busily harvesting water chestnuts, singing on the lake.

onger there, only an iron ox in the Douye Pavilion

Town of Songs

Shaobo is known as a town of songs and at planting time, as local women toil under the hot sun, they sing "work songs" to keep themselves going. The songs are rich in rural culture and provide excellent opportunities for folklore researchers.

Qingtong Town 溱潼镇

The Song Dynasty Water Town

On fertile land surrounded by water, Qintong Town, known as "A Pearl on Water", is a beautiful place with an agreeable climate. When walking into Qintong, you will find a town that boasts a long history and rich culture.

Huitong Town, Jiangyan, Taizhou City, Jiangsu Province

江苏省泰州市姜堰市溱潼镇

Nearest City: Nanjing or Shanghai

From Nanjing

Direct flight connections to cities across China serve Nanjing Lukou International Airport. High-speed trains arrive at the Nanjing Railway Station and regular trains at Nanjing South Station.

Take a train from Nanjing Station to Taizhou Railway Station (扬州站, two hours). From Taizhou Railway Station, scheduled buses depart about every 15 minutes for Qintong (30 minutes).

From Shanghai

Shanghai is served by Pudong International Airport and Hongqiao Shanghai Airport. Shanghai Station is the city's main rail terminus, with services to around 70 cities in China. Trains to Hangzhou leave from the South Station. From Shanghai Xujiahui Bus Station (上海徐家汇汽车站, a 20-minute taxi ride from the Shanghai Bund), there are two buses daily that go to Huitong Town (7:00am and 9:30am). The journey takes about three hours.

In the Southern Song Dynasty, Yue Fei (a famous general who defended the empire against invaders from the north, but was framed by a notorious courtier and sentenced to death by the emperor) stationed his troops in Qintong Village. The place name "Qintong" was officially adopted more than 400 years ago during the Wanli years of the Ming Dynasty. The Yangtze and Huaihe river systems join in Qintong. Taidong River, which flows across the northern part of the town, and Jiangxing River, which runs through the eastern part of the town, wrap together like two jade ribbons around a pearl.

During the Qianlong years of the Qing Dynasty, Sun Jinnian, a Jinshi (the title for a person who passed the imperial examinations) from Sun Village of Qintong Town, wrote seven-character-quatrains about the beauty of the Qin Lake area. The sites highlighted in his poems include the "East Taoist Temple where fishing boats return" (东观归渔) and "shaded flowers by a clear spring" (花影清皋).

The East Taoist Temple was built in the late Jin Dynasty. An expanse of clear water in front of the temple serves as a bay for fishing boats to berth. "Shaded flowers by a clear spring" refers to a camellia tree planted in the late Song Dynasty in a residential courtyard located in the urban district of the town.

More than 2,000 square metres of ancient

Qintong Boat Festival

buildings from the Ming and Qing dynasties are preserved in Qintong Town, including the Former Residence of an Academician (院士旧居), the Green Tree Monastery (绿树禅寺), the Folk Customs Museum (民俗风情馆), the Title Deeds Pavillion (契约文书馆) and the Marriage Customs Pavilion (婚俗馆). Ancient wells are found in many residential courtyards. The roads are generally cobblestone-paved paths.

In downtown Qinton, rivers weave together and islands dot the bluish-green waves of the lake. The legendary Magpie Lake is one of the few water bodies that is free from pollution in the whole province and is a good place for swimming, fishing, and bird-watching.

Qintong has long attracted teachers and scholars to its riverbanks. Chu Quan, an official in the Ming Dynasty, once studied in the Water

Cloud Pavilion (水云楼) of the ancient town. Jiang Lutan, a renowned poet and scholar of the Qing Dynasty, lived here for years. The Water Cloud Pavilion was particularly inspiring for the poets. "Draw up water from the lake, so that fresh tea can be made. Buy the Wu Mountain, and use it as a screen", wrote Zheng Banqiao, a calligrapher, artist and writer at the pavilion.

Watery Temple Fair

The Qintong Boat Festival has a history that can be traced back nearly 1,000 years, when the army under Song Dynasty general Yue Fei fought the Jin army on Qin Lake. Since that battle, locals have taken boats out on the lake every Tomb-Sweeping Day to hold a memorial ceremony for soldiers that died in that battle. The festival is supposedly the only authentic well-preserved temple fair on water in China. It is an annual spectacle, with breathtaking competitions and performances.

Wu Town 乌镇

The Poster Town of Southern China

Wu Town ("Raven Town"), with its beautiful water landscape, unique food, folk festivals and ways of life that can be traced back more than 1,000 years, is a living fossil of ancient civilization and culture.

Wu Town, Tongxiang County, Jiaxing City, Zhenjiang Province
浙江省桐乡市乌镇
Nearest city: Hangzhou or Shanghai
From Hangzhou
Hangzhou Xiaoshan International Airport offers a wide selection of routes. Direct trains link Hangzhou to more than 20 cities, including a high-speed service from Shanghai that takes about 1 hour and 15 minutes.
From Hangzhou East Bus Station(杭州汽车东站, a 20-minute taxi ride from Hangzhou Railway Station) buses to Wuzhen Town take about one hour.

From Shanghai
Shanghai is served by Pudong International Airport and Hongqiao Shanghai Airport. Shanghai Station is the city's main rail terminus, with services to around 70 cities in China. Trains to Hangzhou leave from the South Station.
From Shanghai Tourism Distribution Centre (上海旅游集散中心, a 16-minute taxi ride from the Shanghai Bund) buses to Wuzhen Town take about two hours.

There are many ancient towns in southern China, but few are as steeped in history and culture as Wu Town. The enchanting bridges, running rivers and households you see when standing at the bow of a Wu Peng Boat (a special boat in southern China which has a black cloth covering the boat's hold) are evocative of the scenery described in Tang poet Li Bai's Midnight Songs (a set of four poems named after the four seasons, written in the voice of a young lady from a southern China town, whose name was Midnight).

It is said all the walls in Wu Town were once covered with black paint. People around Tong County used the character Wu (meaning "raven") as a metaphor for the color "black", hence the town's name. According to archeological finds, there were people living in Wu Town more than 7,000 years ago. The name of Wu Town was officially adopted in the Xian Tong years of the Tang Dynasty. The town took its present shape in the Song Dynasty, when skillful craftsmen came to build gardens here.

Waterside houses

The most unique feature of Wu Town is its "water chamber" households built alongside the rivers. Standing out from the river bed and facing the water, the homes rest on the river. Windows are set on three sides of the chambers so that views of the town and river can be enjoyed from inside. These water chambers are the soul of Wu Town. They are both functional and aesthetic, and give the town a romantic feel.

Wu Town is a world of water. The broad Shi River cuts through it, dividing the East Palisade (东栅) sightseeing district from the leisurely West Palisade (西栅). The East Shi River runs from east to west through the East Palisade, creating an authentic water town atmosphere.

Bridges form a maze crisscrossing the town's rivers. The number of bridges totalled 140 at one time, and now there are still 30 ancient bridges preserved in the town. Among the ancient structures, the "bridge within a bridge" is the most remarkable attraction. It was created by the combination of two imposing arch bridges, the Tongji Bridge (通济桥) and the Renji Bridge (仁济桥). Each bridge can be seen from the arch of the other, like the moon reflecting in a well.

Wu Town owes much of its modern fame to its native son Mao Dun, a celebrated twentieth century writer whose real name was Shen Dehong. Mao Dun spent his childhood here. His former residence is a two-story wooden building with double courtyards and four traditional homes. The residence has the serene air of a scholar's home. The former Aspiration Academy (立志书院) lies to the east of Mao Dun's former home, which has now been turned into a museum honouring him.

The town is home to a few other interesting museums. The Southern China Hundred Beds Museum (江南百床馆) is the first museum in China that collects ancient beds of the region, and features several dozen boutique beds from the Ming and Qing dynasties. The Southern China Folk Custom Museum (江南民俗馆) exhibits vivid representations of birthday celebrations, weddings, and festivals. The Hundred Flower Hall (百花厅) is famous for its exquisite wood carvings. Human figures, animals, and beasts grace the door sashes and widows frames.

Located beside the Grand Canal, the West Palisade consists of a dozen islands are surrounded by bluish green waters. The islands can be visited on ferries. More than 250,000 square metres of structures from the Ming and Qing eras are scattered throughout the area, as well as 1.8 kilometres of the ancient West Palisade Street and 72 well-preserved stone bridges.

The Spiritual Water Garden (灵水居) is the largest

site in the West Palisade — it's a serene place that radiates simple beauty. Mao Dun's memorial museum is located deep in the maze of the grounds. There are many other sights here, including Zhaoming Academy (昭明书院), the Old Post Office (老邮局), Storytelling Theatre (评书场), the Hall on a Hall (厅上厅), White Lotus Tower (白莲塔), the Hengyitang Pharmacist (恒益堂药店), the Water Stage (水上戏台), and the Floating Market (水上集市).

Several workshops in the West Palisade are worth visiting. The first is the soy sauce factory (叙昌酱园), where visitors can see how the town's special brown sauce is made. The sauce is only sold in Wu Town, and is not cheap at a price of 25 yuan per bottle. The town's iron workshop (亦昌冶坊) is also interesting. The Yida Silk Store (益大丝号) allows visitors to operate an old silk-reeling machine.

Wu Town has a colourful variety of folk customs, such as the Flower Drum Opera and the bridge walking ritual held during the Lantern Festival. Other cultural happenings in the town include shadow plays, boxing matches on boats, and acrobatics shows. Singing performances can be found at the Grand Theatre from 13:00-15:00. Flower Drum Operas are put on from 19:00-20:00 on the Water Stage in the West Palisade. There are also evening storytelling shows. Next to the White Lotus Tower River in the West Palisade lies Tea Street (茶市街), a small road which extends for only 168 metres but is still worth a visit for those interested in the arts.

General Plague

One custom with an interesting background is the memorial ceremony for General Plague. Folklore says that General Plague was a young man who learned of a plot between two ghosts to contaminate the well in the West Palisade. The young man stood by the well to prevent the townspeople from drawing the poisoned water, but was misunderstood and beaten to death for being a troublemaker.

A peaceful corner of Wu Town

Xitang Town 西塘镇

River Sheds and Deep Alleys

Xitang Town was established in the first year of the Tang Dynasty (618) and during the Ming and Qing dynasties it became an important craft centre. The town is located close to the boundaries of Jiangsu, Zhejiang and Shanghai, and for hundreds of years it was a hub of culture and transport.

Xitang Town, Jiashan County, Jiaxing City, Zhejiang Province
浙江省嘉兴市嘉善县西塘镇
Nearest city: Shanghai
Shanghai is served by Pudong International Airport and Hongqiao Shanghai Airport. Shanghai Station is the city's main rail terminus, with services to around 70 cities in China. Trains to Hangzhou leave from the South Station.
Take the high-speed train from Shanghai Hongqiao Station (上海虹桥站) to Jiaxing South Railway Station (嘉兴南站, about 30 minutes, then a 30-minute taxi ride will take you to Jiaxing North Bus Station (嘉兴汽车北站). Then transfer to a shuttle bus to Xitang Town (about 40 minutes.) At weekends, buses head directly from Shanghai Indoor Stadium (上海体育馆, a 20-minute taxi ride from the Bund) to Xitang Town (about 50 minutes).

Xitang Town is located on flat land at the meeting point for nine rivers, dividing it into eight zones. The topography has been characterised as "nine dragons holding a pearl" (九龙捧珠). There are more than 100 bridges in Xitang.

River "sheds" are a unique architectural feature of Jiangnan. The town's streets run along the river, with shops concentrated on the riverside. In the past, local farmers and traders used boats exclusively for transportation; transactions were carried out on the riverbank. The river's commercial zone gave birth to the "sheds", which connect the river to shops, shielding visitors from the sun and rain. The sheds were passed down generation to generation and became a symbol of the town.

Dragon Bridge (卧龙桥) is the oldest bridge in town, with exquisite vertical arches. Happiness Bridge, (五福桥位) located in the harbour, is a site for burning incense. The covered Childbirth Bridge (送子来凤桥) faces the river sheds of the south. Town elders say that if a couple walks over the bridge, they will be blessed with a child. They will have a son if they walk south and a daughter if they walk north. The Eternal Peace Bridge (永宁桥) has a fitting name, as it is the best place to quietly view the scenery of the town. Standing on the arched Anjing Bridge (安境桥), you can enjoy a panoramic view of three types of bridges, including the flat Eternal Peace Bridge and the twisting Long Peace Bridge (万安桥).

The town has 122 alleys, which for the most part are peaceful and long. The most famous is Stone Skin Alley (石皮弄), which runs between Honour Hall (尊闻堂) and Seed of Fortune Hall (种福堂). The unusual name comes from the thin stone used on the lane — thin as skin, residents say. The alley is only around a meter wide, leaving a sliver of sky above the walkway. The Four Virtues Temple Alley (四贤祠弄) is the longest alley in town at 236 metres. The shortest is in Yuqing Hall (余庆堂, which contains a Ming and Qing Dynasty carving wood museum), and it is only 3 metres long. The widest alley is near the harbour beside the Li House and is wide enough for five people to walk side by side. Wildcat Alley (野猫弄) by Huanxiu Bridge is less than 0.3 metres wide — the narrowest in town.

West Street (西街) is the main east-west street in Xitang, and is structured like a typical water town lane. The narrowest part of the road is only wide enough for a farmer to carry a shoulder pole. The tourist spots on the street include Zhongfu Hall, West Garden, the Button Museum, and the Jiangnan Stone Cover Museum (瓦当). East Pond Street (塘东街) was one of the most bustling streets of old Xitang. On the street are many restaurants, and the 100-year-old pharmacy Zhongjiefu (钟介福). A poem on the gate reads, "I'd rather the medicine be covered with dust, and wish the country has no sickness". The street is also the site of clothing store Yuanyuan (源源绸布庄), where famed Communist revolutionary Chen Yun stayed during the Fengjing riots of 1928.

Xitang has preserved the folk traditions of Jiangnan water towns. "Field songs" (田歌) were passed down from generation to generation and are still sung in parts of Jiangsu, Zhejiang, and greater Shanghai. On the third day

River sheds

Old house interior in Xitang

of the fourth month on the lunar calendar (usually late April or early May) is the birthday of the patron saint of the Xitang people, or their "seventh grandpa". Parades and performances are held for three days at the "Temple of Seventh Grandpa" (老爷庙).

Nights in Xitang are picturesque, with families strolling along the river and lighting lanterns.

Xitang food uses fresh, healthy ingredients and includes dishes such as steamed fish (清蒸白丝鱼), dried vegetables with meat (霉干菜扣肉), soybeans and water chestnuts (毛豆菱角), wonton stew (馄饨老鸭煲), and snails in soy sauce (酱爆螺蛳).

Xitang Nights

From May to October every year, Xitang holds night tours of boat and three tourist spots — the Zhangzheng Root Carving Museum, Button Museum, and West Garden. The night tours run from 17:00–20:30 and finish with performances on a water stage.

Nanxun Town 南浔镇

Town of the Four Elephants

East meets west in Nanxun, and there are gorgeous views everywhere. Historic relics compliment the town's natural beauty, which brims with the poetic charm of old towns of the Yangtze river.

Nanxun Town, Nanxun District, Huzhou City, Zhejiang Province
浙江省湖州市南浔区南浔镇
Nearest city: Hangzhou
Hangzhou Xiaoshan International Airport offers a wide selection of routes. Direct trains link Hangzhou to more than 20 cities, including a high-speed service from Shanghai that takes about 1 hour and 15 minutes. Proceed to Hangzhou North Bus Station (杭州汽车北站, a 30-minute taxi ride from Hangzhou Railway Station). Buses depart about every 30 minutes for Nanxun Town (90 minutes).

Located in the central part of the Hangjiahu Plain, Nanxun has a history of over 700 years. It has been a place of great wealth since the Southern Song Dynasty, although the town's name has changed. The village was originally named Xunxi (浔溪) after a river in the area, but later changed to Nanlin, or "Southern Forest" (南林). Only in 1252 was Nanlin was designated a town and its name changed to Nanxun (南浔), formed by a combination of the characters from its previous names.

Thanks to the rise of silk industry and the development of its commercial economy, Nanxun was prosperous from 1573 to the middle of Qing Dynasty. In the late Qing and early Republic of China period, it became China's silk trade centre. Suddenly, Nanxun had become the strongest town in the Jiangsu and Zhejiang area (江浙地区) with hundreds of wealthy families. The most famous residents were the "four elephants" — a reference to four of the wealthiest families in town — whose combined annual income supposedly exceeded the entire annual tax revenues collected by the Qing treasury.

White wall, blue tiles, ports, old bridges — typical Yangtze scenery.

One Hundred Building in Nanxun

Nanxun has become a model for heritage towns in the southern Yangtze region because of its unique setup, good preservation, and rich cultural background. It has been commended for "outstanding protection" by UNESCO because of its well-maintained architecture, including great mansions which combine western and eastern styles.

The "One Hundred Building" is said to have been built by Dong Fen, a senior Ming Dynasty official, for his nannies and servants. It was named "One Hundred" because it has close to 100 rooms. The unique building zigzags along the river and is linked to stone bridges. The 400-metre-long building features white walls, blue tiles, long corridors, ports, flower walls, gates, veranda eaves, a running river, and boats chugging alongside. The nearby "Three Old Bridges of Nanxun" —Tongjin Bridge (通津桥), Hongji Bridge (洪济桥), and Guanghui Bridge (广惠桥) — add to the scene.

The Book Depository in Jiaye Hall (嘉业堂) is one of the four largest book storage buildings in the southern Yangtze region. It was built by scholar Liu Chenggan between 1920 and 1924. At its peak, there were more than 600,000 books in the store, making it the largest private book collection in China. Its lotus pool, manmade mountains, pavilions, and hollow white pillars embody the delicacy of Yangtze gardens. The western-style chandeliers reveal the wealth of its owners. One great treasure of the town is a Song Dynasty block-print edition of the first of the of the " Twenty-four Histories" (a collection of Chinese historical books covering the period from 3000 BC to the Ming Dynasty in the 17th century).

Nanxun has five large gardens and dozens of smaller ones — more than the celebrated Suzhou. Close to Jiaye Hall, there is Little Lotus Grange, a private garden that belonged to Liu Yong (one of the "Four Elephants" of Nanxun in the late Qing Dynasty). The garden houses Liu Yong's domestic temple and hospital. It has a lotus pool at its centre, and has both an inner and outer garden. In the centre of the lotus pool, there is a zigzag bridge. Also in the pool is a beautiful pavilion, where you can sit and take in the scene. Separated by plaster walls and connected by ornamental perforated windows, the inner and outer garden are separate but still feel connected.

The Zhang Shiming Old House (张石铭 旧宅) showcases Ming and Qing styles with western touches. Zhang Shiming (张石铭, also named Junheng钧衡) was the oldest grandson of Zhang Songxian (1817-1892), who passed the imperial examinations in 1894. He was a businessman and amassed a great fortune. His cousin, Zhang Jingjiang, was one of the four patriarchs of the Kuomintang. The Zhang family was also one of the "Four Elephants". The former residence of Zhang Jingjiang has become a museum.

Virtue Hall (崇德堂), also referred as the town's "Red House", was the residence of Liu Yong's third son, Liu Ansheng (刘安泩). The middle part of the home was built according to traditional Confucian principles, while the southern and northern combine Chinese and Roman styles. The northern part, with a European facade, is majestic. Visitors can watch Chinese folk troupe performances here.

100-Year Old Store

Famous snacks on sale at "Wild Chufa" (野荸荠) a more than 100-year-old store) include orange cakes, "win" cakes, bean tea, stinky tofu, and "Lin sisters' cookies". The village also boasts of its four famous dim sum dishes: Zhou Sheng'e dumplings, Ding Lianfang's buns, Zhenyuan Tongsu candy, and Brother Zhu's rice dumplings. Meanwhile Nanxun has an abundance of bamboo shoots, which feature prominently in the town's cooking.

Xinshi Town 新市镇

The Immortals' Town

The Grand Canal passes through Xinshi, which lies in the middle of the Hangjia Lake Plain. Taoist scholar Lu Xiujing built a home here during the Southern Song Dynasty after falling in love with the scenery.

Xinshi Town, Deqing County, Huzhou City, Zhejiang Province
浙江省湖州市德清县新市镇
Nearest city: Hangzhou
Hangzhou Xiaoshan International Airport offers a wide selection of routes. Direct trains link Hangzhou to more than 20 cities, including a high-speed service from Shanghai that takes about 1 hour and 15 minutes.
Many scheduled buses head to Xinshi Town from Hangzhou Long-distance West Bus Station(杭州长途汽车西站, a 20 minutes taxi ride from Hangzhou Railway Station). The journey takes about 1hour.

Taoist scholar Lu's house is near the pond by the east gate (东栅古潭). Once, after Lu spent three days playing by the pond, the townspeople hailed him a Taoist immortal and renamed his resting spot "Fairy Pond" (仙潭), which became another name for Xinshi.

Immortal Pond (三潭), also known as the Chen Family Pond (仙潭), is one of the three main bodies of water in Xinshi, and was also named for the afore-mentioned scholar Lu. The history museum by the pond occupies the former site of a famous Qing-era pawn shop, Deyuan Pawn Shop (德源当). In the front hall of the museum there is a map of how Xinshi looked in the late Qing dynasty, and upstairs you will find information about famous town residents, and archaeological finds that tell the story of the town's long history. Around the Immortal Pond are three stone bridges built before the Song Dynasty. The three bridges are named Immortal's Arrival Bridge (驾仙桥), Meet the Immortal Bridge (会仙桥) and Gaze at the Immortal Bridge (望仙桥).

The West River Mouth (西河口) is a 1,000-year-old street. Most of the old houses and buildings here were built in the late Qing Dynasty and the Republic of China. Ther are docks and stone steps every 10 metres. Most docks double as a place for villagers to do their laundry. There are dozens of well-preserved homes with white walls and black tiles in Xinshi. The most beautiful are Lucky House (俞吉祥), Uncle Fang's House (方伯第), Love and Respect Hall (爱敬堂), and the Qian Residence

(钱宅).

The Fairy Pond Museum of Folk Arts (仙潭民间艺术馆) on Siqian Street (司前街) is the old residence of renowned Qing Dynasty alchemist Zhou Guangtong. In the hall there is a display about worshiping the silkworm (轧蚕花), a ritual from the Qing Dynasty. Across from the Fairy Pond Museum is the Lord Liu Temple (刘王庙), built in memory of Liu Qi, a famous general from the Southern Song who fought against intruders from the Jin Dynasty.

Rouge Alley (胭脂弄), at the north end of the Siqian Street, was the red-light district of the Ming Dynasty town. The Xiyong Temple Front Alley (西通寺前弄) connects to the Tang Family Taoist Land (唐家道地) in the east.

The Juehai Temple (觉海寺) is also 1,000 years old. Located in the north of Xinshi, the temple is topped by an 8-metre-high bell tower with a delicate copper bell that weighs 1,500 kilograms. Every year during the Qingming Festival Silkworm Temple Fair (清明蚕花庙会), people flock to the temple to worship the goddess of silkworms.

The South Yangtze River Area Silkworm Culture Museum (江南蚕文化馆) is found in the alley in front of the Juehai Temple. In the hall, you can see representations of the elegant goddess of silkworms, Ma Mingwang, and learn about Xinshi's silkworm culture.

Silkworms

The Silkworm Temple Fair (蚕花庙会) has a long history. It is said that when Xi Shi, the beauty of Yue Kingdom, travelled to Gusu from Huiji to deliver silkworms, she passed by Xinshi and saw two farm girls dancing in front of her sedan. She was deeply moved by their dance and presented them with colourful silk flowers. After that, Xinshi became prosperous and has always had bountiful silkworm harvests. Every Qingming Festival, the people of Xinshi hold the temple fair in honour of Xishi.

The criss-crossing rivers, old bridges, and black and white houses in Xinshi are typical of southern China riverside towns.

Longmen Town 龙门镇

Hometown of Sun Quan

In Longmen Town you can learn about the traditions and culture of the family of Sun Quan (emperor of the Wu country in the Three Kingdoms period), and enjoy the scenery of Longmen Mountain, which attracted the famous hermit Yan Ziling.

Longmen Town, Fuyang City, Zhejiang Province
浙江省富阳市龙门镇
Nearest city: Hangzhou
Hangzhou Xiaoshan International Airport offers a wide selection of routes. Direct trains link Hangzhou to more than 20 cities, including a high-speed service from Shanghai that takes about 1 hour and 15 minutes.
Take a taxi from Hangzhou Long-distance West Bus Station (杭州长途汽车西站) to Wangjiang East Road Bus stop station(望江东路公交站, about 20 minutes).Then transfer to a No. 514 bus directly to Fuyang Town (about 50 minutes).

Longmen Town is at the foot of Longmen Mountain in the Fuchun River area and is surrounded by mountains on all sides. The Shan River (剡溪) joins the Longmen River (龙门溪) in the north part of town. In the Eastern Han Dynasty, the hermit Yan Ziling visited the area and said it reminded him of a place with the name "Longmen". The moniker stuck.

Going up along the Longmen River, you will see the Longmen Mountain Waterfall (龙门山瀑布), with a fall of hundreds of metres into Dragon Pond (龙潭).

Around 90% of the townspeople have the family name Sun (孙),which they say makes them descendants of Wu Emperor Sun Quan. Two Sun family temples stand in the centre of the town, surrounded by more than 40 Sun family halls, three brick archways, an ancient tower and a temple, named Yuqing Hall (余庆堂, the Sun Family Temple), an important place for the whole town to hold ceremonies, worship ancestors, discuss clan issues, and celebrate and entertain.

The unique structure of the corridor in "One Hundred Steps Hall" (百步厅) and the marvellous appearance of the

Bamboo horse in the ancient town of Longmen

buildings is still apparent, though time has left its mark.

Another attraction in Longmen is the town's 400-metre-long pebble street. The ancient alley is paved by stones and lined by dimly lit stores with old signboards hanging outside, while inside shop owners tally their earnings on abacuses.

The hills surrounding the town contain various sites of interest. The Jiguang Puzhao Temple (寂光普照寺) built in the Tang Dynasty is situated on Longmen Mountain, and the Longmen Temple (龙门寺) built in the Jin Dynasty at the foot is one of the oldest temples in Fuyang County. The northernmost hill on the slope of Longmen Mountain is supposedly shaped like a dragon's head and the rest of the line is like the body, protecting the descendants of the emperor Sun Quan. The hill is named Dragon Mountain (洋龙山).

Tong Xing Tower (同兴塔) is on Stone Tower Mountain (石塔山) 1.5 kilometres west of town. The pavilion-like white tower is made of bricks and was built by Sun Chang, a Qing Dynasty resident of Longmen. The tower is beautifully shaped, tall and old. It is one of the best-

Gluten

Local cuisine is distinguished by its use of gluten. Specialty dishes include braised gluten with meat (红烧三鲜面筋), gluten and trotters in a clay pot (面筋猪蹄煲), gluten and duck in a clay pot (面筋老鸭煲), and fried gluten (油炸面筋). Wentai bean noodles (文台粉条) are also a tasty treat while Guotai tofu (国太豆腐) is fresh, tender and delicious.

preserved ancient towers in Fuyang County.

On the first day of the ninth month of the lunar calendar (usually in October), the Longmen Temple Fair (龙门庙会) is held. The fair has been held for 1,000 years, with traditions being passed down through the Sun family since the Northern Song Dynasty. At the fair townspeople hold a big feast for all their friends and family. Other traditional activities include the "Same Age Meeting" (同年会), ancestor worship (祭祖) and the Lantern Festival (元宵节), which lasts for five days.

Paths, folk houses and halls on the approach to Longmen Town

Cicheng Town 慈城镇

The Ancient County Town

Cicheng Town lies at a latitude of 30 degrees north, linking it to mystical places like the Bermuda Triangle and the Egyptian pyramids. Locals consider this a favourable geomantic omen, making the area fit for rich culture, great talents, and favourable weather for crops.

Cicheng Town, Jiangbei District, Ningbo City, Zhejiang Province
浙江省宁波市江北区慈城镇
Nearest city: Hangzhou
Hangzhou Xiaoshan International Airport offers a wide selection of routes. Direct trains link Hangzhou to more than 20 cities, including a high-speed service from Shanghai that takes about 1 hour and 15 minutes.
Take a high-speed train from Hangzhou Railway Station to Ningbo East Railway Station (宁波东站, two hours). Several bus routes heading from Ningbo East Railway Station to Yuyao City and other destinations will pass by Cicheng Town (about 40 minutes). A combined entry ticket for the Confucian Temple, Bachelor Masion and Qingdao Temple (清道观) is only 75 yuan.

There are mountains on three sides of Cicheng and a plain to the south. During Kind Lake (慈溪) in the north of the town is a highlight. In the Qianglong reign (1735-1796) of the Qing Dynasty, Shigu Pavilion (师古亭) was built on the embankment in the centre of the lake. On the hill southwest of the lake, there is a stone monument where US military leader Frederick Townsend Ward was shot to death in the Taiping Rebellion.

One kilometre west of the lake is Dabao Mountain, where General Zhu Gui and hundreds of soldiers fought British invaders in 1842 during the Opium Wars, and where Zhugui Temple stands now. Dabao Mountain (大宝山), Lion Mountain (狮子山), and Qingdao Mountain (清道山) add an imposing feel to Cicheng, while the Cloud Lake Reservoir (云湖水库) provides city people an ideal place to relax on holidays.

During the Tang Dynasty, the layout of the town was like a chessboard. A great number of old buildings are well-preserved. In the west part of town, there is Danai Hall (大耐堂), Osmanthus Hall (桂花厅), the Liu Family Temple (刘家祠堂), Taiping Heavenly Kingdom Mansion (太平天国公馆), and the former residence of Zhou Xinfang (周信芳故居). The east features the Jiaoshi House (校士馆) where children took imperial examinations, an old gate with the Chinese character "福" (fu, meaning good fortune 福字门头), and a slew of traditional homes.. There is a Confucian Temple (¤Õ庙) in the middle of town, along with a few more old homes. On the hill southeast of town is a Qingdao Taoist Temple (²M¹D观), famous for its large bell.

The Confucius Temple (孔庙) is at No. 55 East Zhuxiang Road (竺巷东路). The imposing temple shows the importance of Confucianism in traditional culture and is the most well-

Ming and Qing Dynasty architectural style in Cicheng

Ancient architecture in Cicheng Town

preserved of its kind in eastern Zhejiang Province. The coloured drawings of Fengyue houses show off Song Dynasty painting styles.

The Jiadi Home (甲第世家), also known as the Qian Residence (钱宅), is located in Jinjiajing Alley (金家井巷). Qian Zhao passed the imperial examinations and became an official of the Ming Dynasty in 1533. Several of his descendants followed in his footsteps, so the family was called the "Jiadi Family" (甲第世家), meaning "family with many scholars". The house faces south and its layout has a characteristic east Zhejiang Ming architectural style.

A gate with the character "fu" (福, meaning good fortune福字门头) is located in the Jinjiajing Alley (金家井巷). The house used to be a part of the former residence of Feng Shuji, the provincial governor in the Jiajing period of the Ming Dynasty (1522-1566). But when Feng's descendents hit hard times, they sold the house to the Ying family. The Yings redesigned the grounds and placed two gates on the east side of the front gate. The screen wall of the second gate is where the brick engraving of "fu" (福) can be found.

There are seven relatively intact archways in town, including Dong Guan Archway (冬官坊), En Rong Archway (恩荣坊), Shi En Archway (世恩坊), the Fengyue Coloured Gate (冯岳彩绘台门). You can also find Song Dynasty stone figures (宋代石翁仲) on the eastern slope of Damiao Mountain (慈湖大庙山东坡). There are also some stone windows, brick engravings, and wood carvings in Cicheng.

A corner of Cicheng

Kind River

The Kind River (慈溪) is one of the many places in Cicheng with a story behind its name. Legend has it when the mother of Han dynasty scholars son Dong An fell ill, he built her a house and carried her water every day from her favourite river until she recovered. Thus the river, and the county surrounding it, was named "Kind".

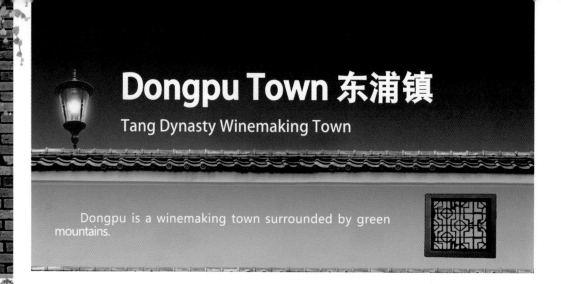

Dongpu Town 东浦镇
Tang Dynasty Winemaking Town

Dongpu is a winemaking town surrounded by green mountains.

Dongpu Town, Yuecheng District, Shaoxing City, Zhejiang Province
浙江省绍兴市越城区东浦镇
Nearest city: Hangzhou
Hangzhou Xiaoshan International Airport offers a wide selection of routes. Direct trains link Hangzhou to more than 20 cities, including a high-speed service from Shanghai that takes about 1 hour and 15 minutes.
Take a shuttle bus from Hangzhou Xiaoshan International Airport (杭州萧山国际机场) to Shaoxing Railway Station (绍兴站, about 45 minutes). You can take a taxi from Shaoxing Railway Station to Shaoxing South bus station(绍兴汽车南站, 10 minutes and 20 yuan). Then transfer to the No. 118 bus, which stops at the Former Residence of Xu Xilin in Dongpu Town.

Dongpu, meaning "eastern pond" was the hometown of the great patriotic poet Luyou (1125-1210, from the Southern Song Dynasty). In his old age, Luyou returned to and lived in his hometown, leaving behind timeless lines about the experience. "Lying down late at night, listening to the rhythms of the wind blowing the rain, cavalry and fierce war come into my dreams".

Dongpu is famous for its lanes and alleys. You can find 72 lanes in the market alone, including many off of Dongpu Old Street, and the village offers typical river town scenery of zigzag streams, whitewashed walls, black tiles, corridors, and homes by the rivers. Dongpu Old Street was established in the Southern Song Dynasty, and was prosperous in the Qing Dynasty. It suffered a great deal of damage during the Cultural Revolution of the 1960s to 1970s, but fortunately many original structures survive, and most of the old stores are relatively well-preserved.

Qingdian Lake (青甸湖) in the east of the town is also called "Mirror Lake" because of the clearness of the water. Many scholars and literati were drawn to the lake's beautiful views, and have spilled ink to discuss the area. "It is like travelling in a mirror while walking up a quiet mountain path" wrote the calligrapher Wang Xizhi (303-361). Famed Tang Dynasty poet Li Bai (701-762) wrote, "I would like to travel to Tianlao Mountain, Yue County in my dream, I saw a bright moon reflected in the lake one night".

The old town has a wide variety of bridges; some are simple, others are majestic. Corridors and pavilions were built on some of them, while others even have temples and stages. The "interchange" bridges are the most interesting. They have an upper level and a lower level on each side, and people walking across can reach out and hold boats' towropes. The

Dongpu Dwellings

Silong Bridge (泗龙桥) over Qingdian Lake has been listed as an officially protected historic site due to its unique design.

Dongpu has been the centre of the winemaking industry since the Song Dynasty and has claimed to be the original home of the famous Shaoxing WIne. The centrality of the wine industry in the town is reflected by the fact that 45 of the 250 shops on Dongpu Old Street are alcohol-selling establishments. The Xiaozhen Wine Shop (孝贞酒坊) on Yuepu Bridge, has been around since ancient times, and the Wuzong Emperor (1491-1521) of the Ming Dynasty and the Qianlong Emperor (1711-1799) from the Qing both tasted Dongpu wine there.

Shaoxing's traditional wine sets come in different styles with colourful patterns. Special crafts include duckbill flasks from the Shangzhou Dynasty, the He (a kind of ancient wine vessel with round top and three or four legs) of the Warring States Period, cockscomb-shaped flasks and cups from the Jin Dynasty, zhangtuo (the wine cup holder) and zhihu (a special type of flask) from the Tang Dynasty, the rhino horn wine vessels of the Ming Dynasty, cup sets of Qing Dynasty, and flasks made of tin and porcelain from early modern times.

Wine Boddhisatva

In the past, the Immortal Wine Ceremony (酒神会) was held at the beginning of the seventh month of the lunar calendar each year (usually early August on the western calendar). The ceremony was held mainly to welcome the wine Bodhisattva. The Bodhisattva Temple is located in the fourth hall of the Rongding Monastery (戒定寺). The wine Bodhisattva is dressed in Tang-style garments, buttoned on the right, with her hair up. Two children sit beside the Bodhisattva, one holding a wine rake, the other a wine jar. Dragon boat races and other performances are also held at the temple.

Dongpu Town, regarded as "the town of water, bridges, wine, and literati"

Anchang Town 安昌镇

Hometown of Private Advisers

In the second year of the Qianning Emperor's reign of the Tang Dynasty (895), a Tang general assembled an army here. Because he managed to pacify a rebellion, the town was named Anchang ("Anchang" means peace and prosperity in Chinese).

Ancheng Town, Shaoxing County, Zhejiang Province
浙江省绍兴县安昌镇
Nearest city: Hangzhou
Hangzhou Xiaoshan International Airport offers a wide selection of routes. Direct trains link Hangzhou to more than 20 cities, including a high-speed service from Shanghai that takes about 1 hour and 15 minutes.
Take a shuttle bus from Hangzhou Xiaoshan International Airport (杭州萧山国际机场) to Shaoxing Railway Station (绍兴站, about 45 minutes). In Shaoxing buses leave from Shaoxing Bus Station (绍兴客运中, a 15-minute taxi ride from the train station) or Shaoxing North Bus Station (绍兴汽车北站, a10-minute walk from the train station), for Anchang Town. The journey takes about 40 minutes.

Anchang is a typical river town, with numerous crisscrossing streams, strings of ancient streets, platforms, doors and arcades with carved beams and painted rafters, deep secluded alleys, diverse stone bridges and river ports. The town also offers theatrical performances and traditional activities such as "boat bride fetching", winemaking, "shuffling boats" and the culinary traditions of New Year cakes, traditional pudding, sausage, and white sugar production.

In the past, Anchang was a flourishing commercial port and had the largest dock on the east Zhejiang ship route. It was also the most important cotton distribution area in all of eastern Zhejiang.

Anchang had a reputation as a cradle for private advisers, who were employed by officials in the Ming and Qing dynasties to help with processing daily affairs. Although

Multiple river crossings, a long string of ancient streets and gallery ter

River scene

they didn't have official positions, they had great influence on local politics, the economy, and the military. Private Advisers Hall (师爷馆), based on the original residence of famous Qing private adviser Lou Xintian (1872-1944), is a good place to visit to understand this special class in late Chinese dynastical society. There is a group of sculptures in the town recreating scenes of local officials trying a court case under the watchful eye of the advisers. The plaintiff and defendant kneel in front of the court, while clerks stand beside them holding sticks. It is clear from the sculpture that the real authority is the private adviser, sitting behind the judge, listening and assessing the evidence and the judge's performance.

The Shuikang Money Shop (穗康钱庄) closed in 1949 after operating for almost 100 years. The wealth god still housed in the shop's shell is interesting as it differs from typical modern representations. In its left hand are three stacked gold ingots, while its right hand is clenched into a fist in front of its chest as it sits in a private adviser's chair, smiling. The old Shuikang Money Shop now features an excellent exhibition of nearly 1,000 kinds of coins and old paper money.

The Anchang Folk Customs House (安昌民俗风情馆) is located beside the river, at the end of the long old street. In the Nanshahuaji Room (南沙哔叽室), there are 12 royal-themed cotton figurines from the Qianlong reign (1711-1799) and several ancient textile machines.

The Naolayue (闹腊月) festival, held in January or February, is one of the most exciting times to see the town. Activities include village plays (社戏), drumming performances, traditional songs, "boat bride fetching" and a birthday party for the town's elders. Tourists can sample local New Year's cakes and traditional pudding, as well as watch craftwork in action as townspeople make buckets, weave bamboo, forge iron, stitch lace, and spin cotton.

Anchang's small bridges are also special. Styles vary, with some featuring pavilions, others arches, and still others roof beams. The most famous bridges are Fulu (福禄), Wan'an (万安), and Ruyi (如意). When a local woman gets married, local custom has her walk across these three bridges.

Qiantong Town 前童镇

A Classic East Zhejiang Small Town

Qiantong is located in the southwest part of Ninghai County in Zhejiang Province, and is one of the best-preserved small towns in east Zhejiang. Among the nearly 10,000 inhabitants, 90% share the family name Tong (童).

Qiantong Town, Ninghai County, Ningbo City, Zhejiang Province
浙江省宁波市宁海县前童镇
Nearest city: Hangzhou
Hangzhou Xiaoshan International Airport offers a wide selection of routes. Direct trains link Hangzhou to more than 20 cities, including a high-speed service from Shanghai that takes about 1 hour and 15 minutes.
Take a high-speed train from Hangzhou Railway Station to Ningbo Railway Station (about two hours). Proceed to Ningbo South Bus Station (宁波汽车南, a five-minute walk from Ningbo Railway Station), and take a bus to Ninghai West Bus Station (宁海汽车西站) or Ninghai South Station (宁海汽车南站, about one hour). From either of these locations, regular buses head to Qiantong Town directly, (about 30 minutes and 40 yuan).

There is an old cobblestone street in town flanked by wooden shop signs. Surrounding the street are blocks of exquisite and well-preserved ancient architecture, including the "Small Bridge Running Water House" (小桥流水宅), "Bright Lion Hall" (狮子明堂), Peaks House (群峰簪笏宅), Sustenance House (欣所寄宅), Gentry House (大夫第) and Cloth Pavilion (着衣亭). Each building is unique in its design, and most date from the Jiaqing and Daoguang reigns of the Qing (1796-1850). Delicate jumping fish gables and wallflowers demonstrate the unique styles of local craftsmen.

The Tong Family Clan Hall (童氏宗祠) was built in the Ming Dynasty, and includes an opera stage, a patio, several halls, and a courtyard. The main hall was built in Ming Dynasty style, but the hall's wooden shelves, drum-shaped and "shrouded basin" pillar foundations, and five-phoenix opera stage are distinctive. These styles originated around the year 500, and were popular in the Sui and Tang dynasties. Due to the village's remoteness, they were preserved into the Ming Dynasty.

Zhisiqi House (职思其居)was built in the Qing Dynasty, with the family motto "Pay as you earn, manage the household industriously and thriftily" (量入为出，勤俭持家) carved into its red steps. The courtyard is a two-storey quadrangle. The patio is spacious, and the cobblestone that covers the ground was designed to look as it the floor was paved by coins. The central hall is empty with no floor slabs, but on the main wall, the red card indicating a "pass" on the provincial civil service exam is still visible.

There are more than 500 household items at the village's Folklore Museum, including furniture, lamps, lanterns, pottery, and costumes. The museum traces the development of the country's cultural history from ancient to modern

The old cobblestone street and ancient buildings with green ivy, white walls and black tiles hint at the town's former prosperity

times.

Legend has it that the Tong family's ancestors piloted the waters from Baixi River into the village, building homes along the way. According to Taoist philosophy, the rippling stream should rush alongside every home, so that the people can wash their clothes and food. Thus Qiantong's homes sit riverside, linked together by cobblestone roads.

There is an ancient camphor tree in the eastern part of town. The large branches spread in five directions, and are known as the "five dragons". The tree is hollow inside, with an inner diameter of six metres, forming a natural wooden "cave" that can hold more than 10 people.

The Qiantong Yuanxiao Temple Fair (前童元宵行会), which dates back to the Ming Dynasty, is a day when everyone in the village bangs gongs, beats drums, and set off fireworks. It is the most traditional folk festival in Qiantong. Other local festivals include Huangyangshi (黄洋市, usually falls in late January), and the Lianghuangjie Temple Fair (梁皇街庙会, usually in April).

The fishing bird and an old man

Tofu Feast

The "tofu family feast" (豆腐家宴), glutinous rice cake (糍粑), and New Year cakes that are popular in Qiantong are all classic Jiangnan fare, but there are also local specialties such as steamed dumplings filled with minced meat and gravy (汤包), dried bean curd, chicken tea (鸡子茶), sticky rice dumplings (糯米园), meat wheat cake (肉麦饼), and wheat plaster (麦糊头).

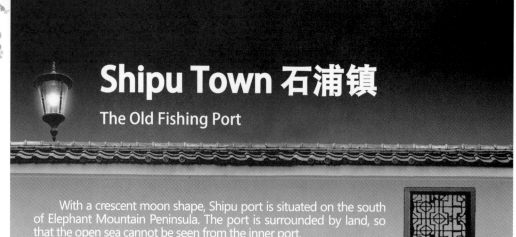

Shipu Town 石浦镇

The Old Fishing Port

With a crescent moon shape, Shipu port is situated on the south of Elephant Mountain Peninsula. The port is surrounded by land, so that the open sea cannot be seen from the inner port.

Shipu Town, Xiangshan County, Ningbo City, Zhejiang Province
浙江省宁波市象山县石浦镇
Nearest city: Hangzhou
Hangzhou Xiaoshan International Airport offers a wide selection of routes. Direct trains link Hangzhou to more than 20 cities, including a high-speed service from Shanghai that takes about 1 hour and 15 minutes.
Take a high-speed train from Hangzhou Railway Station to Ningbo Railway Station (about two hours). Ningbo South Bus Station (宁波汽车南站, a 5-minute walk from Ningbo train station) has direct buses heading to Shipu Town (about two hours).

Shipu Town has been strategically important throughout history, and as one of China's four main ancient fishing ports, it offers shelters, supplies, markets, and processing bases. A comprehensive defence system like the one in Shipu is rare in China. Dating back to the Yuan Dynasty, but especially from 1368, nearly 60 great military sites were set, creating a huge defence net along the coastal line. These military facilities were the "great steel walls" of an era without gunpowder.

Old weapon facilities, ancient city gates, and stone inscriptions all testify to former days of war. The most well-preserved emplacement is the one on Golden Pheasant Mountain (金鸡山), which guarded three directions. The Second Bay cliff side inscription is on the eastern crag of Second Bay in Shipu. Most inscriptions were engraved by military officers during the Sino-Japanese war in the Ming Dynasty, and express their firm resolve to fight their enemies.

Shipu Old Street (石浦老街) is a little run-down but pleasant, and includes Wanxing Street¡],ɹˌæµó), Fujian Street

One of the 4 largest fishing ports in China — Shipu Fishing Port

(富健街), Middle Street (中街), and Back Street (后街). The streets are all quite well-preserved. The stores have wooden walls, which contrasts with the brick-constructed homes in the alleys. This is actually a unique feature of coastal towns in the southern Yangtze region, and Shipu's Middle Street, constructed in the Ming Dynasty, is one of the best examples of the style.

Walking to the iconic Weng Castle (瓮城) you will come to Middle Street (中街), where you will see the God of War Temple (关帝庙). The temple's roof looks like a snow-covered mountain, and the beams and columns are beautifully carved and painted. Old shops line both sides of the street. The Yuansheng Money House's (源生钱庄) funny exhibit is entertaining and worth a visit. The basement of the Hongzhang Silk House (宏章绸庄) has an exhibit on the past prosperity of the silk house, featuring old photos from the area's formerly booming silk trade. The upper floor of the house is a workshop where 600 kinds of silk and 1,000 styles of Chinese buttons are made. The "All Go Spring" pharmacy (皆大春药店) allows visitors to experience the feel of an ancient Chinese medicine house. The Zaixing Cigarette House (栽兴烟宅) was actually a place for smoking opium, and has an exhibition of old paraphernalia. The segregated smoking rooms for the rich and poor remind visitors of the extreme class divisions in ancient China.

Built during the reign of the Hong Wu Emperor (1368-1398), the City God Temple (城隍庙) of Shipu is covered with delicate carvings and craftwork. It is one of the best-preserved large buildings from the Ming and Qing dynasties in the town. The edge of the opera platform in the temple looks like there are horns rising out of it, and has vivid carvings of characters from popular dramas.

A pleasant spot is the Royal City Beach (皇城沙滩), located in the northeast part of town. It houses fields of villas on the seashore, a market selling shells and seafood, and some old-style boats.

A rich culture has developed around Shipu's fishing industry over the centuries. Local fishermen pray to goddess Matsu, as well as worship Lord Guan (a general of the Three Kingdoms era), and the Dragon King (the ruler of the sea). Activities centred around fishing culture include "stepping on the beach" (三月三踏沙滩, usually late April or early May), the "welcome the gods competition" (六月六迎神赛会, usually late July or early August), and the "drifting sea lamps" event (七月半放海灯, usually in late August or early September). Locals also perform the ancient ceremony of making offerings to the sea.

Sandalwood Mountain

Tantou Mountain Island (檀头山岛), located in the east port of Shipu, is a unique tourist attraction. Natural views on the island are marvellous, and fragrant plants line the coasts. The island has earned the moniker "Sandalwood Mountain of China".

Fotang Town 佛堂镇

Hall of the Buddha

With an over 1,000-year history, Fotang Town became a prosperous commercial centre thanks to its broad trade network — derived from the development of water transportation on the Wu River - and the Shuanglin Temple.

Ancient China: Towns

Fotang Town, Yiwu City, Jinhua City, Zhejiang Province
浙江省金华市义乌市佛堂镇
Nearest city: Jinhua
Jinhua Yiwu International Airport has routes to a limited number of key Chinese cities. The city is also an intersection point for three railways lines.
The simplest way to reach the town from Jinhua is by taxi. You can hire a cab to Fotang Town directly from Jinhua Yiwu International Airport (金华义乌国际机场, about 30 minutes).

During the Ming and Qing dynasties, Fotang was a major regional trading port and distribution centre for agricultural products, and its well-developed port economy has bequeathed rich material and cultural legacies.

During the first year of the Liang Pu Emperor of the Southern Dynasty , the Indian monk Bodhidharma visited the Shuanglin Temple (双林寺) . According to legend, he used a chime stone to help locals cross the river when trapped by flooding. The decedents of the town built the Du Qing Temple, which indicates Bodhidharma's kindness for helping them cross the river.). The name of the town was then changed to Fotang, or "Hall of the Buddha".

The Qing Dynasty and Republic of China architecture on both sides of Fotang's ancient street are mostly two-storey wooden structures, whose carved wood and painted corridors are surrounded by elegant eaves. The twisting, narrow alleys preserve the appearance of the town as it was millennia ago.

The Moral Cultivation Hall (培德堂) is an ancient structure consisting of delicate wood, brick and stone

Fotang Temple

Seven Fairies Fotang

carvings located in the Tian Sixin Village area （田心四村）of Fotang. The hall was named by Lin Zexu, a Chinese official known for his efforts to eradicate the opium epidemic in the 19th century.

Hu Gong Palace (胡公殿) in Fotang is reputed as a location where Bodhidharma bathed, and the waters of the wells are still filled with a high-quality mineral spring. Lake Mountain Palace (湖山殿) is said to have once been used as a shelter for Zhu Yuanzhang, the first Emperor of the Ming Dynasty, to avoid enemies. After he became emperor, he ordered the palace to be built as a gift, naming it the "River-facing House".

Shuanglin Temple (双林寺), despite centuries of renovations, essentially belongs to the Ming and Qing dynasties. Along the main axis of the temple are dooryards with three entrances and 10 palaces. Buddha Palace （释迦殿） is the main hall of the front courtyard. There is a "mountain-style" roof that consists of gray tiles and the door lies in front of the middle erecting beam, called Ming Jian (明间). In the middle of the hall rests a stele in which four Chinese characters invoke the "spirit of a vulture" (灵鹫遗风).

Great Hero Treasure Palace (大雄宝殿), the tallest building on the temple grounds, is the second main hall. The roof of the hall has eaves topped by a long ridge, and under the eaves is the dougong (a system of brackets inserted between the top of a column and a beam in the hall).

More than 2,000 coloured clay sculptures are preserved in the temple. The artwork is impressive, covering a period from the Tang Dynasty to the Song, Liao, Jin, and Yuan dynasties. The most ancient stele preserved in the temple — the Stele of Gugu, is 1,400 years old.

The Buddha sculpture of Fotang

Fantan Town 皤滩镇

Hidden between Mountains and Water

Fantan Town, located in Taizhou City, is about 40 kilometres west of Xianju County. Fantan is also the meeting point of Wanzhu Creek, Zhumu Creek, Huang Yuken, Nine-city Port and Yongan Creek.

Ancient China: Towns

Pantan Town, Xianju County, Taizhou City, Zhejiang Province
浙江省台州市仙居县皤滩镇
Nearest ctiy: Hangzhou
Hangzhou Xiaoshan International Airport offers a wide selection of routes. Direct trains link Hangzhou to more than 20 cities, including a high-speed service from Shanghai that takes about 1 hour and 15 minutes.
Hangzhou East Bus Station (杭州汽车东站), a 20-minute taxi ride from Hangzhou Train Station (杭州火车站), has regular scheduled bus services to Xianju County (a three-hour trip). At Xianju County transfer to a bus to Hengxi Town (横溪镇), which will pass by Fantan Town (about 30 minutes). The admission ticket for the Ancient Street of Pantan costs 25 yuan; entrance to the Tongxiang Academy costs 20 yuan.

Today Fantan is peaceful — a town whose cobblestone streets are rose-coloured, the result of salt that was deposited on the ground hundreds of years ago. It is in many ways the quintessential ancient town of the southern regions of the Yangtze River, and is a valuable resource for studying the ups and downs of ancient towns in China.

Fantan has preserved its three-mile "dragon-shaped" ancient cobblestone street. The town is also home to many ancient residences built during the Tang, Song, Yuan, Ming, and Qing dynasties, as well as the Republic of China period. Their imposing presence and delicate structures make them typical examples of houses built for wealthy people in ancient China.

The town is also home to many steles — one of the most attractive hangs in Yihou Hall (贻厚堂), at the entrance of the south of the street's wall. The stele was given by scholar Zhang Ruozhen of Tong Chen School (桐城派) and is well-preserved, resting at the top of the middle hall. Another

stele that hangs above the front door of the hall reads in large and imposing Chinese characters "Luo She Ming Gao" (洛社名高), conveying to visitors the social position and good conduct of the owner of the house.

At the back of each ancient shops on Jiuqu Street (九曲古街) are residences, with a hall in the front and a quadrangle courtyard to the rear. Behind the courtyards are high dooryards, indicating the busy lives of Fantan's vendors.

Besides ancient shops, the old street also features the homes of literary families. The most outstanding of these are the Long Door House (长门堂) and He Family Inner Door House (何氏里门堂). The latter has a stele made of real gold that reads "university scholar" (大学士). The building consists of connected buildings and rooms encircled by corridors, carved beams and painted columns.

Tong River Academy (桐江书院), built during the Song Dynasty, is surrounded by mountains, clean water, and green forests with trees even older than the town. A scholar from the Southern Song Dynasty named the academy and sent his child to study here, and the academy earned a reputation in the southern Yangtze River region as the second-most prestigious academic institution there. The academy is now a popular local tourist attraction.

Fantan's Boneless Lantern Embroidery Festival (针刺无骨花灯) is a celebration of a unique Chinese craft. The lanterns are distinguished by a lack of any internal support, and are embroidered with the patterns of different flowers.

Fantan ancient street

Fantan Town

Bats and Fish

Fengshui has had a significant influence on the development of Fantan. On the gate of each ancient house in the town are arrangements of Chinese characters or decorations that have auspicious implications. Some feature bats, as the Chinese word for the animal is a homonym for a phrase that brings luck; deer, implying a high social position; or the character for "fish", which sounds similar to the word for "prosperity". All the images of animals are displayed in carvings or sculptures. Other decorations involve characters from local stories or plays.

YantouTown 岩头镇

Rock Head Town

Yantou Town boasts a history of half a millennium. It is laid out in blocks of buildings built to a standard pattern: three entrances and two courtyards. It is also known for its comprehensive irrigation system, making Yantou a valuable model of ancient village planning.

Yantou Town, Yongjia County, Wenzhou City, Zhejiang Province
浙江省温州市永嘉县岩头镇
Nearest ctiy: Hangzhou
Hangzhou Xiaoshan International Airport offers a wide selection of routes. Direct trains link Hangzhou to more than 20 cities, including a high-speed service from Shanghai that takes about 1 hour and 15 minutes.
Take a high-speed train from Hangzhou Station to Wenzhou Station (about three hours). Then take the No. 33 bus to Anlan Pavilion Port (安澜亭码头, 20 minutes), and then a ferry to Oubei Town (瓯北镇). Scheduled buses from the port will go to Yantou Town (one hour and 10 yuan). In the town it is possible to hire pedicabs for sightseeing tours of the town.

Yantou Town, or "Rock Head Town", was founded in the early Tang Dynasty. The town got its name from its location in front of three rocks where hibiscus grows. Among the more than 200 ancient villages and towns along the Nanxi River, Yantou is the only one that features comprehensive water conservancy infrastructure.

Yantou Village's main entrance is a door to the north, known as "Mercy Door" (仁道门). By the west side of Inner-Door Street is the Jin's Family Grand Ancestral Hall (大宗祠). Across the street is the stone Chastity Memorial Arch (贞节坊). In front of the ancestral hall is the magnificent Scholars' Archway (进士牌楼), granted by Ming Emperor Shizong (世宗) to the scholar Jin Zhao. It is a three-room, four-pillar wooden structure. The Mercy Door, Grand Ancestral Hall, Chastity Memorial Arch and Scholars' Archway form the ancient heart of Yantou Town.

The water storage dam in the eastern village was built in the years of Jiajing's rein, when local clan regulations stipulated that dams could only be used for growing flowers, planting trees, and building pavilions. Business activities were prohibited. During the Qing Dynasty, Yaotou's dam became a passing-through for dealers carrying salt on shoulder poles. By the end of the Qing Dynasty, a commercial street had developed around the dam, forming the 300-meter Beautiful Water Street (丽水街). Both sides of the street are lined by 90 two-storey shops; in front of the stores are eaves that protect pedestrians from both sun and rain. All the town's buildings face east, while the gates open to the west.

The well-known Tower Lake Temple Scenic Area (塔湖庙) is located to the south of Beautiful Water Street. The area contains lakes, one of which is home to Qin Island. Eight of Yantou's "10 Scenic Spots" are in this area: Long Spring Dam

The mist and rain of Yantou

(长堤春晓), Lotus-watching Bridge (丽桥观荷), "watching fish in clear water" (清沼观鱼), the Qin Island birds (琴屿流莺), "Tall, Green Pen Hill" (笔峰耸翠), "Autumn Moon in the Water Pavilion" (水亭秋月), "water surrounded by jade" (曲流环碧), and "moon's reflection in Tower Lake" (塔湖印月).

Perhaps the most special place in the ancient town is the country garden, which mainly consists of Beautiful Water Lake and Beautiful Water Street. Around the lake are tall hibiscus plants.

Beautiful Water Bridge was built with 48 long stone bricks, meaning Yantou is one of the "48 Cities" (四十八都). By the end of the bridge sits a mighty old banyan tree. Walking along the gallery to the Wind-riding Pavilion (乘风亭), on which an inscription reads, "autumn wind comes in the fifth month (of the lunar calendar), spring is not coming back". Further on is Greeting Officer Pavilion (接官亭), also known as Judgment Pavilion (评理亭), built in the Ming Dynasty. It is also known as the Flower Pavilion (花亭) due to the lotus pond south of Beautiful Water Street. There are four pillars in all, with a five-tiered arch that forms an octagon caisson, a visual metaphor of the five elements and eight trigrams in Chinese cosmology. Along with the eight spines of the double roof there are the statue "Old man Zhang Guolao riding a white donkey" (张果老骑白驴), as well as a portrait: "Liu Hai presents the money" (刘海献钱).

Water Pavilion Temple

The Water Pavilion Temple (水亭祠) is located in the southern section of Yantou's centre street. It was once the largest college along the Naxi River, but now only one hall remains. In front of the hall is a large pool, with a pavilion at its centre, and a 16-square-metre stone base remains. To the south of the pavilion is Tang Mountain (汤山), home to Wenfeng Tower (文峰塔), built at roughly the same time as the temple.

Yantou Ancient Town

Nianbadu Town 廿八都镇
The Twenty-Eighth City Town

Nianbadu Town is hidden in the mountains and remains largely unknown to the world. Preserving the town's ancient feel are Anhui-style horse-head walls, roofs and beams in the Zhejiang tradition, as well as Fujian-style walls, cobblestone streets, magnificent houses and temples, and elegant murals.

Ancient China Towns

Nianbadu Town, Jiangshan City, Quzhou City , Zhejiang Province
浙江省衢州市江山市廿八都镇
Nearest city: Hangzhou
Hangzhou Xiaoshan International Airport offers a wide selection of routes. Direct trains link Hangzhou to more than 20 cities, including a high-speed service from Shanghai that takes about 1 hour and 15 minutes.
Hangzhou South Bus Station (杭州汽车南站, a 15-minute taxi ride from Hangzhou Train Station), has about 10 scheduled buses a day to Nianbadu Town (three hours).

Nianbadu Town was once known as Daocheng (道成). During the Song Dynasty there were a total of 44 cities in Jiangshan (江山), and the town became known as the "28th City".

Roughly 1,100 years ago, military leader Huangchao sent troops south, opening a trail in the mountains between Zhejiang and Fujian. The 1,000-year-old trail became an important commercial route throughout the Qing Dynasty. Cloth and goods from Jiangsu and Zhejiang provinces were transported by road for delivery to Fujian and Jiangxi via 28th City Town.

Local products from Fujian and Jiangxi were also transported to Shanghai, Hangzhou and other cities. 28th City Town for hundreds of years enjoyed the status of the wealthiest business town in the border region of the three provinces.

However "28th City Town", due to its strategic significance, was often fought over bitterly and many armies have been stationed here throughout history.

Today, the town still has many well-preserved Ming and Qing dynasty buildings. On the Maple River (枫溪) Old Street, most stores are also merchants' houses, with stores up front and houses behind. The most striking of 28th City Town's stores are the Grand Station (大站) and Gatehouse (门楼). The residential style of the houses make their external walls appear large.

The Four Happiness Gate (happiness, richness, long-live and joy福禄寿僖) is quietly located on the old Maple River.

On Maple River Street there is also Peach Flower Lane (桃花弄), in which a house features three zigzagging courtyards. This was an embodiment of the principle that a successful businessperson should not show their riches; the design also offered added security during wartime. Now however, only three empty courtyards remain.

Maple River is the major artery of 28th City Town, and several ancient bridges cross it. The stone-arch Water Peace Bridge (水安桥) was built in 1864. Above the bridge are galleries and three double-eave pavilions with hollow windows facing in four directions.

Maple River Bridge (枫溪桥) has an even longer history than Water Peace Bridge. It is built from black bricks, offering exquisite carvings on its fences. At the nearby water port, the half-circle arch and its reflection form a full circle. As the water ripples, the sight evokes a bright full moon. Also on Maple River Bridge is Water Star Temple (水星庙), built in the seventh year of the Tongzhi reign of the Qing Dynasty. There is a

theatre stage in front, while behind is the Grand Hall of the Zhengwu Emperor (真武大帝) and representations of Taoist gods.

There are close to 150 surnames among the 10,000 inhabitants of 28th City Town. Throughout history, people from all over China have gathered here, bringing together dialects from various regions. Nine dialects from Zhejiang, Jiangxi, Fujian and Huizhou are in use in the town, making it a picture of China's linguistic variety. The differing dialects have led to the development of a local language spoken only in 28th City Town.

Immigrant Culture

The "immigrant culture" of 28th City Town is very different from other ancient towns. Popular in the town are traditional customs such as improvised folk songs, paper cutting, puppeteering, stilt-walking, and the building of dragon lanterns and boats. Dragon dances have been performed in the town for hundreds of years, with locals usually using paper dragons made up of seven or 13 parts.

Ancient covered bridge in 28th City Town

Sanhe Town 三河镇

The Commercial Corridor of Central Anhui

Sanhe Town, located along the junction of Hefei, Liuan and Chaohu, was originally called Magpie Coast. Three rivers — Happy Harvest River, ,Hang Port River, and Little South River - run through the town.

Sanhe Town, Feixi County, Hefei City, Anhui Province
安徽省合肥市肥西县三河镇
Nearest city: Hefei
There are two airports in Hefei — Hefei Luogang Airport (合肥骆岗机场) and Hefei Xinqiao International Airport (合肥新桥国际机场). Both offer a wide variety of domestic routes. High-speed rail routes are served by Hefei South Train Station (合肥高铁南站), while regular trains run from Hefei Station. From Hefei Bus Station (near Hefei Rail Station), regular buses depart for Sanhe Town (one hour and 10 yuan).

The town's main street is surrounded by water, and the ancient buildings that stand there are characterised by exquisite carved pillars. Outside the town wafts the sweet smell of rice flowers.

Sanhe has throughout history been a military target, and also a gathering place for businesspeople. It is home to the "Eight Ancients of Sanhe", including ancient streets, bridges, alleys, forts, houses, city walls, and teahouses.

The town has several bridges. The Little South River alone is crossed by nine bridges, including Jigong Bridge (济公桥), Natural Bridge (天然桥), Magic Turtle Bridge (仙龟桥), Three Countries Bridge (三县桥), Magpie Coast Bridge (鹊渚桥), Double Dragon Bridge (二龙桥), and Mosquito Free Bridge (无蚊桥). The most famous is Three Countries Bridge, also known as Stone Head Bridge (石头大桥), which features a three-pole stone arch. Moon-Watching Bridge (望月桥), meanwhile, is also called Dream Bridge (圆梦桥) — it is said that by each full moon wishes made there will come true.

Crane Cottage (鹤庐), located on the Ancient South Street, is the former residence of the Sichuan Governor Liu Bingzhang. In the display hall are some of the former governor's weapons, pictures and other documents and exhibits. Liu used to own hundreds of homes in Sanhe, but only this one remains and has been redecorated.

Also in the ancient town are the scenic spots of Liutong Xinglongzhuang (刘同兴隆庄), an old store; Quintessence House (国粹楼); Fairy House (仙姑楼), where the seven fairies who deliver children are worshiped; Xinyue Court (鑫樾阁); and Wannan Buddhist Temple (万年禅寺). Peach Blossom Island (桃花岛) is also a beautiful sight.

Sanhe has also made its mark in history as a spiritual place. Taiping army leader Chen Yucheng and Li Xiucheng fought the Qing army in the town, scoring the famous Sanhe victory. Now in the town are the remains of King Ying House (英王府), Victory Gate (大捷门), The Main Camp (大本营), Ancient Wall (古城墙), and Ancient Fort (古炮台).

Sanhe is also the birthplace of Lu Opera (庐剧), a style of Chinese opera local to Anhui Province. On holidays Lu Opera performances are common in Sanhe.

Water town

Anhui Cuisine

Sanhe food is based on Anhui-style cuisine. Recommended dishes include Sanhe shrimp paste (三河虾糊), crisp duck yuanbao (酥鸭元宝), and crispy chicken (八宝酥鸡). Fried rice dumplings (油炸粑粑) and fried shaomai (烧卖) are also popular.

Moon-Watching House

Riverside Streets

Xucun Town 许村镇

The Examination Village

Throughout history, Xucun Town has drawn poets and other literary figures. Li Bai, one of the most famous poets of the Tang Dynasty, once complimented the town poetically, writing: "Drifting in the water is the long sandy beach; elegant and quiet are the cliffs to the east and west".

Xucun Town, Shexian County, Huangshan City , Anhui Province
安徽省黄山市歙县许村镇
Nearest city: Huangshan
Huangshan Tunxi Airport offers connections to major cities across China. Huangshan Railway Station on the Jianxi-Anhui line is linked to regional centres such as Nanjing and Hangzhou.
From downtown Huangshan's Tunxi Bus Station (屯溪汽车, near Huangshan Railway Station), take a bus to Shexian Bus Station (歙县汽车站, about 40 minutes). Then transfer to a bus heading to Xucun Town (about 40 minutes and 40 yuan).

The origins of Xucun can be traced to the Eastern Han Dynasty, when it was named Fu Zili (富资里, or Rich Native Village). After the Tang Dynasty, the Xu family moved to the town, and it was later occupied mostly by their descendants. The village was thus renamed.

Xucun has been designed with fengshui in mind. Its history is marked by well-preserved ancient architecture from the Ming and Qing dynasties.

There are close to 200 ancient residences in Xucun, and many feature architecture from the Ming and Qing dynasties. These include Zhang House (章宅), Xu Shoushan House (许寿山宅), Xu Shengyuan House (许声远宅), Xu Jiaze House (许家泽宅), Xu Xianting House (许献廷宅), and Xu Shelin House (许社林民宅). There are also buildings typical of the Hui (微) style (a reference to Huizhou), as well as Horse-Head Walls — 马头墙; high walls that make like rearing horses.

At the entrance of the village lies the granite Shengping Bridge (昇平桥), built in the Ming Dynasty. Retrace your steps along Fang Creek and you will arrive at the centre of the village, where you can see Gaoyang Bridge (高阳桥), built in Yuan Dynasty, and the lanterns that are hung in its corridor. A Buddha throne is set inside, as well. Walk across the bridge, and the remnants of an ancient port can be seen.

Nearby is the Daguan Pavilion (大观亭), built during the reign of the Jiajing Emperor of the Ming Dynasty for the gathering of scholars. It is said that while standing on the pavilion one can see broad views of remote mountains, nearby rivers, farming fields and other ancient residences. To the north of the pavilion is the Five Horses Archway (五马坊). The archway features a well-preserved early Ming Dynasty pattern, making it an important specimen for the study of ancient architecture. Inside the village are many other

Gaoyang Bridge

Sword Games

Xucun's unique cultural activities include the Lion Dance（舞狮）; the Grass Dragon Dance on the 15th of the 8th month of lunar calendar, (八月十五舞草龙, usually in October); Performance of the Playing Sword (舞大刀); Festive Lanterns Appreciation （嬉花灯）and others. The Performance of the Playing Sword (舞大刀) is regarded as an expression of loyalty and success, and is also a perfect display of the artistry involved in martial arts.

A few minutes' walk from Five Horses Archway is a famous local place, Qiangli Door （墙里门）. The story of the town's ancestral hall has been recorded on the bricks of the door, and the hall is now a museum to the history of Xucun. Dabangbo (大邦伯祠堂), a branch of the hall built in the Ming Dynasty, consists of three dooryards and three doors.

The architecture of Yigeng Little School (仪耕小学堂) differs from that of surrounding buildings. It has three entrance doors and sweet osmanthus fully blossom inside its courtyard. On the stone steles is an introduction to the school's history: it was the first western-style institution built in Weizhou.

archways, including the Weisheng Archway (薇省坊), Sanchao Dianhan Archway (三朝典翰坊), Pure and Noble Archway (冰清玉洁坊), and Double Section Archway (双节坊).

Shengping Bridge

Wan'an Town 万安镇

Home of the Compass

Wan'an Town is home to the relics of Wang Wang Palace, which belonged to the Hui Lord-protector of the Tang Dynasty; and the Fairy Cave, once the hideout of the first Ming Dynasty emperor. Also well-known is the dragon boat festival held during the 5th month of the lunar calendar (usually May or June).

Wan'an Town, Huangshan City, Anhui Province
安徽省黄山市休宁县万安镇
Nearest city: Huangshan
Huangshan Tunxi Airport offers connections to major cities across China. Huangshan Railway Station on the Jianxi-Anhui line is linked to regional centres such as Nanjing and Hangzhou.
Buses from Tunxi Coach Station (屯溪汽车站, near Huangshan Railway Station) to Yi County (黟县) will pass by Wanan Town(2 yuan and 30 minutes). There is no entrance fee for Wanan Town, but a charge of 30 yuan is applied for the Ancient Stone City (古城岩).

Wan'an sits about 6 kilometres east of Xiuning County (休宁县). The water of the Heng River flows in the shape of a horse's hoof across the town, from west to east.

The town used to be one of the most important water and land ports in ancient Huizhou (微州). It developed along the Heng River (横江), the water of which flows east to eventually each the city of Hangzhou (杭州). Go west along the Heng River (横江) and pass Xiuning County (休宁县) and you will come to Dayi County Fishing Pavilion. The fishbone-shaped layout of the road system consists of commercial streets and busy lanes. Wan'an Old Street (万安老街) was the town's main street during both the Ming and Qing dynasties, receiving praise in a popular phrase: "Small is Xiuning County, Big is Wan'an Street".

Old Town Rock (古城岩), a chain of low-rising mountains that lies east of Wan'an, is known for its abundant ancient relics, historic inheritance and view of the "Morning Sun on Longevity Mountain" (寿山旭日). Today, people regard the rock as a cultural symbol of the history, customs and legends of Huizhou. Three ancient towers

Residence on Old Town Rock

Old Town Bridge (古城桥), also called Gaogong Bridge (高公桥), is situated below the Old Town Rock in the town's east. The bridge crosses the flowing water of the Heng River (横江) and reaches South Water Village (水南村). Together with nearby places of interest, the bridge makes for an elegant scene. Other bridges in the town are Wealth Bridge (富来桥), Carriage Bridge (轮车桥), and Guanyin Bridge (观音桥).

Usnea tea (松萝茶) finds its origins at Usnea Mountain (松萝山) in Wan'an's Blessing Temple Village (福寺村). The famous tea is one of the earliest to have been cultivated in China, earning prominence in the Ming Dynasty. Qing Dynasty poet Zheng Banqiao complimented the tea by writing: "Making a bottle of fresh Usnea Tea and sharing it with visitors that come to rest at night is the most delightful event".

Usnea leaves are thick, with clear leaf veins and a uniform green colour. After being mixed with water, the tea gives out a faint scent. It tastes bitter at first, but the aftertaste is savoury and mellow.

and four ancient bridges have been preserved in the town itself. The Old Town Tower (古城塔) on Old Town Rock is also known as Longevity Tower (万寿塔). The seven-storey tower's base is made from red granite, though its body consists mostly of bricks. The up-curling corners of its eaves are carved with patterns of flowers, grass and waves. The tower's top, which weighs about 2,400 kilograms, fell off in 1958.

Xunfeng Tower (巽峰塔), the best-preserved of Wan'an's towers, is located on the eastern side of Yuji Mountain (玉几山). It is 35 metres tall and also seven storeys; 168 steps spiral upward inside the tower, extending to its top floor. Its design evokes Buddhist pagodas from the Tang Dynasty. Murals in Xunfeng Tower are still clear enough to be recognized.

The final ancient tower is Fulang Tower (富琅塔), located at the front of Fulang Village (富琅村) and opposite Old Town Tower and Xunfeng Tower. Although its interior has been damaged, the structure of the tower remains exquisite, with well-arranged bricks and decorated eaves. On the Chinese characters indicate that the tower was built during the reign of the Wanli Emperor of the Ming Dynasty.

Compass

Wan'an also hosts the Wan'an compass, the only wooden compass still known to exist in China. Compass-making began in Wan'an in the late Yuan Dynasty and beginning of the Ming Dynasty, mostly developing during the latter and prospering in the middle of the Qing Dynasty.

Wan'an Carved Memorial Archway

Shuidong Town 水东镇

Home of Chinese Dates

The ancient town of Shuidong grew alongside the development of the Shuiyang River. The ancient granite streets of the town have been well preserved and the elegant Hui architecture of the Anhui Province area contrast to bring a poetic air to the town.

Shuidong Town, Xuanzhou District, Xuancheng City, Anhui Province
安徽省宣城市宣州区水东镇
Nearest city: Huangshan
Huangshan Tunxi Airport offers connections to major cities across China. Huangshan Railway Station on the Jianxi-Anhui line is linked to regional centres such as Nanjing and Hangzhou.
Take a train from Huangshan Station to Xuancheng Station (宣城站, three hours). Take a cab to Xuanchen West Bus Station (宣城汽车西站, 15 minutes. From there buses go to Ningguo City (宁国市) and will pass Shuitdong Town (40 minutes). Entrance to the ancient town is free, but there is a 15-yuan charge for Dragon-Spring Cave.

Shuidong is more than 1,100 years old, established in the Sui-Tang period. The town's name in Chinese means "east of the water". During the Ming and Qing dynasties, the town developed into a prosperous commercial port of the Shuiyang River (水阳江). The current preserved ancient street stretches for nearly 750 metres. It is home to other mazes of streets — including Up Street, Down Street, Front Street, Horizontal Street, Shopping Street, Wang Zi Street and Shen Family Alley — which crisscross and diverge to form the ancient Shuidong downtown area. On both sides of the granite streets are black bricks and tiles, wooden eaves, "horse-head walls" (high walls of local buildings with tops that look like a horse's rearing head), giving the town its unique look. Most of the large ancient houses are based on architecture from the Ming and Qing dynasties, with simple and balanced inner structures and artistic decorative carvings on columns. The most representative pieces of architecture are the Mansion of Da Fu (大夫第), referring to a senior official in feudal China), Wulong Yard (乌龙院), Fireproof Bell Tower (防火钟楼), Wangtong Hair Oil Workshop (汪同发油坊), and Qing Changren Pawnshop (庆昌仁当铺.

At the entrance to the ancient streets is the oldest temple in Xuanzhou (宣州), Ningdong Temple (宁东寺, also known as Three Officers Palace 三官殿), built in the Tang Dynasty. The 18 Steps (十八踏) and Five Wells (五道井) are the most unique historic relics on the street. An elegant two-storey archway sets the 18 Steps, under which is a square-shaped ancient well made from black brick. The well is connected to a pond more than 20 metres

long.

The Saint Maria cathedral, located on the ancient street,

Xiaohu Village

Shuidong's Ancient Street

is a Gothic building that covers an area of 700 square metres. One of the two largest cathedrals in China's six eastern provinces, the Saint Maria is laid out in the shape of a cross. Its inner structure consists of bricks and wood, giving a sense of antiquity and elegance. There are two important days in the cathedral each year: "Help of Christians" and "Patron Saint Mary", both occasions on which Christians from nearby cities including Shanghai (上海), Hefei（合肥）, and Wuhu（芜湖）attend ceremonies there. The influence of the ceremony extends to parts of Southeast Asia as well.

Green Mountain Dragon Spring Cavern (碧山龙泉洞) is located at Green Mountain (碧山), which lies 6 kilometres east of the town. Experts say that the Dragon Spring formed into limestone caverns roughly 3 million years ago. Outside the spring cavern is a mountainous area consisting of greenery accompanied by the sound of a bubbling spring. Travel services including cafeterias, tea houses, and hostels have been set up, set in the flourishing woods and tall bamboo.

The ancient Dongsheng Xiaohu Village (东胜小胡村) lies about 8 kilometres south of Shuidong. Its design is reflective of Song Dynasty architecture — construction with wood, black bricks, and gray tiles.

The mouth of Dragon Spring Cavern

Gourmet Dates

Shuidong is also known as "Home of Dates" (枣乡). The famed Shuidong green date can be traced back to the Ming Dynasty, while the "golden amber date" (金丝琥珀枣) has been frequently regarded as a gourmet treat.

Maotanchang Town 毛坦厂镇

A Water Town in the Mountains

It is said that after Zhu Yuanzhang, the first emperor of the Ming Dynasty, had taken Nanjing and enthroned himself in the early Ming Dynasty, he ordered war horses to be kept in towns around Suwan (Jiangsu and Anhui provinces today) as a defence against the riders from a county to the north.

Maotanchang Town, Jin'an District, Liuan City, Anhui Province
安徽省六安市金安区毛坦厂镇
Nearest ctiy: Hefei
There are two airports in Hefei — Hefei Luogang Airport (合肥骆岗机场) and Hefei Xinqiao International Airport (合肥新桥国际机场). Both offer a wide variety of domestic routes. High-speed rail routes are served by Hefei South Train Station (合肥高铁南站), while regular trains run from Hefei Station.
Each day two buses head to Maotanchang Town from Hefei Tourism Bus Station (合肥旅游汽车站, located beside Hefei Train Station). The services depart at 8:00 and 15:00, and take 2.5 hours.

Maotanchang Town lies at the southern end of Jian District in Liuan City, 100 kilometres from Hefei City. There was at the time an open grassy plain in the mountain area of southern Liuan that served as a perfect herding area. Following the Emperor's orders, officers set up stud farms there and named the place "Maotanchang" (茅滩厂), meaning "stud farm on a grassy breach". Later, "Maotanchang" (毛坦厂) was adopted as a homophone for the original and has been used ever since.

On Maotanchang's Old Street (老街), from the Ming and Qing dynasties, are some of the best preserved ancient residences in western Anhui. Two watchtowers stand on either side of the street, which runs 1,000 metres from south to north. Though already beaten by the weathering of wind and rain, their past glory can still be gleaned from the grand frames that remain. The moss-mottled cobblestone path, with ancient Ming and Qing pavilions lined on either side, looks like a deep valley. The crowded market, on the other hand, can evoke scenes of a noisy medieval castle.

One of the most important ancient buildings in Mantanchang, the Tu Ancestral Hall (涂氏祠堂) is said to have been built by Tu Zongying, a famous minister from the late Qing Dynasty, in the classical style of Hui Zhou architecture. The structure applied a design rarely used among ancestral halls, with a familial ancestral temple in the front and public temple behind. The hall's compact layout, as well as its beams and columns carved with delicate patterns, are splendid.

The Zhang Family War Museum

A Pavilion

was built in Tu Ancestral Hall more than 50 years ago in memory of a successful strategic counteroffensive made by Communist Party luminaries Liu Shaoqi and Deng Xiaoping. The main Ancestral Hall still stands in the back courtyard and houses "red" relics.

Newly built in the hall is the Dabie Mountain Folk Custom Museum, which introduces local trade and industry, culture, food, and folk arts, vividly representing the life and work of people in west Anhui.

The Integrity and Piety Chamber (节孝坊) is a token of the glory of the Tu (涂) family. Characters on the chamber are carved in a unique style: the Imperial Edict plaque hanging on top of the chamber uses the Yang engraving (relief) method; characters bulge out from the plaque. Poetic couplets on both sides of the chamber use the Yin engraving method, with characters incised into the surface. Characters used in the main hall of the chamber, however, are carved using a combination technique known as "yin and yang" engraving, with the edges of the strokes incised into the surface and the middle stroke bulging out.

Operatta is a traditional form of entertainment still enjoyed by residents of Maotanchang. During their leisure time, small groups of townspeople head to the local theatre, carrying their own seats. When excited by a performance, audience members leave money in front of the stage. Dragon Lanterns and Lion Dances are also among local favourite cultural activities.

A View of the East Stalagmite Scenic Region

Rooftops of Maotanchang

Mighty Stalagmite

The East Stalagmite Scenic Region (东石笋风景区) located 15 kilometres to the south of Maotanchang, is a major travel destination. Among the towering mountains, crisscrossing brooks, tall ancient trees, and the unbroken green sea of bamboo, there is a famous spectacle known as the most impressive stalagmite in China. It is a striking 38 metres tall, in the shape of a sharp sword pointing to the heavens.

Zhujiajiao Town 朱家角镇
Venice in Shanghai

The ancient town of Zhujiajiao is located at the west end of Shanghai, and sits next to beautiful Dianshan Lake. Surrounded by lakes and crisscrossing rivers, it is a typical water town of southern China, with a long history.

Zhujiajiao Town, Qingpu District, Shanghai
上海市青浦区朱家角镇
Nearest city: Shanghai
Shanghai is served by Pudong International Airport and Hongqiao Shanghai Airport. Shanghai Station is the city's main rail terminus, with services to around 70 cities in China. Trains to Hangzhou leave from the South Station.
Take the No. 4 bus from Shanghai Stadium (上海体育场) to Zhujiajiao Town directly (about one hour). Another option is a special tourist bus that you can take from the south side of People Square (Pu'an Road,普安路), which stops at Zhujiajiao Town (about one hour).

Markets formed in Zhujiajiao during the Song and Yuan dynasties, and the town boomed in the Wanli Years of the Ming Dynasty. It developed into a commercial centre following the end of the Qing Dynasty. In the Republic of China period, its rice business became so prosperous that the river was jammed every harvesting season with ships carrying rice.

Known as "the best Ming and Qing dynasty street in Shanghai", Grand North Street in the central area of Zhujiajiao harbours a collection of typical structures from the two dynasties. Grand North Street lies along the Caogang River near "Release Bridge".

In ancient times merchants gathered here and brought here with them "business that beats all other towns". Teahouses, wine bars, grocery stores, rice shops and butcher shops sprung up and there was said to once be 1,000 shops on a 3-kilometre street. Many vintage stores can still be found in the streets, such as the century-old Han Dalong Sauce Store (涵大隆酱园), newly opened vintage restaurant Mao Sun Place (茂荪馆), and "Ancient Town Vintage Teahouse" (古镇老茶馆), often called the best teahouse in suburban Shanghai.

Local dishes include chestnut and meat dumplings (黄栗肉粽), bound braised pork (红烧扎肉), spiral shells, scented alfalfa with rice wine (酒香草头), green peas, peanuts with bamboo shoots (笋香花生), and salted shrimp (盐水虾).

There are also traditional workshops and a dazzling array of shops selling craft products such as ceramics, works of calligraphy and Chinese traditional paintings, as well as food.

Yet water is the soul of the ancient town. The nine long

Study and Cultivation Garden

good by releasing captive animals". According to the rules fixed by a Buddhist monk called Xing Chao, no fishing is allowed under the bridge. It is a place where fish and turtles should be sent back to their homes in nature.

Other famous bridges in the town are the triple-arch "Nine Peaks Bridge" (九峰桥) and the high-arch Taian Bridge (泰安桥).

The Garden of Study and Cultivation (课植园) located by West Well Street (西井街) in the north of Zhujiajiao offers serenity and beauty. Its name suggests that one should "never abandon cultivation between studying time". The exquisite design and well-proportioned arrangement make the garden a prime example of private garden design.

streets along the crisscrossing rivers and the numerous branches of the Caogang River extend in a shape not unlike an open folding fan. Every household in the town can be visited by boat, hence its nickname: the Venice of Shanghai. Most homes are constructed with bricks and wood, sitting near rivers and bridges. Some even rest on the water itself. These homes are "suspended" midair over the rippling water.

A total of 36 bridges were built in this ancient town during past dynasties; the biggest is the "Release Bridge", the largest five-arch stone bridge in the Yangtze Delta region. As its name implies, it is known as a place where people "do

Qing Post Office

The Zhujiajiao Qing Post Office (大清邮局) is the best-preserved Qing Dynasty post office in eastern China. Many visitors take photos and send them to their families or friends through the postal service.

Bridge on the Caogang River

Fengjing Town 枫泾镇

Gate in the Southwest

Fengjing is a typical southern Chinese ancient town. Rivers and alleyways crisscross Fengjing, dividing the town into 29 blocks. It houses serene water, bridges, and trees.

Fengjing Town, Jinshan District, Shanghai
上海市金山区枫泾镇
Nearest city: Shanghai
Shanghai is served by Pudong International Airport and Hongqiao Shanghai Airport. Shanghai Station is the city's main rail terminus, with services to around 70 cities in China. Trains to Hangzhou leave from the South Station.
From Shanghai Southwest Bus Station (上海西南汽车站) take the "Feng-Mei Line"(枫梅线) to Fengjing Town (about 45 minutes).

Fengjing Town lies in the southwest of the greater Shanghai area; Fengjing is more than 1,500 years old. It was initially formed as a village in the Song Dynasty, and reached the size of a town during the Yuan Dynasty. Because of its location at the joining of the Wu and Yue (vassal states in the Spring and Autumn Period), Fengjing has been referred to as the "Gate in the Southwest" of Shanghai, leading to the provinces of the country's southwest.

With four well-preserved ancient streets — Peaceful Street, Production Street, Grand North Street, and Friendship Street — Fengjing is a large and intact ancient water town. It features numerous bridges on crisscrossing rivers, including Cool Breeze Bridge, Bamboo Path Bridge, and Bei Feng Bridge, which together form a line.

Like the preface of a great work, the Fengjing Memorial Archway (枫泾牌坊) provides a basic introduction to Fengjing's rich history and culture. Throughout history, half of the ancient town belonged to Jiangsu Province, while the other

"Two bridges in three strides and ten alleys in a single glance".

The ancient stage in Fengjing

half lay in the jurisdiction of Zhejiang Province. These boundaries were clearly demarcated by two landmarks: the boundary river to the west and the archway to the east.

Walking out of the History and Culture Exhibition Museum (枫泾历史文化陈列馆), you will step into the Fengjing Corridor (枫泾长廊), a structure typical of water-centred towns in China. The corridor stretches for 300 metres from the Zhihe Bridge in the south to the Bamboo Walk Bridge, connecting the corridor on Production Road. It used to be the most prosperous commercial strip in the Wu and Yue region, often sheltering vendors and shoppers from heavy rain and the scorching sun.

Continuing north along the Fengxi Corridor (枫溪长廊), you will arrive at the North Town Tourist Area. There, Production Road Corridor will greet you first. The neat and broad walkway extends to the east along the Fengjing City River. To its south are scenic spots like the Ancient

Stage, where traditional opera performances are shown every morning and afternoon, and East Region Fire Committee (火政会), an early-modern fire station.

Past the Taiping Bridge is Peaceful Street (和平街). To its north is the Family Exhibition Hall of Peasant Paintings, the original site of a People's Commune, and the 300 Garden (三百园), a grand household built in the Song Dynasty. The garden is a record of its owner, Chen Shunyu.

Following Peaceful Street westward and walking past the Beifeng Bridge, you will arrive at a street filled with manual workshops — North Grand Street (北大街). The manual workshops in Fengjing's North Grand Street provide visitors a chance to understand how clothing, weaving and iron forging were carried out in times past, and how herbal medicines and various instruments were made.

Also near the street is King Shi's Temple (施王庙). The king, originally known as Shi Quan, was a solider under the command of Southern Song Dynasty general Yue Fei.

Fengjing has a colourful variety of folk activities. Among them are trotting horse lanterns (a lantern adorned with a revolving circle of paper horses), stilts shows, and folk songs and stories. The Lantern Riddle Art Festival is held in the first month of the lunar year (late January or early February), and the unique weddings of the Wu and Yue area can usually be seen in the ninth month (usually October).

Fengjing is also called "feasting town" for its unique food culture. The "four teasures" of Fengjing — diced pig's feet (枫泾丁蹄), golden maple yellow wine (金枫黄酒), scented dry tofu (天香豆腐干), and zhuangyuan cake (枫泾状元糕) — all make for good eats.

Cartoons

The Ding Cong Cartoon Exhibition Museumn (丁聪漫画陈列馆) is near Peaceful Street. Born in 1916, Ding Cong was one of China's most famous cartoonists. His caricatures were published in newspapers and magazines under his pen name, "Ding Jr".

Jiading Town 嘉定镇

Ancient Garden Town

On the top of the Fahua Pagoda, built in the Song Dynasty, you can glimpse a picture of the whole of Jiading Town. Beside the pond is Kuixing Tower, characterised by multi-layer eaves.

Jiading Town, Jiading District, Shanghai
上海市嘉定区嘉定镇
Nearest city: Shanghai
Shanghai is served by Pudong International Airport and Hongqiao Shanghai Airport. Shanghai Station is the city's main rail terminus, with services to around 70 cities in China. Trains to Hangzhou leave from the South Station.
The special Jiading bus line (嘉定专线) from Chengdu North Road (at the crossing of Nanjing West Road,南京西路路口) or the Hujia Special bus Line (沪嘉专线) that departs from the Southwest of People Square (人民广场) will both take you to Jiading Town Bus Station (嘉定客运中心).

The north-south Hengli River crosses the east-west Lianqi River in the centre of Jiading Town. The two rivers and the ring-shaped moat form a "cross and ring" pattern that is rare in towns south of the Yangtze River. Signs of human activities have been discovered from even before the Spring and Autumn and Warring States periods.

The Ancient City Wall of Jiading (嘉定古城墙) sits by the Jiading Moat. First built in the Song Dynasty, the remaining wall is about 240 metres long and divided into two parts — the south gate (南门) and west gate (西门). It is the longest and most well-preserved ancient city wall in Shanghai. The west gate includes Xishui Pass (西水关).

In the centre of the town is Zhouqiao Old Street (州桥老街). It is the "root of Jiading" and the most prosperous old block, surrounded by ancient towers, temples and gardens from the Song, Yuan, Ming and Qing dynasties.

The Jiading Confucius Temple (官方译法嘉定孔庙) was first built in the Southern Song Dynasty. It is now part of the Shanghai Museum of the Chinese Imperial Examination System (官方译法中国科举博物馆), a museum dedicated to China's imperial examination. Along the Huilongtan Pond (官方译法汇龙潭) are stone columns with carvings of 72 different

Jiading bamboo carving

lions, representing Confucius' 72 best students. In front of the temple's Dacheng Gate (大成门) are seven turtle pedestals, on which stands a large stone tablet recording the history of the temple's construction, going back to the 13th century. The temple contains an examination room that allows people to see firsthand how the imperial examination system worked. The Shanhu Academy in the temple vividly recreates scenes from an imperial examination.

Hidden by trees on the nearby mountain is the Siyi Pavilion (四宜亭), an aesthetic response to the decorative archway of the lecture hall of the Confucius Temple.

Walk out of the Confucius Temple and cross Binxing Bridge, built in the Song Dynasty, and you arrive at Huilongtan Park (官方译法汇龙潭公园) on No. 299 Zhentacheng Street. The park has become famous for the Huilongtan Pond that sits in front of it. Dredged in the Ming Dynasty, it was named Huilong ("converging dragons") because five rivers, like zigzagging dragons, converge at the pond. The park also houses historical sites and cultural relics such as stone pavilions and towers from the Song, Yuan, Ming and Qing dynasties

Located at No. 314 Dingzhen East Street, Qiuxia Garden (官方译法秋霞圃) is one of Shanghai's five classical gardens. It used to be the private garden of the mansion of Gong Hong, Minister of Works of the Ming Dynasty.. The garden is designed artistically and delicately

Fahua Pagoda

with pavilions, buildings, ponds, paths, trees, bamboos, bridges, springs, and stones.

Dongdajie Street's Jiading Chenghuang Temple (官方译法嘉定城隍庙) is named after Chenghuang, the god of water and earth that defends the town, according to Taoist doctrine. The temple was built in 1218, the same year that Jiading was officially named a county. The temple's design, with conjoined halls and separate roofs, is rare among ancient temples in southern China.

Bamboo

Jiading bamboo carving has a long history and is a treasure of Chinese engraving arts. According to records, bamboo carving began in the Ming Dynasty and developed into two major centres — Jiading and Jinling.

The meshing of manmade and natural landscapes in Huilongtan Park.

Xinchang Town (Shanghai) 上海新场镇

Little Suzhou

During the Yuan Dynasty, local salt works were moved to Shisun Beach, since renamed Xinchang Town. Experts have described Xinchang as an "ecological museum of the aboriginal Pudong people".

Xinchang Town, Pudong New Area, Shanghai
上海市浦东新区新场镇
Nearest city: Shanghai
Shanghai is served by Pudong International Airport and Hongqiao Shanghai Airport. Shanghai Station is the city's main rail terminus, with services to around 70 cities in China. Trains to Hangzhou leave from the South Station.
Take Express Bus Line 4 from Pudong Bailingjing Bus Station(浦东白莲泾汽车站), or the Longdong Express Line from the Longyang Road Metro Station(龙阳路地铁站). Both stop at Xinchang Town (40 minutes and 30 minutes, respectively).

The names of several places in Shanghai's Pudong area have something in common: the names Liuzao (six stoves), Ertuan (two regiments), and Sandun (three groups) are all related to salt.

According to records, the land on which Xinchang Town is built on was reclaimed roughly 1,300 years ago, in the mid-Tang Dynasty. During the Song and Yuan dynasties, Xinchang gradually developed into a town. The attractions of the town for visitors include stone arch bridges featuring exquisite carvings, traditional homes by the river, tall stone walls, saddle bridges, and the Shisunli archway.

First built in the Kangxi reign of the Qing Dynasty, Qianqiu Bridge (千秋桥) was originally known as Zhangyi Bridge. The arch of the bridge reaches 6 metres high. Couplets are engraved on both the north and south sides of the bridge. "May more good people be born, may more good things be done", says the one facing south. "Helping others to help yourself, planting virtues to harvest fortune", reads the other.

The stone quay walls differ from those of other water towns. First, they are much older. The walls — stretching over 2,000 metres — were built in the Yuan, Ming and Qing dynasties. They are also continuous: from Baoqiao Port to Hongqiao Port, the quay walls at the east bank of the Houshi River are hardly broken. The walls' stone "ox noses", also called "lead cows", used to tie ships safely to shore, are delicately inscribed with various patterns.

The Xi Family Hall (奚家厅) on Hongdong Street was built in the late Ming and early Qing. There are four yards, three of which still have gates featuring elegant carvings. Yet the Pan Family House (潘氏住宅) on No. 302 Xinchang Big Street has a completely different style. The house has five yards, each with a patio. It houses gold-painted wood columns in its main hall and spectacular fireproof walls on both sides.

No. 1 Teahouse (第一楼茶园), beside the Hong Bridge, was built in the late years of the Tongzhi reign of the Qing Dynasty. It was originally a bungalow that was made into a three-storey building in 1916. The first floor used to be a restaurant, while the second floor provided performance rooms and the third housed the bedrooms. There are still performances today and tea is sold for just 2 yuan per person. Some tables and chairs are almost 100 years old. Looking down from the teahouse, you can see striking views of the town with its "bridges, rivers and households".

The Guo Family Temple (郭家庙) is located at No. 6 Station Road. First built in the Ming Dynasty, 12 halls remain following several

reconstructions. The main hall enshrines the East Mountain Emperor and other gods, such as the Dragon King, Town God, Guanyin, Zhaotian, and Sanguan. There are two remaining Chan Tings (忏亭) — tall pillar decorations assembled with high-quality timber — that are over 140 years old. Painted with gold, the Chan Tings are valued for the skills employed to achieve their intricate relief sculptures, suspended carvings and casting carvings.

Nanshan Temple (南山寺) in Xinchang was built in the Yuan Dynasty. The two ginkgo trees behind the temple are almost 700 years old. The 670-year-old Leiyin Temple (雷音寺), meanwhile, has experienced many boughts of turmoil. Some of its halls remain nevertheless. The Leitan Bridge (雷坛桥) in the south has also witnessed a similar history.

The old houses, streets, and ancient style of Xinchang have attracted film directors and producers: the Ang Lee film Lust, Caution — based on a novel by Chinese writer Eileen Chang — was partly shot in the town.

Qianqiu Bridge

The Ancient Town of Xinchang

巴 蜀 古 镇
Bashu Towns
(Sichuan and Guizhou)
Mountains and Legends

Huanglongxi Town 黄龙溪镇

The Yellow Stream Hiding A Dragon

"The 1,000-year-old banyan tree covers the ancient temple, you will hear the sound of the bell and drum in the night. The charming jade trees and bright moon makes travellers forget their way home," reads an ancient poem about Huanglongxi .

Huanglongxi Town, Shuangliu County, Chengdu City, Sichuan Province
四川省成都市双流县黄龙溪镇。
Nearest city: Chengdu
Chengdu Shuangliu International Airport is the busiest airport in Central and Western China. The city is also a major rail terminus with four railway stations.
From New South Gate Bus Station (新南门车站, a 20-minute taxi ride from Chengdu Train Station成都站) there are direct buses to Huanglongxi Town (10 yuan and one hour). If you start from Huayang Transit Centre Station (华阳客运中心, an hour's drive from Chengdu train station), you can take the No. 1821 bus to Huanglongxi Town (about 50 minutes.)

Huanglongxi is located 40 kilometres south of Chengdu next to the Fu River (or Jin River) in the east. The town's history can be traced back to the year 216. An old proverb said, "The yellow stream running with the clear Jin River looks like it is hiding a dragon," hence the town became known as Huanglong ("yellow dragon"). The prime minister of the Shuhan Kingdom (221-263), Zhu Geliang (a legendary military strategist of the Three Kingdoms period) made Huanglongxi the starting point for his famed southern expedition, and massive forces were stationed here as he prepared to consolidate the Shu Kingdom.

Huanglongxi is made up of seven old streets. The main street is the most well-preserved and bustling of the seven. In the middle of it is an open boat mooring site where you can see a large banyan tree on the opposite bank. Under the

Yamen (buildings for ancient feudal officials) of three counties

tree, there is an open-air teahouse. At both ends of the main street there are temples, the northern one is called Zhenjiang Temple (镇江寺), and the southern one is Gulong Temple (古龙寺).

Zhengjiang Temple is at the north end of the main street, and is built on the site of a 1,000-year-old wharf. Walk down the stone steps on the right side and you will see the running Jin River. Zhenjiang Temple was called the "Lord Temple" in the early Qing Dynasty, and locals believed worshipping there helped protect them from floods.

Gulong Temple, located on the south end of the main street, consecrates the Dragon Emperor (Huanglong). The front gate is low-rise, but after you enter it, there are magnificent halls, exquisite pagodas, an old government office, and a spacious courtyard. There are two big banyan trees on the grounds that are each more than 800 years old. Their thick trunks require 10 people to embrace, and a miniature temple has been constructed on the branches.

A 300-year-old stage called Wanniantai (万年台, meaning a stage with a long history) is located at the entry of Ancient Dragon Temple (古龙寺), and is relatively well-preserved. A Qing-era wooden stage is a rare site in Sichuan

Ancient China: Tow

Huanlongxi houses with wooden columns, grey-green tiles and hanging eaves, constructed during the Ming and Qing dynasties

Province. In the middle of the roof ridge sits a representation of the Maitreya Buddha between some ornamental figures of fish and dragons. The stage was traditionally used for thanking the gods and entertaining guest.

Another symbol of the town are the teahouses which seem to be everywhere. The tables, chairs, and stools are often all made from bamboo and the atmosphere is relaxed, making them a great place for a mid-afternoon break.

The most well-known and traditional cultural activity in Huanglongxi is the Dragon Lantern Burning (烧火龙) held during the Chinese New Year (in late January or early February). The festival dates back to the Southern Song Dynasty and has a history of more than 800 years. Now it attracts visitors from all over the world.

Old houses built on the riverbanks

During the Dragon Lantern Burning, there are a number of other shows and activities going on in the town, including dragon burning (烧火龙), dragon dancing (彩龙), lion dancing (南狮表演), river lantern floating (漂河灯), Kongming Lantern Burning (燃放孔明灯), fireworks and firecracker shows, Sichuan operas and so on and so forth. The festivities were described in the poem Shangyuan Ye (上元夜, The Sparkling Night of the Lantern Festival) by Cui Ye (崔液, a Chinese poet in the Tang Dynasty). "On seeing the moon, everyone stops to appreciate it, and on seeing the lanterns, everyone is lost in its sparkling beauty" (谁家见月能闲坐，何处闻灯不看来).

Serious About Tea

For the locals, having tea is as essential as having meals, and the tea ritual is taken seriously. Locally grown jasmine is often added to the tea. In some of the teahouses, excellent Sichuan green teas are served, such as zhuyeqing (竹叶青), e'mei xuerui (峨眉雪蕊). The teas are generally inexpensive, at around 2 to 3 yuan.

Luodai Town 洛带镇

The Western China Hakka Town

The well-preserved streets of Luodai Town harbour groups of Hakka dwellings and provincial guildhalls in the styles of the Ming and Qing dynasties, and 1,000 years of history and diverse culture are waiting to be slowly savoured by you in the misty western Chinese drizzle.

Luodai Town, Longquan District, Chengdu City, Sichuan Province
四川省成都市龙泉驿区洛带镇
Nearest city: Chengdu
Chengdu Shuangliu International Airport is the busiest airport in Central and Western China. The city is also a major rail terminus with four railway stations.
From Luodai Transit Centre Station (洛带汽车站, a 40-minute taxi ride from Chengdu Station), take the No. 1219 bus to Luodai Town (two stops). You can also hire a taxi directly from the train station to Luodai town (about one hour).

Located about 18 kilometres east of Chengdu, Luodai was originally known as Zhenzichang (甄子场) and its current name has a tale hiding behind it. The town once boasted a well, named Bajiao Well (八角井). Carp from the east lived in the water and people believed that whoever ate the carp could achieve longevity. Once, the King of the Shu Kingdom Liu Chang came to seek the mysterious carp but fell into the well by accident. Fortunately, he was saved, but his jade belt was lost in the well. Therefore, the town was renamed Luodai Town (Dropped Belt Town).

There are two major types of Hakka dwellings in Luodai: ancestral homes and common houses. Located at No. 15 Dafu Mansion Lane, the Dafu Mansion (大夫第) is the ancestral home of the Wu family (巫), and is the oldest and best-preserved Hakka dwelling in Luodai Town. Built late in the reign of the Emperor Qianlong (1711-1799) and the early reign of Emperor Jiaqing (1796-1820), the house was given the name Dafu Mansion in honour of its early owner Wu Zuojiang, who was awarded the posthumous title of Fengzhi Dafu (a senior official post in dynastical China) by the emperor after his death. The hall and garden of the mansion have been destroyed, but the main buildings of this mansion still stand in good condition.

The common dwellings in Luodai are simple but elegant. They are single quadrangle courtyards with two principal halls. There is an area for drying things in front of the door and a courtyard inside the walls. Directly behind the courtyard is the central hall. With a good natural draft and lighting, the homes are cool in summer and warm in winter.

Hakka people in Luodai, originally coming from Guangdong, Hubei, Jiangxi,

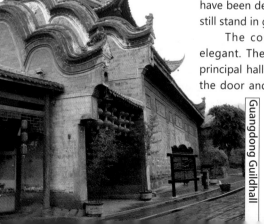

Guangdong Guildhall

The Five-Phoenix Tower

north of Sichuan, and other places, still adhere to their traditions, customs, and use their native language even after many generations, which makes them distinctive among Sichuan people. Many Hakka-style guildhalls have been well-preserved.

Among these guildhalls, the largest was built by Hakka people originating from Guangdong in 1746. Known as Nanhua Palace (南华宫), it is an important landmark in Luodai. Its main structure consists of an opera stage, musical building, side buildings, and three halls lined up in a row. With its double quadrangle courtyard structure and the only fire-sealed style building in Sichuan, the whole hall is splendid and magnificent. The stone couplets in the hall, which are beautifully written and demonstrate exquisite calligraphy and carving skills, are still in good condition.

Located on Xia (Lower) Street (下街), Huguang Guildhall (湖广会馆) was built in 1746 by Hakka people originating from Hunan and Hubei. Because it also serves as a temple dedicated to the ancient King Dayu, it is also known as Dayu Palace. The hall has a solemn and magnificent door. Entering the hall, you will see an opera stage at the hall's focal point, wing rooms on the left and right sides, a main hall under the stage and a spacious courtyard in the middle.

Hakka Park (客家公园), located on Park Lane,

was originally built in 1928. Its main structures include four halls, three pavilions, one ancestral temple and a lake. The most distinctive building in the park is the Lady's Teahouse, which specialized in services for Hakka women. The original Lady's Teahouse no longer exists, but a big teahouse for both sexes has been built on the same site.

Opened in March 2003, the Sichuan Hakka Museum (四川客家博物馆) is one of the major museums of Hakka culture in China. The Hakka people's migration, settlement, and business development is extensively exhibited. The cultural relics displayed in the museum mainly consist of copper wares, pottery, ironware, carved stones, pottery figurines and iron coins from different dynasties that were unearthed in the Longquanyi District, as well as relics from Randeng Temple.

Fire Dragon

The Fire Dragon Festival is a traditional festival of the Hakka people, which is said to have been introduced to Luodai and surrounding areas by the Liu family from Jiangxi. The Liu family still lives in Baosheng Village (宝胜村) of Luodai and run a business of creating dragon art and dragon dances. They have created a unique set of dragon dances, including "inviting the dragon", "sacrificing the chicken and beginning the main dance", and "painting the eye of the dragon".

Anren Town 安仁镇

Chengdu Plains Town

Many of the current buildings of Anren were constructed in the early 1900s and possess both traditional Chinese and modern European characteristics. Various architectural styles blend together here, and the old town as a whole is quite distinct.

Ancient China: Towns

Anren Town, Dayi County, Chengdu City, Sichuan Province
四川省成都市大邑县安仁镇
Nearest city: Chengdu
Chengdu Shuangliu International Airport is the busiest airport in Central and Western China. The city is also a major rail terminus with four railway stations.
From Chengdu North Bus Station (成都城北客运中心, adjacent to Chengdu Station) there are regular buses to Anren Town (about one hour). Admission to the Garden of Liu's Family is 50 yuan; the Folklore Museum of Sichuan is 10 yuan.

Thirteen kilometres to the southeast of Dayi County (大邑县), Anren was founded in 620 (the third year of the reign of Li Yuan, the and first emperor of the Tang Dynasty). With a history of more than 1,000 years, the town was named Anren (安仁) in reference to Confucius' teachings that "the virtuous rest in virtue".

Anren town can now generally be divided into three regions: Liu's Manor (刘氏庄园), the Jianchuan Museum District (建川博物馆聚落), and the historical and cultural old district.

Well-preserved streets include Weixing Street (维星街), Yumin Street (裕民街), and Shuren Street (树人街). On each side of these streets stand old wooden buildings with tiles.

The old residence of Liu's Manor (刘氏庄园老公馆) lies 500 metres east to Anren Town and dates back to the 1920s. During the Cultural Revolution, it was renamed Rent Collectors' Courtyard (收租院) and served as a site for communist social class education. Today the residence is a cultural and historical museum. Constructed in an irregular polygon shape, the building is surrounded by high walls. Inside there is a living room, reception room, a workers' courtyard (雇工院), the "lady's attic" (小姐楼), the rent collectors' courtyard (收租院), a garden, and a worshipping hall. The walls surrounding the manor are so high that the residence seems to be covered in a huge shadow. The rent collectors' courtyard (收租院) is famous for its vivid carvings of landlords exploiting farmers before the communist victory in 1949.

Established in the early 1940s, the new residence of Liu's Manor (刘氏庄园新公馆) is located on Guwan Street (古玩街, a street with a number of antique stores), 300 metres north of the old residence. The residence has been turned into the Museum of Local Traditions and Customs of Western Sichuan (川西民俗博物馆), featuring exhibitions of wedding traditions (婚俗厅), daily life (生产生活厅), and folk art and culture (民间工艺及民间文化厅).

Constructed in 1923, General Liu Xiang's (1888-1938) former residence (刘湘将军故居) is located on Jixiang Street (吉祥街) in the old town. Liu was an iron-fisted general in Sichuan during the Republic of China era. Although the sealed-off residence appears unremarkable at first glance, there are some notable features inside. Starting with the renovated entry, a babbling stream flows throughout the typical traditional three-hall building (三进式布局). The most outstanding features, however, are the walls, made of flowers rather than stones, and serving as borders between neighbouring courtyards and the central garden. The magnificent courtyard is known as the best courtyard home in western Sichuan Province, and has red wall columns, painted beams and carved pillars.

The Jianchuan Museum Cluster (建川博物馆聚落) has a large collection of antiques, pictures and historical records from the Sino-Japanese War (1937-1945). It also features antiques from the Cultural Revolution.

A traditional festival held in the town every year at spring equinox (春分会, usually in April) dates back to more than a century ago. At the fair, there are tasty dishes and activities, such as circus shows, singing and dancing, acrobats, Sichuan operas, and games. Other spring equinox activities include a parade and burning dragon lanterns (烧龙灯).

Dough Art

Dough figurines (面人黄) are one of the most interesting traditional folk arts in Anren, which have been passed on from generation to generation. The delicate figurines are made from wheat meal, which has been steamed, boiled, kneaded, formed, and eventually painted with different colours.

Anren Town has attracted numerous film-makers

Xinchang Town 新场镇

Water Town in the West Sichuan hills

The ancient buildings of Xinchang exhibit Ming and Qing dynasty styles with western Sichuan touches. The town has long gathered Confucians, Buddhists, and Taoists, and due to its location, was a main stop on China's ancient tea route.

Xinchang Town, Dayi County, Chengdu City, Sichuan Province
四川省成都大邑县新场镇
Nearest city: Chengdu
Chengdu Shuangliu International Airport is the busiest airport in Central and Western China. The city is also a major rail terminus with four railway stations.
From Chengdu Jinsha Bus Station (成都金沙汽车站, about a 15-minute taxi ride from Chengdu Station) there are regular direct buses to Dayi County (大邑县, about one hour). At Dayi Country, transfer to a minbus to Xinchang Town (20 minutes).

First built in the Eastern Han Dynasty, the ancient town of Xinchang is located in the Longmen Mountains, 58km south of Chengdu, and borders Xiling Snow Mountain National Park (西岭雪山) to the north.

Xinchang has been a prosperous market town for hundreds of years, trading lumber, coal, tea, rice, and other crops.

According to the Xinchang Annals, Touyan Village within Xinchang was first called "Fan Market" and is the oldest example of Xinchang's market culture. Touyan is at the foot of Guanyin Bank (观音岩), which is the north bank of the Touyan River's mouth. During the Jiajing reign of the Ming Dynasty (1521-1567), some houses and streets were built on the narrow strip of land. This area gradually became the town's trading centre. Because the area is shaped like a fan, it was named "Fan Market". During the Kangxi reign of the Qing Dynasty (1661-1722), the town was formally planned and built, with the crisscrossed streets resembling a "#". The Qing streets and alleys are well-preserved, and include Shangzheng Street (上正街), Taipingheng Street (太平横街), Xiangshi Street (香市街) and Hebei Street (河坝街).

There are 15 relatively intact Ming-Qing folk houses in the town, including the Li Family Ancient House (李氏古宅), the Luck Comes Club (福临社), and the Yellow Crane Tower (黄鹤楼). The structures are built with wooden and grey tiles, with stores on the first floor, residential and store rooms on the second floor and patios in back by the river. They feature exquisite carvings and paintings and ornamentally carved windows. The Ming Dynasty Chuanwang Palace (川王宫) by the Tiger Jump River

Ancient houses in Xinchang

(虎跳河) is the most characteristic building of the style. It was built during the Ming Dynasty in memory of King Li Bing, who made great contribution to water control. Later, the palace was turned into a temple.

In the main hall of Chuanwang Palace is a statue of former Sichuan King Li Bing, while the other halls are dedicated to Buddhist, Taoist and Confucian deities. The halls on both sides have memorial tablets for the ancestors of the townspeople.

The river below the nearby Buddha Cliff (佛子岩) is wide, smooth, and clear, and crossed by a primitive rope bridge. Walking on the unstable bridge provides great views but requires nerves of steel. During the Ming Dynasty, skilful craftsmen carved Buddhist images on the rocky scarps and built temples here for good luck. There are 40 grottoes dispersed over a 50-metre expanse of the nearby Buddha Cliff (佛子崖). Access to the cliff is free and open to the public and while some grottos were blown up to build a road, a number of stone engravings remain. The carvings on the precipice are covered by lichens and bushes, and some can only be seen from the river.

Buddha Cliff

Big Temple

Lingguan Big Temple (灵官大殿) was rebuilt in the stone carvings corridor. Inside the temple there is a beautiful stone-carved Guanyin Buddha, and the Turtle Prime Minister of the Dragon King.

Pingle Town 平乐镇

Silk Road River Town

The Baimo River runs from west to north through Pingle Town. The town is like a living version of *Along the River During the Qingming Festival* (a famous panoramic painting by Song Dynasty artist Zhang Zeduan) with rivers, birds, bamboos, west Sichuan style riverside buildings and 1,000-year-old banyans.

Pingle Town, Qionglai City, Chengdu City, Sichuan Province
四川省成都邛崃市平乐镇
Nearest city: Chengdu
Chengdu Shuangliu International Airport is the busiest airport in Central and Western China. The city is also a major rail terminus with four railway stations.
From Chengdu New South Gate Bus Station, a 20-minute taxi ride from Chengdu Station (成都站), take a bus to Qionglai Bus Station (邛崃汽车站, one hour). There is a regular service from Qionglai Bus Station (the shuttle bus leaves every 15 minutes) to Pingle Town. The trip takes 30 minutes.

Pingle is situated in a flat green basin surrounded by mountains, 18 kilometres southwest of Qionglai City. It was originally called Pingluo. The area has been settled since prehistoric times, and the name Pingluo means settlement on flat ground. Pingle Town is famous for its Qin and Han dynasty cultural legacy, and its scenery, shaped by centuries of water conservation.

Time has stripped away the town's prosperity, but left characteristic folk houses and its "block" style. Most of the streets in the town sit along the river in a fishbone pattern with different lengths and curvatures. The stilted buildings along the riverside have long pillars. There are two bridges connecting the east and west bank – the Leshan Bridge (乐善桥) in the upper reaches and the Xingle Bridge (兴乐桥) in the lower section. A dock was built between the bridges and you can go straight down to the streets through the stone steps

Pingle Town with western Sichuan water village style

Pingle street scene

layout, which lacks the traditional middle line of symmetry. The whole building supposedly absorbs spiritual winds from all directions and has great natural lighting and ventilation.

Pingle was a famous papermaking base in the Ming and Qing dynasties, with the area's paper being sold north and south of the Yangtze River. The Yin family was an important local family of paper merchants who opened the Yinfuxing paper store in Chengdu.

Located at the foot of the Qilong Mountain in the east of the town, Guanyin Yard was built in the early Tang Dynasty. There are lively copper statues of the Buddha Guanyin and 33 total representations of Guanyin, including Thousand-hand Guanyin (千手观音), Jade Jar Guanyin (净瓶观音), Riding Dragon Guanyin (骑龙观音), Riding Tiger Guanyin (骑虎观音), and so on. Three-hundred metres ahead of Guanyin Yard, you will find a part of the South Silk Road – the Ancient Post Road of the Qin and Han dynasties (秦汉古驿道).

From the top of Huajiu Mountain (花揪山), in the north of the town, there are panoramic views of surrounding mountain chains. If you are weary from your climb, you can go to the Li Family Yard (李家大院) hidden in the bamboos on the mountaintop. There, you can sample Huajiu tea (花揪贡茶), brewed with spring water, listen to folk songs, and admire the scenery.

alley.

The 120 meters long Leshan Bridge is 120 meters long was built in the first year of the Tongzhi reign of the Qing Dynasty (1862). Instead of having a traditional semi-circle shape, the arches of the bridge were built into an onion shape. This arch shape is very rare in western Sichuan. Historically, Pingle has had two main handicraft industries – papermaking and smelting iron. There is a family-run blacksmith's shop on Badian Street which has been around for 16 generations.

Changqing Street (长庆街) is right beside the river and is famous for selling bamboo wares. Walking on the red stone slabs, you can see bamboo baskets, dustpans, sieves, shoulder-poles, and brooms. Some stores have exquisite items on sale, such as bamboo-thread woven vases with porcelain as the roughcast, tea sets, and wine sets. The whole street carries a faint scent of bamboos.

The Yin Family Yard (银家大院) is the most intact Ming and Qing dynasty architecture in the ancient town. It has seven patios, leading many to say it resembles "seven stars surrounding the moon". The yard is a classic western Sichuan quadrangle dwelling, with interesting design and exquisite decorations. The dragon gate sits in the west and faces east, the main hall north-south. It is clear that a geomancer was responsible for the design of the

On The River

There are many folk performances on the streets of Pingle, such as the lion lantern (狮灯), ox lantern (牛儿灯), female dragon lantern (女子龙灯) and waist drum lantern (腰鼓灯) shows. You can also board a bamboo raft to enjoy the waterscape. In the evening, there are barbecues by the riverside and performances with rich local colour, such as Zhuma folk songs (竹麻号子).

Xishi Town 仙市镇

Dock on the Ancient Salt Path

Xishi Town ("Immortals Market" Town) is located in a deep green landscape in southern Sichuan. The town's ancient ancestral temples, houses and towers have witnessed its many ups and downs but their charm and attraction remain.

Xianshi Town, Yantan District, Zigong City, Sichuan Province
四川省自贡市沿滩区仙市镇
Nearest city: Chengdu
Chengdu Shuangliu International Airport is the busiest airport in Central and Western China. The city is also a major rail terminus with four railway stations.
From Chengdu Jinsha Bus Station (成都金沙汽车站, about a 15-minute taxi ride from Chengdu Railway Station) direct buses head for Xianshi Town at 8:15am every day (about 3.5 hours).

Beside the Fu River (釜溪), Xishi Town (仙市) is located 11 kilometres to the east of Zigong City (自贡市). The old town was built more than 1,400 year ago during the Sui Dynasty and has developed from the birth of the well salt industry, its main source of income.

In ancient times, Xishi was one of the most important docks on the Fu River. It has numerous temples that are still well-preserved. Xishi Town was on the route for Zigong well salt to be transported out of Sichuan. It is toured by the local tourist authority as "the bright pearl on the ancient salt path", because of its fine architecture and, flourishing Buddhist culture, and its "four streets, four warehouses, five temples, three docks, one carp, three memorial arches, nine steles and 10 lands"..

An archway marks the entrance to the old town. Simple and elegant, it has four pillars and three gates. Through the archway is the main street. To the right of the entrance, there was once a temple, named Jiangxi Temple, which no longer exits but has been rebuilt as residences. Beside the old temple grounds there is a small well which is still used by some residents.

There are five railed gates in Xishi. The dock is not far from the lower section of the main street, where boats moor every day. Passing through the gate, the main street is lined with food shops

Rooftops

A corner of a residence of Xishi Town

and restaurants. There is also a blacksmith's workshop and two stores selling tea.

The Chen Ancestral Temple （陈家祠堂） on New River Street was a site for the merchant Chen families to get together. Walk into the main gate and pass through a hallway, and you come to a patio well-stocked with various plants. Continue your walk down a few stone steps and you will find a larger hallway and patio. The buildings have high walls and tilted eaves, but the main house is situated at the highest level to show its status.

The town's five famous temples — Nanhua Palace (南华宫), Sky Palace (天上宫), Master of Sichuan Temple (川主庙), Hunan and Guangdong Temple (湖广庙), and Jiangxi temple (江西庙) — in the old town epitomize salt merchant culture. The Master of Sichuan and Hunan and Guangdong temples were destroyed and the Jiangxi Temple is in ruins, but the names of the temples still suggest the splendour and prosperity of the scene as the salt merchants gathered and competed for sales.

The name of the town, which literally means "immortals market", originated from a calming legend: The daughter of the Jade Emperor god was attracted by the beautiful scenery in the human realm, so she descended to the world, lay down beside the Fu River, and fell asleep. In honour of her, the riverside is called Fairy Beach. Buddhist culture has retained a strong influence in the town. The

Golden Bridge Temple (also known as Nanhua Palace) built in 1692 and the Sky Palace built in 1850 are representative of the phenomenon with their red walls, blue tiles, tilted eaves, wood-carved animals, flowers, and fish. It is said that the Golden Bridge Temple was built by merchants from Fujian and Guangdong who did salt business at Fairy Market. Later, some monks moved into the temple, and its name was changed to Golden Bridge Temple. Unusually, part of the street passes through the temple. On that long and narrow street, there is a theatre stage. When people use the street for ceremonies or just on their way to the market, they often wear traditional aprons and carry large buckets of Buddhist oil.

Coming out the back door and passing through a hall in the Golden Bridge Temple （金桥寺）, you will come to a riverside. Along the river, there some stone tables and benches where retired people like to relax and chat.

Sleeping Beauty

The name of the town, which literally means "immortals market", originated from a legend: The daughter of the Jade Emperor god was attracted by the beautiful scenery in the human realm, so she descended to the world, lay down beside the Fu River, and fell asleep. In honour of her, the riverside is called Fairy Beach.

The main street of Fairy Market

Zhaohua Town 昭化镇

The Birthplace of Empress Wu Zetian

Situated at the foot of Cattle's Head Mountain and surrounded by the Jialing, White Dragon and Clear rivers on the east, south and north, Zhaohua Town has a natural moat. In ancient times it had to be passed through when entering Sichuan, thus it was called "the throat and key of Sichuan",

Shaohua Town, Yuanba District, Guangyuan City, Sichuan Province
四川省广元市元坝区昭化镇
Nearest city: Chengdu
Chengdu Shuangliu International Airport is the busiest airport in Central and Western China. The city is also a major rail terminus with four railway stations.
From Chengdu Zhaojue Temple Bus Station (成都昭觉寺汽车站, about a 10-minute taxi ride from Chengdu Station), take a bus to Guangyuan City (广元市 about three hours). From Guanyuan, your best option is to hire a taxi to Shaohua Town (about 30 minutes and 30 kilometres).

Zhaohua Town has more than 2,320 years of history and is the oldest town in northern Sichuan. It was founded in 316 BC when Qin Country destroyed Bashu Country and established Jiayin County (葭萌县) in its place.

Due to its strategic location and its antiquity, numerous significant historical events have happened in Zhaohua. In the Three Kingdoms period, the Shu leader Liu Bei (刘备) once stationed his troops here to fight. Indeed, many stories in the epic Romance of the Three Kingdoms (三国演义) are set in the town, including "Zhang Fei fights with Ma Chao at night" (张飞挑灯夜战马超) and "Jiang Wei fails on Cattle's Head Mountain" (姜维兵败牛头山). Unsurprisingly, the town is a popular destination for domestic tourists and others on a "Three Kingdoms" tour.

The ancient military walls were established at the end of the East Han Dynasty. In the Ming Zhengde reign, Zhaohua's walls and moats were laid out in the shape of a calabash with city gates facing in all four directions. In the Qianlong reign of the Qing, the southern gate was shut to prevent floods, and now the relic near the southern gate is its only remnant. Three gates — Admiring Phoenix Gate (瞻凤楼), Linqing Gate (临清门), and Gongji Gate (拱极门) — in the east, west and north survive. Linqing Gate was a "marriage gate". Traditionally, when a woman married, her groom had to pick her up at that gate. The custom is still observed by many today.

Coming out of the western gate of Zhaohua and climbing along the Shu Path (蜀道) on the mountain for about 7 kilometres, you will see Cattle's Head Mountain. This was the location of Romance of the Three Kingdom's "Jiang Wei's troops are besieged at Cattle's Head Mountain" scene. The mountain is shaped like a huge cattle head, hence its name.

Before the ruins of the ancient temple on Cattle's Head Mountain, there is an old oval-shaped well named Jiang Wei Well (姜维井). When Jiang Wei's troops were besieged on Cattle's Head Mountain, his soldiers had no water to drink. That night, Jiang's prime minister Zhuge Liang appeared to him in a dream and told him that he should set up an altar and pray for water. Immediately after waking up, Jiang commanded his soldiers to dig a well and set up an altar to pray with incense. After a day had passed, he sent two soldiers to look at the well, but they reported "no water". Jiang Wei killed them at once. He sent another soldier to the well. That soldier also found no water, but he studied the well's wall and noticed a water mark. He gathered some villagers to help dig, and within two hours they struck flowing spring water and the water filled up half the well. Jiang was delighted and said, "A half-full well is enough". From then on, it is said that the water has always remained at half level, never being full or dry.

Dragon Gate College in the west of the city was first established in the Qianlong reign of the Qing Dynasty. The full Chinese name means "a fish leaping over the dragon's gate" and symbolizes praying for success. In the Daoguang reign, the Qing government made the school an official test site for the civil service examination. A stone bearing the three characters "拴马石" (stone for tethering horses) reveals the school's past, as exam hopefuls would travel great distances to reach the site by horse.

Daughters' Festival

The Jialing River in front of the Nuhuang Jimiao Huanze Temple (meaning "the queen is thankful for the love of the king"皇泽寺) is where the great Empress Wu Zetian was born (利州江潭). Women in Zhaohua come to the temple to worship and celebrate at the start of the lunar year (traditionally on Wu Zetian's birthday). Every September, there is the Daughters Festival, which commemorates Wu — the only female emperor in Chinese history.

Dragon Gate College features a fish leaping over a dragon gate, symbolizing hope for success

Enyang Town 恩阳镇

A Land Where Two Rivers Meet

EnyangTown is surrounded by green mountains, with Dengke Temple (登科寺) on the eastern mountain, and White Cloud Temple (白云寺) on the northern mountain. Thousand Buddha Rock (千佛岩) inserts itself into the river from the south.

Enyang Town, Bazhou District, Bazhong City, Sichuan Province
四川省巴中市巴州区恩阳镇
Nearest city: Chengdu
Chengdu Shuangliu International Airport is the busiest airport in Central and Western China. The city is also a major rail terminus with four railway stations.
From Chengdu Railway Station (成都火车站) take a train to Bazhong Railway Station (巴中站, eight hours). From the bus station beside Bazhong Railway station many direct buses leave for Enyang Town (40 minutes.)

Around 17 kilometres to the southwest of Bazhong City (巴中市), Enyang has a history of more than 1,400 years and has numerous historical sites. It was established as Yiyang County in the year 525, during the Liang Putong reign.

In its golden age, Enyang boasted 37 streets, of which nine remain. The street with the most Ming Dynasty buildings is named Old Market Street (老场街) and is very distinctive About 50 residents live on the street, and most of the homes have two storeys and attics with wooden carved decorations The upper parts of the carvings are used as a firewall. The old street was built along the riverside.

Other distinctive streets include Upper Main Street (上正街) and Lower Main Street (下正街). You can find Red Army relics on both. In December of 1932, area troops from the Communist army switched their focus from Hubei,

View of Enyang Town

Henan, and Anhui provinces and moved through Shanxi to Bashan. Bazhong was taken over and the Sichuan and Shanxi revolutionary base area was established. On the 400-metre street, there 13 sites with Red Army relics, including various administration offices such as the former Yilang County committee of the Chinese Communist Party (原中共川陕省仪阆县委), and courthouses. Stone-carved slogans, such as, "The Red Army will win" and "Destroy forces in Sichuan and Shanxi" bring visitors back to the turmoil of the Chinese Civil War.

Enyang Large Bridge

The old buildings are built in the rich residential style of northern Sichuan and have the traditional layout of buildings in the Ming and Qing dynasties. Most are wooden and earthen structures, with pillars but no beams. They typically have one to three rooms and all are surfaced with blue tiles. Among them, Wenchuang Tower (文昌阁), King Yu Palace (禹王宫), Warrior Palace (武圣宫) and Longevity Palace are the most representative. Built in the Ming, Wenchuang Tower (文昌阁) is a landmark of Enyang.

The tilted buildings near the mountain and by the river are the most famous residences in the old town. They are mainly concentrated near the Oil Workshop Street (油坊街) beside the Neiling River (内邻河). They were popular in the Tang Dynasty and flourished in the Ming and Qing. Tilted eaves on the attics, carved beams and painted rafters extend from the roofs. Most of the buildings are two or three storeys, with the tallest having four floors.

Water is the town's soul. Enyang is situated beside the Ba River (巴河), and the water's dock was prosperous for a time. The Phoenix Flying Bridge (起凤桥) beside the dock was built in the middle of Qing Dynasty and is paved with blue stones. Enyang Large Bridge is located on the outskirts of town. On the inner side of the bridge is Lute Beach and the General Stone. Five huge stones sit on the lower part of the beach, with heights of about 6 to 7 metres, in the shape of a lute.

Enyang town has a very long history. Its dragon boat races (赛龙舟), weddings (娶亲), the lantern festival (灯会), temple fairs (庙会), and other folk activities are all well-known in the region.

Tilted buildings near the mountains and by the river

Buddhist Stronghold

Buddhist culture remains strong in the town, as is apparent from the White Clouds Temple (白云寺) in the north, the Wenzhi Mountain Camp (文治寨) and Qianfo Rock in the west, Dengke Temple (登科寺) in the east, and Great Yiyang Mountain and Puxian Temple in the southeast.

Laoguan Town 老观镇

The Ancient County Seat

At an elevation of 700 metres, Laoguan Town is nearly always cloudy and foggy. It has been 1,500 years since Emperor Liangwu of the Southern Dynasty officially founded Baima Yiyang County. Over the subsequent centuries, the ancient town has accumulated a rich historical culture and legacy.

Laoguan Town, Langzhong City, Sichuan Province
四川省阆中市老观镇
Nearest city: Chengdu
Chengdu Shuangliu International Airport is the busiest airport in Central and Western China. The city is also a major rail terminus with four railway stations.
From Chengdu South Gate Bus Station (成都新南门车站, a 20-minute cab ride from Chengdu Station), there are direct buses to Langzhong City (four hours). From Langzhong, regular buses travel the route to Laoguan Town (one hour).

Laoguan is located in the northeast section of Langzhong City. It has always been a critical military and commercial hub of northern Sichuan Province, which is one reason why the Emperor Liangwu set up the county here. The administration of Laoguan has become more and more local over the past 1,500 years.

According to records, Laoguan Court is the site of the county seat of the ancient Feng Kingdom (古奉国县城). The ancient street is more than 1,000 metres long with ancient folk houses, temples, marvellous towers, archways, stately stone lions from the Northern Wei Dynasty and red culture signs on both sides.

At the Laoguan Market (老观集市) there are remains from a rare Qing Dynasty wooden granary (古木仓). Laoguan gets plenty of sunshine, so the rice produced here is high-quality and was thus used as tribute to the emperor. The

Qing Dynasty Wooden Granary

Old Street of Laoguan

which originated in Laoguan, has 400 years of history and has become a famous cultural feature of Laoguan. Since ancient times, Laoguan's people have enjoyed acting in, watching, and talking about lantern operas. It's no wonder Laoguan is considered a heartland of antern opera.

Qing granary is 9 metres long, 4 meters wide with a capacity of more than 200 tons. Carved into the beam of the 160-year-old granary are the Chinese characters for "built in the Daoguang reign of the Qing Dynasty".

The granary (古木仓) is well-designed. It is surrounded by pillars, has double-layered clapboard between rooms, and bridges for transportation supported by beams. There are stairs in the granary and wooden funnels at the bottom of every room. The grains automatically come out after opening the plug board, which leads to a significant reduction of human labour and material resources.

To become more waterproof and rat-resistant, stone columns were built under the granary, lifting it about 1 metre off the ground. The granary has good ventilation, and it is dry all year round.

Qiaoxuan Temple (谯玄庙) is no longer standing, but was important in the town's history. The year Qiao Xuan (a famous minister in the Han Dynasty) died in his hometown, the Emperor Guangwu ordered local officials to build a temple for him. Though the temple is gone, Qiao Xuan is still remembered, as Qiaomiaozi Village (谯庙子村) was named after him.

Laoguan has a rich culture of folk songs which has been supplemented in more recent times with songs about the Red Army. Meanwhile the northern Sichuan lantern opera,

Hanging Clothes

"Climbing up the mountain in the morning, pick up a leaf and play with it. When girls hear the sound of the leaf, they come out and pretend to hang their clothes". This lyric is from a traditional northern Sichuan folk song called Hanging Clothes 《晾衣裳》. The song is sung by people in Laoguan and is regarded as a classic Chinese folk song.

Laoguan folk houses

Luoquan Town 罗泉镇

The Dragon Town in Central Sichuan

The ancient houses of Laoquan are well-preserved. There is a 2.5 kilometre street in the town with bamboo, wood and mud buildings on both sides. Because the long street is shaped like a dragon, Luoquan claims the title of the "No. 1 dragon town in central Sichuan".

Luoquan Town, Zizhong County, Neijiang City, Sichuan Province
四川省内江市资中县罗泉镇
Nearest city: Chengdu
Chengdu Shuangliu International Airport is the busiest airport in Central and Western China. The city is also a major rail terminus with four railway stations.
From Chengdu Bus Station (成都汽车总站) take a shuttle bus to Zizhong South Bus Station (资中城南汽车站, about two hours). There are shuttle buses to Luoquan Town before 15:00 every day (45 minutes).

Luoquan Town, located 88 kilometres northwest of Neijing City, dates back to the Qin Dynasty. The black-tile buildings of the town's ancient street have stores on the first floor, carged beams, painted rafters and cornices.

The town's salt wells (罗泉井盐) also have a long history: the industry began in the Qin, and by the Qing the number of salt wells in town reached 1,500. Luoquan well salt won first prize at the 1925 World Expo held in Paris, France.

There were famously "nine palaces, one Buddhist temple and eight temples" in the town. However, the Salt God Temple (盐神庙) is the most intact, and the only temple enshrining Guan Zhong, the god of salt. In 1869, during the

Ancient Luoquan buildings with carved beams, painted rafters and cornices.

Tongzhi reign, salt merchants raised money to build the Salt God Temple near the corner of Zilai Bridge, (where the head of the dragon is). The gate, archway, stage, wing buildings, main hall, side rooms, corridors, and courtyards are carefully constructed, and elaborately designed. The main hall enshrines Guan Zhong, Guan Yu (the god of war), and Zhu Rong (the god of fire). There is a painting of dragons playing with treasure on the roof of the main hall which is still vivid after hundreds of years.

The Salt God Temple (盐神庙) is now a place for locals to get together and soak up the sun. Passing through the old stage (旧戏台) after entering the hall, you will arrive at the spacious temple square (庙前广场). The wing buildings, side rooms and corridors have already lost their colours. Stepping into the main hall, you can see the blue sky through the patio.

Around the corner of Banbian Street in the middle of town is Fuyin Hall, built in the Guangxu reign of the Qing Dynasty (1875-1909). The hall is striking for its characteristic Chongyan Xieshan roof style. In the summer of 1911, people in Sichuan started the Boalu Movement to fight for the right to build railways themselves. Long Mingjian and Wang Tianjie, members of the Chinese United League (a secret society and underground resistance movement formed by Sun Yat-sen), held a meeting to raise an army and plan an armed insurrection. The meeting brought Fuyin Hall fame. Sun Yat-sun said, "If there wasn't a Baolu Movement, the Wuchang Uprising (which triggered the 1911 revolution that brought down the Qing Dynasty) would have been delayed for a year".

Chenghuang originally referred to the god who guards the city (in other words, the moat), so Chenghuang Temples (城隍庙) are among the most important in town. The Luoquan Chenghuang Temple is located at the end of the Zilai Bridge (子来桥) and the Salt God Temple (盐神庙) is at the other end. The Chenghuang Temple used to be a busy place, but now you can see the weeds inside through a crack in the rusty door.

Luoquan folk houses

Unique Tofu

Luoquan has a unique tofu dish (豆腐筵席) – the soybeans for making the tofu are ground with a special grinder. The tofu is white and soft and makes for a spicy meal after adding some local seasonings.

Salt God Temple

Fengsheng Town 丰盛镇

Longevity Town

Fengsheng is an ancient rural commercial town with a rich cultural legacy. The town is located in a mountain area, 500 metres above sea level, which means it has fresh air and pleasant weather.

Fengsheng Town, Ba'nan District, Chongqing Municipality
重庆市巴南区丰盛镇
Nearest city: Chongqing
Flights from all over China serve Chongqing's Wanzhou Wuqiao Airport, while Chongqing Railway Station is a high-speed rail hub.
From Chongqing Nanping Bus Station (重庆南坪汽车站, a 20-minute drive from Chongqing Station) there are two buses at day (at 8:00am and 2:00pm) that head directly for Fengsheng Town (about four hours).

Fengsheng Town is in the east part of the Banan District of the greater Chongqing region, although it is 60 kilometres from Chongqing City. According to the Ba County Annals, Fengsheng was built in the Song Dynasty. During the Ming and Qing dynasties, it became a prosperous business centre which attracted merchants and stores, and was known as the most important trading and distribution centre in the Yangtze River".

There are 13 ancient mountain fortress ruins in Fengsheng, including Tianping (天平寨), Gongshan (共山寨), Laoya (老鸦寨), Tiewa (铁瓦寨), Guanshan (关山寨) and Shengping (升平寨) fortresses. The Guanshan Fortress has three old folk houses, and is the most intact. The Tiewa Fortress has the most beautiful views of the group. The scenery is especially spectacular at dawn. Standing on the 815-meter-high fort, you get splendid views of the surrounding mountains. To the west is a huge reclining Buddha. Other historic temples in town include Ziyun (紫云寺), Tiewa (铁瓦寺), Yunxiang (云香寺), Fazu (法祖寺), Guanfang (官房寺), Xingfu (兴福寺), Wen (文庙), Nuwang (女王庙), and Jiangxi (江西庙).

Fengsheng has a unique geographical position, hidden in the mountains of a border region, making it a target for enemies. Diaolou (碉楼, meaning "watchtowers") were a line of defence and living quarters. The most famous is the 130-year-old European Watchtower (欧式碉楼) built in the late Qing Dynasty. The building is divided into two parts. The lower section was used for housing. Built with big stones, it is sturdy and safe. The upper part has lookouts and embrasures, so that the enemies could be spotted and attacked immediately.

Walking into the European watchtower, you find that

Pastoral Fengsheng

the front gate and lintel were crafted in late Renaissance style. The lower part of the gate is Gothic and the decorations on the windows are inspired by Asia Minor. The cabbage illustrations on the pillars on the top floor are Corinthian. The whole tower is delicate and well-designed.

Pleasant weather and a stable lifestyle apparently help the people of Fengsheng people live longer. According to experts, each year three to four people in the town celebrate their 100 birthday, while many people over 90 can still carry heavy bags of fertilizer, hoe, farm, and do business. Over 1,500 people in the town are over 70 years old.

The town's underground river is 1 kilometre southeast of the town's centre, and is formed by four springs — Sanchaoshui (三潮水), Gandong (干洞), Longtan (龙潭), and Mofangwan (磨坊湾). The Sanchaoshui gushes intermittently and is special for its long high tides and neaps tides in the spring. Usually the underground tidal stream appears from 10:00 to 13:00, and the Sanchaoshui from 14:00 to 17:00.

The Xiangshui Lake and Waterfalls (响水湖及其瀑布群) are 3 kilometres away from the town government, connected by a highway. The lake covers an area of 300,000 square metres, and there are up to 20-metre-high 12-level waterfalls and a pool nearby.

Fengsheng Old Street

Jindaoxia Town 金刀峡镇

"Little Jiangnan"

Jindaoxia town is located at the southern foot of Huaying Mountain. Stepping across the bridge in the middle of the town, you will feel like you are walking into a scroll painting from the Ming or Qing dynasty. The streets, paved with black bricks, run along the edge of the flowing waters of Dark Water Beach River.

Ancient China: Towns

Jindaoxia Town, Beipei District, Chongqing City, Sichuan Province
重庆市北碚区金刀峡镇
Nearest city: Chongqing
Flights from all over China serve Chongqing's Wanzhou Wuqiao Airport, while Chongqing Railway Station is a high-speed rail hub.
From Chongqing North Bus Station (重庆汽车北站, a 15-minute taxi ride from Chongqing Station), there are direct buses to Jindaoxia Town (about 2.5 hours). The hotline for the Chongqing Dadi Travel company is: 023-63500329.

The ancient part of Jindaoxia town, (金刀峡古镇), is today known as Pianyan Ancient Town (偏岩古镇) . Pianyan was built during a turbulent period of the reign of the Kangxi Emperor of the early Qing dynasty. Fearing for their safety, the Huguang family were forced to move, founding Pianyan and turning its empty fields deep within the mountain range into a prosperous economic and trading hub in eastern Sichuan Province. Three hundred years later, the town is well-preserved. Its original name comes from the obliquely slanting cliff to the north of the town ("Pianyan" means "slanting cliff").

In the middle of the ancient town a bridge made from black brick sweeps across the brook. Taking the bridge as a boundary, the main street is divided into the upper-street (上街) and lower street (下街). Shops on both sides of the street are built from wood and bamboo, or walled using wooden boards or fences made of white-brushed bamboo. To the north of the upper-street is a public area that houses the Wu Temple (武庙), King Yu Temple (禹王庙) and Opera Building (戏楼).

At the centre of the street is Qiu Hezhai, a well-known shop. The partly derelict building consists of three stories: the first floor is an open hall with stairs that connect to the dooryard-like second floor in the middle. In the front of the second floor is a pavilion with winding corridors and staircases. The exquisite sculptures and carvings on the windows and handrails testify to the past glory of the ancient town.

King Yu Temple and the Opera Platform are popular gathering places for the public. The temple uses gray tiles and white-brushed walls, making the structure simple but elegant. King Yu's stele and statue are set in the hall. In front of King Yu Temple is the Opera Platform. The upper floor of the platform is open and the surrounding columns are carved with delicate representations of scenes from ancient operas.

The architecture of the ancient town has several unique details. For example, the walls of Wu Temple, located on the north side of the upper-street, are solid at the bottom. This design allows light to seep into the house. The three-storey Jiuhe Zhan (九合栈) is supported by outseams and the design of the functional area of the building is perfectly fitted to the space between hoisting beams.

At 880 metres high, the town has kept the magic and natural scenery of its ancient valley intact. The main view of the valley, which is about 100 million years old, offers a picture of its depth and features its karst.   Jindao Valley offers idyllic views of sunrise and sunset.. The lower valley can be divided into two parts. In the upper part there is the deep gully of the valley, peeled cliffs and two connected mountains. The lower part features a group of caves and waterfalls and ancient stalactites. Hidden Sword Cave (藏刀洞) in the upper valley, and tourist spots in the lower valley, offer interesting attractions. There are many colourfully-named tourist spots for travellers to climb and hike, including Tusk Cave (獠牙洞), Rhinoceros Cave (犀牛洞), and Three-stage Long Waterfall (三级长瀑).

Apart from the excellent views, local folk customs make the place particularly special. In the evening, you can rest in a local camp, watch the folk dances, and try out local barbecue and wine.

Sword

There is a tale for the name of the Jindao Valley: it is said that a brave solider from the late Ming Dynasty, known as Zhang Kun and also called Zhang Jindao once obtained a treasured sword in the valley and then entered the service of King Xia. Since then, the valley has been called Jindao, after the soldier

Pianyan Ancient Residence

Zouma Town 走马镇

A Town of Folktales

In ancient times, travelers and horses that set off for Chengdu from Chongqing would stay overnight in Zouma Town, or "traveling by horse" town. The travelers would exchange tales of the road and over time these stories were integrated gradually into the memories of local people.

Jindaoxia Town, Jiulongpo District, Chongqing City, Sichuan Province
重庆市九龙坡区走马镇
Nearest city: Chongqing
Flights from all over China serve Chongqing's Wanzhou Wuqiao Airport, while Chongqing Railway Station is a high-speed rail hub.
Take a bus from Chongqing Nanping Bus Station(重庆南坪汽车, about 20mins ride
from Chongqing Station) to Zouma Town. The journey takes about 40mins.

Originally, Zouma was part of Ba County (巴县), the territory of Ancient Ba Country (an ancient country located in Sichuan province during the Pre-Qin period). In the middle of the Ming Dynasty, the ancient town was little more than a bazaar and a staging post on the way to Chengdu from Chongqing。 Because of its association with traveler's tales, over the centuries Zouma has earned the title of the "Home of Folk Literature". The mountain songs, tales and anecdotes told by travelers overnighting here have been passed from generations to generation, becoming part of the town's culture.

Zouma Town

If you step into a few of centuries-old shops along Zouma's ancient main street, you will notice that polished square tables (八仙桌, an old-fashioned square table that seats eight people) are still situated at the back of many. The age-old eaves of the ancient houses have been darkened by smoke.

You can follow along the street to Shengwu Opera Building (圣武戏楼), built in the early Qing Dynasty. The carvings and sculptures in the building are vivid and attractive, and its layout has similarities with Beijing's Summer Palace (北京颐和园).

The ruins of a stone archway are situated by the side of a small road in the town. An upper inscription reading "Road to High Position" (青云得路) can be seen. The gateway represents both the ancient prosperity of the town and traditional Confucian values. The town's elderly say there was once a stone here inscribed with the words "officers alight from a sedan; generals from a horse" (文官下轿，武将下马). The stone, named Heart Stone by locals, was set as a memorial to some successful candidates in the imperial examinations of the town.

Peach Flowers in Zouma

Tell Me A Story

Zouma native son Wei Xiande, the son of a street performer, is one China's leading experts in Chinese folktales. By the time he was 22, he was able to tell more than 5,000 folktales. After the Communist revolution in 1949, he went back to his hometown and focused on reassembling the 1,500 tales of Bayu culture (the ancient culture of Ba Country.) Folktales of different kinds in Zouma town include tales of fairies, animals, and other mythological wonders.

Zouma street scene

Laitan Town 涞滩镇

The Opera Town

Beautiful Laitan Town, on the banks of the Qu River, is renowned for its Tang stone carvings, as well as for its Ming and Qing dynasty-style buildings. It is also recognized for its local opera culture, represented by Wenchang Palace Theatre.

Laitan Town, Hechuan District, Chongqing City, Sichuan Province
重庆市合川市涞滩镇
Nearest city: Chongqing
Flights from all over China serve Chongqing's Wanzhou Wuqiao Airport, while Chongqing Railway Station is a high-speed rail hub.
From Chongqing Railway Station (成都火车站) take the No. 1508 express bus service to Ta'ermen Bus Station (塔尔门汽车站, about one hour.) At Ta'ermen, transfer to a minibus to Laitan Town (10 yuan).

Laitan was built in the late Tang Dynasty, but only took much of its current shape during the Song Dynasty.

The town is not big, consisting of Upper Laitan and Lower Laitan. Lower Laitan is centred by the Qu River, near the Qu River pier. This area's main artery is an old street made from bluestone, which is full of bumps and hollows. Wooden residential buildings with white walls and black wooden gates stand on both sides of the street. Their roofs are covered with locally-made small blue tiles and the eaves reach out for more than 1 metre, with the ridged tiles arranged in

The town's Old Street

abstract patterns. The white walls and black wooden gates and windows provide a striking contrast.

Upper Laitan is much larger than Lower Laitan, and is located on Jiufeng Mountain, with views of the Qu River. The half-circle Laitan Barbican (涞滩瓮城) was built in 1862. The well-preserved defensive military building boasts eight gates and makes a valuable contribution to local history and art. While the ancient walls no longer exist, the spirit of what remains reminds people of the war years.

Wenchang Palace Theatre (文昌宫戏楼), built in the Qing Dynasty, is a symbol of the ancient town. The theatre was built along the cliff in a courtyard style. On the eaves of the theatre are exquisite carvings of stories from the Three Kingdoms period.

The 1,000-year-old Song Dynasty Second Buddha Temple (二佛寺), with its constantly burning incense, preserves the biggest Zen Stone Rock statue group in China. There are 42 well-preserved cave shrines, and more than 1,700 statues carved in the south, north and west cliffs of the lower hall of the temple. The main Buddha statue is 12.5 metres tall, the largest in the temple. According to the inscriptional records of the temple, dated from the Zhengde reign of the Ming Dynasty, "There are three great Buddha statues in Sichuan, and Laitan Jiufeng Mountain boasts the second-largest of them". The statue was built on a cliff, and depicts Buddha wearing a belt-style cassock and stroking its knee with its left hand. The right hand is in the posture of speaking Dharma, and two legs down are crossed in the lotus position. The huge head and shoulder are detached from the cliff, but have been stable for hundreds of years

If you have time, it is possible to stay a night in the Second Buddha Temple. When the evening comes, a bright moon is reflected on the quiet river. The Upper Hall of the Second Buddha Temple, located on the top of the Jiufeng Mountain, is a magnificent courtyard building, covering 5181 square metres. Along the central axis to the top there are: Mountain Gate, Heaven Emperor Hall, Main Hall, and Buddhisatva Hall. By the left and right sides are a warehouse, Buddha room and other buildings. The stone-built Mountain Gate is 7 metres high and is vividly carved with more than 100 animals and characters.

Double Dragon Lake in the town's west is a broad artificial body of water built in 1983, with a twisting shoreline. There are four islands, 147 peninsulas, and more than 100 harbours, and it makes for a good place to escape the summer heat.

Inn With A View

The "Ancient Town Inn" in Laitan (古镇客栈) offers good evening views of the town. Standing on the rooftop of the fourth floor of the inn, the whole town comes into view. In the east along the gray tile roofs, you can see the quiet Qu River flowing like silk, while the west is filled with a setting sun.

Anju Town 安居镇

A Town Surrounded By Water

Anju Town lies in a beautiful landscape where small households cluster below swirling clouds, along rivers and around docks and bays. The stone stairways extend down into bluish-green water.

Anju Town, Tongliang County, Chongqing City, Sichuan Province
重庆市铜梁县安居镇
Nearest city: Chongqing
Flights from all over China serve Chongqing's Wanzhou Wuqiao Airport, while Chongqing Railway Station is a high-speed rail hub.
From Chongqing North Bus Station (重庆汽车北站, a 15-minute taxi ride from Chongqing Station) there are direct buses to Tongliang County, (about one hour). You can then transfer to a service to Anju Town (about 30 minutes).

"A town surrounded by water on three sides" — a line from a Tang Dynasty poem — perfectly describes Anju's surroundings. Anju was officially made a town roughly 240 years ago but it had already developed into a prosperous distribution centre by the early Ming Dynasty, transporting goods from Tongliang, Dazu, Tongnan, Hechuan, and many other towns.

Named after the Grand An River (or the Qiong River), which flows through its territory, Anju occupies a location considered strategically important since ancient times. Anju has throughout history been used as a military base; the traces of many expeditionary forces can still be found today. It also remains a commercial hub, with its silks, bamboo, hemp fabrics, rice, wine and other products sold to faraway areas of China. The town exhibits China's usual synergetic religious practices, with buildings such as the Buddhist Bolun Temple, the Daoist Tianyuan Chamber, and the Mazu Temple (dedicated to a deity worshipped mainly by sailors, merchants, fishermen and seafarers.) The town also houses Imperial Academies and Ancestral Halls.

According to local legend, Anju originally had eight gates, built for military purposes. Only two gates remain, both on Crossing Road. One of them, 15-metre-tall Yinfengmen (引凤门), was built in the Ming Dynasty. The Dragon Meeting Bridge (会龙桥) was built in the Hongzhi Period of the Ming Dynasty. The abutments were initially built with bricks, but were later replaced with stone. The name of the bridge reflects the wishes of people at that time of building to befriend a dragon. The bridge also offers splendid views of the town.

Originally the Fujian Provincial Guild, the Mazu Temple (妈祖庙) is where fishermen pray for blessings from the Goddess Mazu. In the golden ages of Anju, many Hakka people moved to the town, eventually building the Mazu Temple. The temple's lofty beam and chuandou (a structure used in traditional Chinese timber buildings, with small columns supporting the upper half of the building), place it in the Anhui style, making it an attractive spot for visitors.

One highlight of the ancient town is Matoushan Wall (马头山墙), an exquisite and complex Anhui-style structure. Hakka stories of the sea can be felt from the perfect arrangement of the courtyards, gardens and balconies.

Located at the centre of the ancient town, two Hanlin Halls (built to commemorate the success of four locals in entering the Imperial Hanlin Academy) — Wang Hanlin and Wu Hanli — stand shoulder to shoulder. It was rare in Chinese history for both father and son to enter the Imperial Academy, as was the case with Wang Loushan and Wang Rujia. Patterns of dragons and phoenixes are carved and painted under each of the eaves; vivid frescos can be found on the walls of the back courtyard. The rooms are furnished with beautiful illustrations, well-preserved wood carvings, paintings, wooden ornaments, gilding flowers, and other small items, all of which reflect the owner's sense of taste.

Located in the town's east is Bolun Temple (波仑寺), which has been developed into a park. It is recorded on the ancient tablet beside Bolun that the temple was built by an unusual monk from the town of Shifang in the first year of the Gaozu Period in the Tang Dynasty. Its Mahavira Hall was constructed

in the Wanli Period of the Ming Dynasty and repaired twice during the Kangxi and Yongzheng Periods of the Qing Dynasty, using funds raised by the monks in the temple. Many historical items and relics can be found inside the temple. An inscription called "The Ace Mountain", written by Mi Fu, a calligrapher from the Song Dynasty, was carved on the stone of Bolun Temple by a local person in the Ming Dynasty.

Bolun Buddhism Temple

109

Bashu

Shuangjiang Town 双江镇

Home Town of a President

The exquisite scenery of Shuangjing's ancient streets, stone bridges and old banyan trees, surrounded by twin brooks and green bamboo, form the unique cultural landscape of an ancient northwestern Chongqing town.

Shuangjiang Town, Tongnan County, Chongqing City, Sichuan Province
重庆市潼南县双江镇
Nearest city: Chongqing
Flights from all over China serve Chongqing's Wanzhou Wuqiao Airport, while Chongqing Railway Station is a high-speed rail hub.
From Chongqing Long-distance Bus Station (重庆长途车站, near Chongqing Railway Station) there are buses to Tongnan County (about two hours). At Tongnan transfer to a bus to Shuangjiang town (one hour).

Shuangjiang Town was founded more than 400 years ago in the late Ming and early Qing dynasties. The ancient town lies downstream of the Fu River, which is navigable year-round and makes Shuangjiang an important gateway to and from northwest Chongqing.

Inside the town, nine ancient streets are preserved today, including Water Alley and Old Swine Alley. There are more than 20 large Qing Dynasty buildings in the ancient town, including King Yu's Palace, Prosper Street Yard, Yuantaihe Yard, and the Post Office Yard.

The former residence of the communist revolutionary Yang Angong (即杨闇公旧居) stands out among the ancient pavilions and courtyards lining the 700 metres of "Qing Street". Its elaborate interior contrasts with its plain exterior, and its architecture style fully embodies the "Bayu" features of the ancient town ("Ba" and "Yu" are both historical names for Chongqing). The home is a chuandou Chinese timber structure with two courtyards and a store facing the street on the ground floor.. Bedrooms are located on both sides of the small patio in the back courtyard, where the Diary of Yang Angong and some pictures are on display.

Located near the mountainside by a dam upstream of Monkey Brook is the "Four Knows" Hall (四知堂) where former Chinese president Yang Shangkun was born. Its architecture applies the traditional design of a "courtyard within courtyard, chamber upon chamber"; every part of the complex is arranged exquisitely. "Four Knows Hall" was named in allusion to the story of Yang Zhen, the Yangs' ancestor in the Eastern Han Dynasty. A man tried to persuade Yang Zhen to accept a bribe by arguing that "nobody knows".

Households in Shuangjiang

Yang Zhen refused, saying: "You know, I know, the heaven knows and the earth knows".

The design of the hall's layout was based on the Chinese character for "four" (四), with five Miankuo chambers (rooms parallel to the purlins) in the front and back hall and four chambers as wing-rooms on the east and west sides. Eight Miankuo chambers are built outside the wing-rooms as outer wing-rooms, which are connected to the inner areas by pathways and courtyards.

Construction materials were carefully chosen for Four Knows Hall. The columns are built with straight round logs, the beams are carved with delicate patterns, the purlins are gilded with golden paint, and the door frames are decorated with golden ornaments. Brightly coloured patterns feature in carvings on the ridge bricks, which depict gods, flowers, and palaces. Decorations on windows and doors are particularly exquisite; patterns of bats (the pronunciation of which is similar to that of "happiness" in Chinese), peonies, peaches and pigmies are engraved or hollowed-out under the eaves and on the columns, reflecting the beautiful wish of the house owner to lead a long, happy, and prosperous life. The superb engraving skills shown on this structure make it a wonderful piece of art in itself.

Though showing the scars of more than 200 years of history, the ancient stage in King Yu's Palace (禹王宫) remains a magnificent and imposing structure, its lofty eaves and bent ridge reflecting a rich cultural history.

The Huguang (referring to the provinces of Hubei and Hunan) Provincial Guilds in Shuangjiang are fairly large due to the considerable number and wealth of people in the Huguang region. The guilds house grand stages, their lofty hipped-gable roofs lifted at corners and decorated with glazed tiles. There are also "wing-pavilions", where noble guests could comfortably enjoy the snacks, tea and opera performances from behind decorated balusters without worry of having their view blocked.

The T-crossing teahouse (字口茶楼) on River Street is a typical commercial building from the Qing Dynasty. All the wooden parts of the structure, such as the tilted supporting, hallways, columns, window frames and door cases, are decorated with exquisite patterns. The common hall is located on the ground floor while the private rooms are upstairs.

In addition to the Qing Dynasty sites, the town houses a number of sites associated with the Kuomintang government of the 1940s, which moved to Chongqing during the war of resistance against Japan. These sites include a guesthouse used by Chiang Kai-shek (蒋介石的行辕), and the Mansion of Bai Chongxi (白崇禧的官邸), a senior Nationalist general.

Jelly Noodles

Shuangjiang's jelly noodles are well-known and renowned for their long history. Among the various types of jelly noodles in Tongnan, Chen's Jelly Noodles (陈凉粉) is the most popular.

Zhongshan Town 中山镇

A Classic Bayu Town

Bamboo Shoot River flows slowly past Zhongshan Town, hidden halfway up a mountain. Looking out from the window of local stilted buildings, you can see fresh green bamboo, old manors, ancient villages, old castles, and time-honoured temples.

Zhongshan Town, Jiangjin City, Chongqing City, Sichuan Province
重庆市江津市中山镇
Nearest city: Chongqing
Flights from all over China serve Chongqing's Wanzhou Wuqiao Airport, while Chongqing Railway Station is a high-speed rail hub.
From Chongqing North Bus Station (重庆汽车北站, a 15-minute taxi ride from Chongqing Station) regular buses go to Jiangjin City (about one hour). At Jiangjin get on a minibus that heads to Zhongshan Town, a trip that takes three hours and costs 10 yuan.

Zhongshan Town was first established in the Southern Song Dynasty, more than 800 years ago. The town is commonly referred to as "Triple Field" (三合场) or "Dragon Hole Field" (龙洞场), and is situated at the mountain of South Jiangjin City, 125 kilometres from Chongqing's city centre. The town is connected to Four Sides Mountain (四面山), a nationally known scenic spot, and is regarded as one of Chongqing's top 10 ancient towns.

Built along rivers, the town is made up of three streets: Dragon Hole (龙洞), Dam in Uncultivated Land (荒中坝), and Promotion Bridge (高升桥). Triple Field Old Street was once

Red lacquer wood, bamboo splint walls with columns for support

Sunset glow in the ancient town of Zhongshan

a prosperous wharf and distribution centre for goods from Sichuan and Chongqing. The town is also home to ancient Han Dynasty tombs.

Inside ancient Zhongshan is a narrow and serene slabstone road. Today it is mostly home to elderly residents, with few young people making a living in the town. Both sides of the street are characterised by Qing Dynasty architecture.

The most representative buildings in the ancient town are commercial shops. Built along the mountain, the town's main commercial street is over 1 kilometre long. The fluctuating climate in eastern Sichuan means that nearly all buildings are designed to be protected from both sun and rain. Double-layered stilted buildings are most common, with the first floor run as a shop and the upper floor used for family life. With blue tile roofs, red lacquer wood, bamboo

splint walls, and round columns for support, the town is an authentic picture of the Sichuan "Bayu" style, which refers to the old names for Chongqing.

Over 200 families live in Zhongshan, and several traditional shops remain, including forges, Chinese pharmacies, and barbers. When the sun is out, the old street's blue slabstones shine, accompanied by the wafting fragrances of herbal medicines and hammering of forging iron.

Roughly 3.5 kilometres from the town is Dragon Hole Reservoir (龙洞水库), the local water power station. The water near its bank is shallow, with soft sands that are especially good for swimming and relaxation. This area also boasts a verdant virgin forest. The precious Alsophila spinulosa trees, taking up an area of over 1,500 hectares, are veritable living fossils.

Smoked Tofu

"Smoked Tofu" is a famous delicacy and local favourite in Zhongshan Town. It is made by putting fresh white tofu on a fine-toothed bamboo comb, and smoked by burning culm underneath. When the tofu turns golden-yellow, the cook prods it with a slim bamboo stick and brushes special chili sauce on both sides. The tofu is crisp on the outside crisp but soft inside.

Tanghe Town 塘河镇

Ming Dynasty Mountain Town

By the side of the serene Tang River and thick bamboo groves is the graceful ancient town of Tanghe.

Tanghe Town, Jiangjin City, Chongqing
重庆市江津市塘河镇
Nearest city: Chongqing
Flights from all over China serve Chongqing's Wanzhou Wuqiao Airport, while Chongqing Railway Station is a high-speed rail hub.
Lots of shuttle buses start from Chongqing North Bus Station (重庆汽车北站, a 15-minute taxi ride from Chongqing Station) to Jiangjin City (one hour and 20 yuan). At Jiangjin get on a minibus to Tanghe Town (15 yuan).

In the southwest Lianchui in Jiangjin District, Tanghe borders Nantan Village in Hejiang County, Sichuan Province. The town was originally established in the Ming Dynasty, and became an important goods distribution centre during the Ming and Qing dynasties. In the town's earliest days, there were just three households — Wang, Sun and Chen — but as commerce took off, the town grew. Today Tanghe is mainly composed of Tanghe Old Street District (塘河古街区), Stone Dragon Door Garden (石龙门园) and Yanchong Temple (延重寺).

At the entrance of the town is a branch of the Tang River and two ancient bridges. The first is River-combining Bridge (江合桥), which links Sichuan Province with the municipality of Chongqing. The other is Kylin Bridge (麒麟桥), reaching across Family Tuo Creek (脱家溪) and surrounded by tall bamboo.

Tanghe Old Street District occupies 2.8 hectares of land, with over 15,000 square metres of ancient architecture in different styles, from both the Ming and Qing. Constructed along the mountain, the old street winds up from the wharf of the bank for a total of roughly 600 metres. The main street is connected with Horizontal Street (横街子), and Temple Lane (庙巷子), with three village doors at the front of each street. Taking the steps, you can see that many houses along the street are in a state of quaint disorder. They are built mainly of bluestone, with beautiful brick and wood walls, unique eaves and dougong (斗拱), carved beams and painted pillars.

Unusually for an ancient Sichuan town, Tanghe contains some Anhui-style buildings. Built in the Ming Dynasty, Chieftain Temple (王爷庙), one such structure, is still well-preserved. The main hall and theatrical stage are both constructed with upward-flying eaves and painted walls. Several inscriptions in graceful Chinese calligraphy, as well as

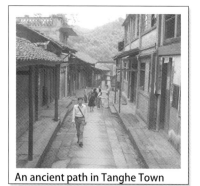

An ancient path in Tanghe Town

Tanghe Town scenery

the preserved pines, bamboo, and plum flowers are still a pleasure to see. Opposite the Chieftain Temple is the Dragon Door (龙门号), once a place of entertainment for scullers. Its horse-head walls, round-ridge roofs and decorated brackets are delicately designed. The western-style Zhu Family Building (朱家洋楼) has a distinctive design, with western and traditional Chinese artistry ingeniously merged.

The Temple of the Sun Family, also called Yanchong Temple (沿重祠), was built during Qing Dynasty Emperor Guangxu's reign. Built in the style of a palace, the ridges are made up of hollow yellow and green glazed bricks, with horse-head walls and double-eaves on both sides.

Two kilometres away from the streets of the ancient town is Stone Dragon Door Manor (石龙门庄园), constructed during the early years of Qing Dynasty Emperor Qianlong's reign. The manor's main halls include nine middle doors forming a complicated "dragon door maze (龙门阵)". In the two side rooms, 18 patios make the magnificent "Eight-fold Maze (八阵图)".

Houses along the street are mainly built from bluestone, with beautiful brick and wood walls, unique eaves and dougong.

Xituo Town 西沱镇

The Tujia Salt Town

As early as the Song Dynasty, Sichuan salt was transported through Xituo to as far away as areas of Hubei Province. Xituo Town was the origin and transfer station for the long salt path, known by ancient people as "Salt Town".

Xituo Town, Tu Nationality Autonomous County, Shizhu District, Chongqing City, Sichuan Province
重庆市石柱土家族自治县西沱镇
Nearest city: Chongqing
Flights from all over China serve Chongqing's Wanzhou Wuqiao Airport, while Chongqing Railway Station is a high-speed rail hub.
Chongqing Chaotianmen Bus Station (重庆朝天门汽车站, a 15-minute ride from Chongqing Station) has direct buses to Xituo Town (60 yuan and about six hours.)

Xituo (Western Inlet) Town is a distribution centre for local produce from the broad mountain areas of the upper branch of the Yangtze — the Dragon River （龙河） — and it is also the only port on the Yangtze in the Tujia autonomous county of the Qian River (黔江).

Docks had already been built in Xituo Town in the Han Dynasty. Its deep water allowed the town to become important for commercial dealings in the Ming and Qing dynasties. Sichuan products — such as salt, silks and embroidery — were transported through Chengdu, Chongqing, and Fuling on the upper stream of the Yangtze to Western Boundary Inlet, then past the old Sichuan path and

Stairs to the Clouds Street

Western Inlet Town

the Qiyao Mountain to the border of Sichuan and Hubei. The old transport line was known as the "long salt path".

Originally built in the Qing and Han dynasties, "Stairs to the Clouds Street" in Xituo Old Town zigzags along the cliff to the riverside and extends to the peak of Dumenzui Mountain (独门嘴山), on the foot of Fangdou Mountain (方斗山). After climbing its over 1,000 steps, standing on the peak of the street and looking down reveals the running water of the Yangtze, and the great Fangdou Mountain and Gem Mountain.

Climbing along the Stairs to the Clouds from the old town, the merchants and peddlers of ancient days are no longer present. Yet the past is suggested by the commercial houses and inns that are very much still running. During the Republic of China period, Yongcheng and Hecheng business houses were the contact points for the underground communists.

Ancient sites, such as the Purple Cloud Palace (紫云宫), King Yu Palace (禹王宫), and Osmanthus Palace (桂花宫), blend with local residences. The well-preserved Han Dynasty bricks, and the huge group of tree fossils all add to a genuine sense of antiquity.

At dusk, standing and looking down from Platform Mountain (月台山), you may see the glowing red sunset, with the residences on the ancient Stairs to the Clouds Street covered by a golden layer of rays, and the clouds' changing colours and shapes.

Xiayan Store (下盐店) is a masterpiece of the town's Qing Dynasty buildings. With mountains to the rear and rivers in front, it faces

the Precious Stone Stockade, a popular tourist resort in Zhong County. The store's main hall and corridors remain, and the tilted white stone firewall is faintly visible. Its other buildings are built from precious wooden materials, such as nanmu (楠木).

The walls of the sealed salt storehouse in Xiayan store are made of wooden blocks; there are hardly any gaps between them. They are delicate and exquisite, with antique flavour and the richness of the Tujia people's style.

The architectural craft of the ancient Tujia is impressive. In the corridors and on the beams of the main hall, there are delicate carvings in various styles, including string carving, three-dimensional carving, flowing carving and lattice carving. There are many different shapes as well: birds, beasts, flowers, plants, insects, dragons, phoenixes, clouds, and fairies.

In 2009, when the water level in the Three Gorges Dam reached 175 metres, parts of Xituo Town were submerged. Yongcheng commercial house, Xianyan Store, the Second Divine Palace, and King Yu Palace in the Stairs to Clouds street were all underwater. Most parts of the street remained intact, however. Xiayan Store has been moved to the upper part of the street, and is kept as an example of traditional residence buildings in eastern Sichuan and a folk culture museum .

Za wine is a favourite drink of the Tujia people, and is always used at receptions. The wine is made from barley and sorghum, stored in a trough and mixed with water. Hosts and guest consume it with straws in turn.

Avenue to the Clouds

Parallel with the old Stairs to Clouds street, is the new Stairs to the Clouds avenue, with 13 platforms and 320 blue stone paved steps, making it rather shorter than the old one. The stores on both sides of the street sell tourist wares with Tujia characteristics. And there is a Tujia folk culture garden for visitors to visit and relax.

Qingyan Town 青岩镇

The Ancient Battle Site

Hidden in the thick soil of Qingyan Cliff is armour from the Ming Dynasty, originally belonging to soldiers guarding the frontier. The deserted residences and rotted wooden carvings on the eaves hint at a former glory, while broken tablets on the street tell of a fantastic past.

Qingyan Town, Huaxi Distrcit, Guiyang City, Guizhou Province
贵州省贵阳市花溪区青岩镇
Nearest city: Guiyang
Guiyang Longdongbao International Airport has routes to other major Chinese cities. Guiyang is also a railway hub of south China, with high-speed connections to Chengdu, Chongqing, Guangzhou, Changsha, and Kunming due to be launched in 2012.
From Guiyang West Terminal Bus Station (贵阳客运西站, a 10- to 14-minute drive from Guiyang Station) take a bus to Huishui County (惠水县). You can then get off at Qingyan Town (about 50 minutes).

The little town of Qingyan, or "blue rock" has a history of more than 600 years. Through this time, and after many renovations and expansions, Qingyan has grown into a complex stone town and one of the most significant ancient towns in Guizhou.

The ancient town is surrounded by walls. To the sides of the winding walls are a watchtower and fort with crenels, where 300,000 troops were encamped in Qingyan in the time of Zhu Yuanzhang, the first Ming Dynasty emperor. The soldiers could see far into the distance from the tower. Nowadays, the tower is open to tourists; standing on the gate, you can enjoy a view of the entire ancient town.

In town's surrounding area features typical Guizhou karst landforms. Most ancient architecture in Qingyan Town was built in the Ming Dynasty's Wanli years. The town reached its peak during the Daoguang reign of the Qing Dynasty. Its highlights include nine Buddhist temples, eight monasteries, three caves, two ancestral halls, a palace, and eight tablets.

The residence of Zhao Yijiong (赵以炯), a leading scholar of Guizhou history, is located in the town's North Street. The layout of the residence's houses and yards, and the exquisite carvings on doors and windowsills maintain the style of a century ago. From the door you can vaguely glimpse a portrait of Zhao hanging on the wall of the main hall. On the walls inside hang his poems and paintings.

Memorial archways are a symbol throughout Qingyan. There were originally eight famous archways in the town, though only three have been well-preserved. Of these is Zhao Caizhang Longevity Memorial Archway (赵彩章百岁坊), which sits outside the town's North Gate. Liu Filial and Chastity Memorial Archway (周王氏媳妇刘氏节孝坊) is situated outside

Qingyan tablets

the central beam of the Liu Filial and Chastity Memorial Archway, you can see two exquisite stone carvings: "Two dragons Fight for Treasure" (二龙抢宝)", as well as "Five Dragons Painting (五龙图)".

The old Buddhist temples and monasteries, and solemn Catholic and Christian churches in town are an example of the unique religious combinations found across China. Standing on the Dingguang Gate and overlooking the steeple churches and majestic memorial archways, the cultures of east and west seem to coexist harmoniously.

the Ding Gate (定门); the third archway, Zhao Lilun Longevity Memorial Archway (赵理伦百岁坊), is next to the South Gate. All of the archways face north and are 9.5 metres high and 9 metres wide. They are in a traditional style that features four pillars, three rooms and Afang roof structures (Afang Palace is a famous Qin Dynasty building). On

Qingyan architecture

Tianlong Town 天龙镇

The Castle-Village Town

For over 600 years, "castle-village" people have lived in the ancient town of Tianlong.

Tianlong Town, Pingba County, Anshun City, Guizhou Province
贵州省安顺市平坝县天龙镇
Nearest city: Guiyang
Guiyang Longdongbao International Airport has routes to other major Chinese cities. Guiyang is also a railway hub of south China, with high-speed connections to Chengdu, Chongqing, Guangzhou, Changsha, and Kunming due to be launched in 2012.
From Guiyang City take a direct tourist bus service to Tiantai Mountain(天台山, 10 yuan and 90 minutes). You can then reach Tianlong Town, which is close to Tiantai Mountain.

Located in the "Golden Channel" of central Guizhou Province, Tianlong castle-village was first a relay station on the Shunyuan ancient road, originally known as "Rice Basket Station" (饭笼驿). It was later renamed to "Tianlong" as the old name was not considered appropriately elegant.

The way Tianlong castle-villagers talk, dress, live, and entertain differs them from other villages in the area. Residents are mostly descendants of a garrison stationed in the town 600 years ago in the Ming Dynasty. People call them "castle-villagers".

The village nonetheless also displays the influences of central Chinese and eastern Chinese culture. Yet the language of the castle-village has remained even after hundreds of years of pressure from dialects spoken nearby.

The dress of castle-village women also shows features of eastern Chinese clothes from the Ming and Qing dynasties. Residents' belief structure focuses on Han gods, and their music has the rhythms of eastern Chinese folk songs.

"Nine-ridge" (九道) is the oldest stone building in Tianlong. Inside it is a maze-like castle. The former residence of General Chen Yunyu (陈蕴瑜, famous for his efforts in the Sino-Japanese War) faces southeast and has a three-courtyard structure, boasting one main hall and two side rooms. It was designed as an updated version of Jiangnan traditional residential architecture and is one of the most stunning contemporary residences on the Guizhou plateau.

In the past, men guarded the town in line with the traditional belief that "men are responsible for the outside, while women are responsible for the family". The women here not only manage daily housework, but also pray to gods to bless the men, who stand ready to fight.

These traditions persist even today. For example, in

Tianlong town has many features of Jiangnan architecture

the Three-religion Temple (三教寺), repaired in the Qianlong reign of the Qing Dynasty, most supplicants are women. They wear traditional blue robes with wide sleeves. After lighting incense and saying prayers, they gather together to chat and do their tasks. The temple is built to honour Confucian, Buddhist and Daoist beliefs, embodying the castle-village's syncretic religious culture.

"Sky Stage Mountain" (天台山) is located toward the rear of the castle-village. There are many carvings on the cliffs and typical Guizhou karst formations. An ancient ginkgo tree sits by the roadside, planted during the Ming Dynasty.

Looking up from the ancient tree to the mountaintop, you can see Five-dragon Temple (伍龙寺), built in the Ming Dynasty's Wanli reign. It was built with wooden boards that are fixed into the mountain.

Performance of a Tianlong local play

Five Dragon Temple

Set on Sky Stage Mountain, the Five Dragon Temple is built with stone. Several small windows open from its walls, which served a military defence function. The internal structures are exquisitely made, especially the vivid wooden carvings in front of the main hall. Given the limited space to work with, the buildings are cleverly designed. The front hall of the temple is consecrated for the Buddha, the back hall worships Yudi (the king in heaven), and the temple was used as a school in the late Qing Dynasty. The temple is also a fantastic viewing spot for looking down from the mountain at the whole of Tianlong.

JiuzhouTown (Anshun) 安顺旧州镇

The Capital of Ancient Anshun

Old Country Town hosts ancient cultural sites including a Palaeolithic bat cave, mysterious cactus-shaped tombs, the Chieftain burial places, Chieftain Palace, and ancient post roads.

Jiuzhou Town, Xixiu District, Anshun city, Guizhou Province
贵州省安顺市西秀区旧州镇
Nearest city: Guiyang
Guiyang Longdongbao International Airport has routes to other major Chinese cities. Guiyang is also a railway hub of south China, with high-speed connections to Chengdu, Chongqing, Guangzhou, Changsha, and Kunming due to be launched in 2012.
From Guiyang Railway Station take a train to Anshun Railway Station (安顺站, one hour). Then, walk 15 minutes to Anshun Bus Station (安顺汽车客运站), from which regular direct buses depart for Jiuzhou Town (about 40 minutes).

The historic ancient town of Anshun's Jiuzhou (Old County) Town is located near Yellow-fruit Tree Falls and 36 kilometres southeast of Anshun, a city in midwest Guizhou Province. Jiuzhou Town was originally called Anshun Country Town, and became the capital of Anshun in the 14th century. In the Ming Dynasty's Chenghua, Anshun Country moved to Adabu (currently Anshun City), where it came under the jurisdiction of Puding prefecture (普定府). People call it "Old Anshun Country", or "Old Country", leading to the saying "the Old Country existed before Anshun".

Jiuzhou Town is surrounded by water on three sides — a mountain graces its fourth side. The construction of streets is based on the principles of yin and yang and the "five elements" in Chinese philosophy. The ancient city walls are shaped like gourds.

Walking through the streets, you will encounter the quiet and quaint Wenchang Pavilion, with the Hefeng Gloriette (河风亭) in the front. The reflection of pavilions in

Jiuzhou is surrounded by water on three sides. The construction of its streets is based on the principles of yin and yang and the "five elements".

water has the depth and beauty of a Jiangnan ink painting.

The Zhan Family Village (詹家屯) is located 3 kilometres south of Old Country Town. It features windows used for firing weapons behind protection, along both sides of the village road. Its location to the southeast of the town means it was frequently fought over throughout history. The ancient buildings in the village are mostly from the Ming and Qing dynasties, and provide castle-village style architectural landscapes. Many of its buildings have multi-cross wooden courtyards, with open yards both to the front and back. In the open yards there are blue stone brick floors. The Ye Family Old House was designed before 1959 by a Nanjing warlord, and the architecture is imposing and exquisite, but was destroyed during the Cultural Revolution. Horse-tethering piles can still be seen in front of its gate. Other sights in Zhan Family Village include Peifeng Temple (培风寺) and "Five Illusion Temple" (五显寺), which boast beautiful carvings and paintings.

Castle-village feasts are elaborate events held for guests, celebrations, family gathering, weddings, and funerals. They include cold dishes, main dishes, refreshments, soup and more, emphasizing the flavour of the raw materials. The dishes can do not need to be heated, meaning they can be eaten by marching soldiers. Examples include spicy chicken, smoky bacon, and salty eggs.

The Jump Flower Festival (跳花节) is the oldest traditional festival of the Anshun Miao people. The word "Jump Flower" is a Han name, named after a slope with flowers. The festival is held in the first month of the lunar calendar. There are still 24 places fixed as flower slopes. Other traditional activities included local plays and dances, flower lantern singing and other colourful folk entertainment.

Old Country fare

Anshun Cuisine

A saying goes: "Guizhou cuisine is best in Anshun, Anshun cuisine is best in Old Country". Ci mushroom (慈菇), sweet rice, braised pork belly, pickles and other specialties are among the town's culinary highlights.

Jiuzhou Town (Huangping) 黄平旧州镇

A Classic Southern Guizhou Town

The ancient town of Jiuzhou has more than 2,300 years of history and is located in a national scenic area next to the Yang Lake — also known as Silver Lake— and the Wuyang River.

Jiuzhou Town, Huangping County, Guizhou Province
贵州省黄平县旧州镇
Nearest city: Guiyang
Guiyang Longdongbao International Airport has routes to other major Chinese cities. Guiyang is also a railway hub of south China, with high-speed connections to Chengdu, Chongqing, Guangzhou, Changsha, and Kunming due to be launched in 2012.
From Guiyang Railway Station (贵阳站) take a train to Kaili Railway Station (凯里站, 2.5 hours). From there transfer to Kaili Bus Station (凯里客车站, a 10-minute walk from Kaili Railway Station), from which there are regular buses to Jiuzhou Town (about 40 minutes).

Jiuzhou Town (Huangping) was founded during the Spring and Autumn period, and is located about 25 kilometres from Huangping County (黄平县). There are four gates in the town, one at each point of the compass, and Jiuzhou is a port for the transfer of goods and products. The town grew prosperous through this bustling trade, and became an important business town in southern Guizhou province.

The broad streets of Jiuzhou are flanked by marshalling posts and panel-structure dwellings on both sides. The high and stern fire seal emits elegant antique beauty. The houses have retained the architectural style of the Ming and Qing dynasties, maintaining their spectacular simplicity. Each house has a fire seal, usually standing 1-metre higher than the dwellings and showcasing beautiful paintings. Wooden window with carvings of dragons, phoenixes, flowers, and fishes, just as with many of the pictures on the walls, make these homes seem like high-class art museums.

Built in 1837, the Fujian Guide Hall, also know as Tianhou Temple (天后宫), is located at Xixia Street (西下街), surrounded by fire seals. There are two main halls, four wing-rooms, and four gardens, mainly dedicated to the Sea God.

Benevolence and Longevity Palace (仁寿宫) was built in 1786 during the Qianlong reign of the Qing Dynasty, and is located in the middle of Jiuzhou. When you come to the main hall and corridor, the excellent carvings and exquisite workmanship stand out.

The three-storey Literature Palace (文昌宫) building is an ancient pavilion about 15 metres tall built during the Ming and Qing dynasties. The palace sits on the water like a pearl set on green ribbons. Visitors can reach the pavilion via a small bridge. Years ago the literati would gather at the

An ancient dwelling in Jiuzhou Town

Jiuzhou Town in Huangping County

pavilion to compose poems and play their lutes with friends. It is now a popular place for the town's elderly to gather.

At the western gate of Jiuzhou is "Five Holes Stone Bridge"(五孔连拱石桥), which crosses the Wuyang River. The original bridge was established by an official named Gu Deheng (古德恒) during the Ming Dynasty. It was destroyed by a flood in 1681, however, and rebuilt into its current state in 1772. The bridge is an important thoroughfare to the cities of Zunyi and Chongqing.

The 6th Group of the Red Army passed Jiuzhou Town after the Central Red Army, so the town offers its share of "red tourism". A map of Guizhou translated by the leader of the 6th Red Army Group and a French preacher named Boshate is preserved in the town's Christian Church. The church, located at the exit of the east gate of Jiuzhou, is a unique combination of Chinese and Western gothic architecture. The prayer house and sitting room make up its main parts. Facing east, the wall of the prayer house is made of orderly rows of bricks. The east wall is 1-metre higher than the ridge, and there are two arch doors below. The west wall has three round windows on its upper part and two small archways below. It can hold up to 400 people for

mass. Six 3-metre pillars extend to the roof inside, and you can see the unique structure of the ceiling, which has been likened to four open umbrellas. There are many arched windows and doors in the east and west side of the living quarters.

Jiuzhou is home to nine palaces, eight temples, three Buddhist convents and four halls. Gutai Fairy Land (鼓台仙境), Wenbo Dragon Pool and the magnificent Red Cliff are all located on the outskirts of town. The town is also within striking distance of the grand Yangtze Gorge, built in recent years, the beautiful landscapes of Guilin and the elegant and gentle Wuyang River.

Post Art

The twelve zodiac sentry posts are exquisitely decorated and rich with symbolic meaning, so the town has been featured as a hometown of sentry post art. Its traditional embroidery and textile technology are also distinctive.

Xijiang Town 西江镇

The Largest Miao Town

The name of Xijiang Town is a transliteration of the Miao word for the village, which translated as "Chicken Speak" (鸡讲). As the largest town lived in by the Miao people, Xijiang's cultural importance is matched only by its beautiful natural setting, with the White Water River passing through the town from east to west.

Xijiang Town, Leishan County, Guizhou Province
贵州省雷山县西江镇
Nearest city: Guiyang
Guiyang Longdongbao International Airport has routes to other major Chinese cities. Guiyang is also a railway hub of south China, with high-speed connections to Chengdu, Chongqing, Guangzhou, Changsha, and Kunming due to be launched in 2012.
From Guiyang Railway Station (贵阳站) take the service to Kaili Railway Station (凯里站) (2.5 hours). At Kaili, transfer to Kaili Bus Station (凯里客车站, a 10-minute walk from Kaili Railway Station) and board a bus to Xijiang Town (about 35 minutes).

Situated in the northeast of Guizhou Province's Leishan County (雷山县), to the northeast of the village is the national preservation area of Leigong Mountian, with its main peak of Miao Ling (苗岭). The residential stockades of Xijiang are characteristic Guizhou wooden diaojiaolou (hanging-foot buildings), made from high-quality cedar wood from the mountain. The wooden architecture buildings are constructed on a slope of 30 to 70 degrees and are based on a two-level trapezoidal platform, with about 2 metres between the levels. Cobblestones were used to stabilise the 100-metre trapezoidal platform, which supports the pillars of the houses. Most of the dwelling houses in Xijiang have five pillars, but the bigger ones may boast up to seven.

The sides of the diaojiaolou buildings are covered with grey tiles and cedar leaves. Normally there are three large rooms — each with two wing offices —partitioned by 7-centimetre wooden boards.

Diaojiaolou buildings are usually three storeys, with the lowest used for cattle and storage. The middle floor is for residents and hosting guests, and also often includes an ancestral shrine. The side rooms are used for sleeping, guest rooms, storage, cooking, or other purposes. The upper floors are used for storing dry food or drying clothes.

The clothes worn by the Miao townsfolk are colourful and diverse, while their silver ornaments display an exquisite workmanship. The women dress up with silver flowers on their heads and silver earrings and necklaces for festivals. Even on regular occasions, the women's' clothes are often adorned with silver flowers on and flower ribbons.

The women are enthusiastic about embroidery. Styles used in Xijiang include flat embroidery, fold embroidery and paste embroidery, though crepe embroidery is the most popular. Embroiderers use 12 coloured threads that are woven into various ribbons then decorated with embroidered flowers, birds, fishes, animals, and other patterns.

The Wind-Rain Bridge (风雨桥) is a highlight of the town, and a venue for feasting days, when a long table is installed. On its corridor, people sightsee from the bridge, and seek shelter from the wind and rain. The buildings on the bridge, established during the end of the Han Dynasty and developed during the Tang Dynasty, were built without any nails or rivets.

There are many traditional festivals in Xijiang Town. In the middle of the 6th month on the lunar calendar is the "Chixin Festival" (吃新节), held to worship ancestors and celebrate the harvest. On the 10th month in the lunar calendar (usually the beginning of October) there is the Lusheng Festival (芦笙节). The Miao people dance while playing the reed-pipe (芦笙舞) when singing folk songs. The "Guzang Festival" (鼓藏节), held once every 13 years, is the most solemn ceremony in Miao culture. During this festival, every family will kill cattle and invite guests to drink. The women dress up and dance and to traditional folk songs played on the reed-pipes. The unmarried youth of the town can participate in youfang (游方), a kind of blind date, where they express through song their hopes of finding a life partner.

The Miao people in Xijiang are hospitable. Regardless of whether it is festival time or a normal day, guests are usually welcomed into local's homes and treated to hot rice wine. During festivals, the treatment is even more lavish.

Sour

There is a saying in Xijiang: "Without eating any sour food for three days, you will lose your way". As this suggests, sour food is important food in the town — its most famous dishes include sour fish, sour pork, sour bird, and sour cucumber, beans and chili. The local glutinous rice and wine are also recommended.

The thousand stockade village of Xijiang

北 方 古 镇
Northern Towns
Walls and Battlegrounds

Yangliuqing Town 杨柳青镇
Cultural Canal Town

The original name of Yangliuqing Town was Liu Kou (流口, later 柳口). It got its current name — which translates to "willow talk" — in the late Yuan Dynasty. Yangliuqing is considered the centre of traditional woodblock New Year's paintings, while other excellent local arts include paper-cutting and black-brick carving.

Yangliuqing Town, Xiqing District, Tianjin City
天津市西青区杨柳青镇
Nearest city: Tianjin
High-speed trains from Beijing South Station arrive at Tianjin Station (30 mins), while other routes are served by Tianjin West Station and Tianjin South Station. Tianjin Binhai International Airport offers a wide variety of domestic connections.
From Tianjin West Station(天津西站), hire a taxi to Yangliuqing Town (about 30 minutes and 40 yuan. You can also take the No. 153 bus. Alternatively, from downtown Tianjin, get on the No. 158, No. 175 or No. 672 buses, which also stop at Yangliuqing Town.

During the Ming and Qing dynasties, Yangliuqing was an important stop along the Grand Canal and a culture and commercial centre in northern China. With its growing commercial prosperity, it cultivated a strong local art culture.

Mingqing Street (明清街) is a tourist hub for those interested in traditional Chinese culture. It is located at the heart of the Yangliuqing Folk Culture Tourism Area (杨柳青民俗旅游区). The long street is built of black bricks and gray tiles — and consists largely of imitation Qing architecture. The buildings are mostly two storeys high, with only a few having one or three floors. There is an old-style bluestone archway on the street, which is considered one of the best in China. Near the street are attractions such as the Shi Family Courtyard (石家大院), Wenchang Pavilion (文昌阁), Gratitude Temple (报恩寺), the God of War Temple (关帝庙), and the An Family Ancestral Hall (安氏祠堂).

The Shi Family Courtyard, built in the late Qing Dynasty and famous for its grand size and exquisite design, is considered by experts to be the best-preserved and largest group of late Qing buildings in China. The whole area contains 12 courtyards. Every detail of the design is rich in meaning — doorsills ascend from the south to north side of the building symbolizing the desire to be promoted to a higher position; gates in every yard have three stairs, which shows the desire to move up three social classes. There are stone and wood sculptures everywhere, which designs such as "Early Morning Phoenix"(丹凤朝阳) and "Advancing Three Ranks" (平升三级), which features a carved screen with three halberds.

The Yangliuqing Museum is located in the Shi Family Courtyard (石家大院) and focuses on the folk art of the town. The exhibition has four sections — New Year's woodblock paintings, brick-carvings of Tianjin, folk customs of Tianjin, and restored woodblock paintings. The museum's collection is rich and is a must-see for visitors.

The Shi Opera House (石府戏楼) in the Shi Family Courtyard is the biggest opera house in northern China. The opera house, archway, and Wenchang Pavilion are known as the "three treasures" of Yangliuqing. Wenchang Pavilion was built during the Wanli Emperor's reign of the Ming Dynasty (1576). The

Ancient Canal of Yangliuqing

Archway of Yangliuqing

pavilion is considered one of the best of its kind in China, and is a bricks-and-wood structure, with three floors and a hexagon shape.

The town's New Year's woodblock painting tradition started in the Song Dynasty, was developed in the Ming, and flourished during the Qianlong reign of the Qing. Once there was a time when "every family knew how to draw and every house knew the art of paint". Putting up a fresh painting around New Year is customary in northern China.

New Year Festival

The Yangliuqing Folk Cultural Tourism Festival (杨柳青民俗文化旅游节) is held annually around Chinese New Year (usually at the end of January to the beginning of February). The festival features yangko performances, lantern riddles, and other activities at the Shi Family Courtyard, Yangliuqing Museum, Yangliuqing Square, and Ming-Qing Street.

New Year's Painting Pavilion

Gu Beikou Town 古北口镇

Under the Great Wall

Since the semi-mythical Xia and Shang Dynasties, Gu Beikou has bourne witness to the Chinese dynastical cycle — an endless succession of wars which never destroyed the town completely.

Gubeikou Town, Miyun County, Beijing
北京市密云县古北口镇
Nearest city: Beijing
From Beijing Qianmen Travel Distribution Centre (北京前门旅游集散中心) a special tourist bus service heads to Simatai Scenic Spot (司马台景区) in Gubeikou Town, a two-hour trip. Keep in mind the service only runs at weekends and holidays. You can also head to Dongzhimen Bus Station (东直门汽车站) and take the No. 980 or No. 970 buses to Miyun Bus Station (密云汽车站, about one hour.) At Miyun, transfer to a tourist bus to Simatai Scenic Spot (司马台景区, one hour). The entrance fee for Simatai Great Wall (司马台长城) is 40 yuan.

Gu Beikou (古北口) in the east and Juyong Gate (居庸关) in the west stand facing each other, marking an important pass between the North China Plain and Inner Mongolia. The pass was well-known in ancient times for its grandness and danger. "The way to our destination is as tough as the desert, but it seems that god has left a key to pass the toughness," according to one ancient traveller.

The Great Wall can be viewed at three places in the town: Crouching Tiger Mountain (卧虎山), Coiling Dragon Mountain (蟠龙山) and Simatai (司马台). Among them, the Coiling Dragon Mountain portion (蟠龙山长城) has suffered the least restoration, and therefore has the most authentic feel. The memorial steles for the Gu Beikou Guardian War (古北口保卫战纪念碑); the Soldiers' Building (将军楼), and other cultural relics on this stretch of the Great Wall are found here. The 24 Eye Building (二十四眼楼) is the heart of the Coiling Dragon Mountain section (蟠龙山长城) and also one of the treasures of the entire wall.

Climbing the Simatai portion of the Great Wall, you are rewarded for the steep and often perilous jaunt with wonderful views of green mountains and crystal-clear lakes. Looking out from the highest part of the wall, you can take in the Wulin Mountains (雾灵主峰) in the east; Coiling Dragon Mountain in the west; the great expanses of the Miyun Reservoir (密云水库) in the south.

Yang Linggong Ancestral Hall, located on Dong Menli (东门里) on the east side of the Gu Beikou River, is a place of beautiful tales. The Auspicious Bell (吉祥钟) sits on the east of the hall, which brings blessings. Standing in the empty field and looking out, the entirety of the splendid Crouching Tiger Mountain (卧虎山) is before you. Every year around mid-September, people from every part of the country come here to pray. Temple fairs and performances are also held in the fall.

The Soldiers' Cemetery (将士公墓) is a big tomb made of yellow sandy soil on the road outside the south gate of the town. The tomb commemorates the more than 300 soldiers who died during the Sino-Japanese War. Many come every year to pay their respects.

On March 4, 1933, the Gu Beikou Battle started — Japanese tanks carved out a way into the region under the protection of warplanes in the sky. Despite huge casualties, seven surviving soldiers of the No. 145 regiment of the Chinese army fought on, with only a machine gun left to defend themselves, on a small mountain named Yi Maoer — a critical point that had to be passed by Japanese forces. The Japanese thought there were dozens of soldiers fighting against them from the top, but after they prevailed found just seven corpses. They built the Tomb of the Seven Brave Chinese Soldiers as a sign of respect for their courage.

Royal Flowers

Gu Beikou has a flower festival, also known as the Longfu Old Festival (隆福老会) in Hexi. Emperor Qianlong of the Qing Dynasty reportedly once passed Gu Beikou and happened to see the festival, which pleased him. He awarded a performance to the Huang Gangxiang Meeting at the festival. The show was performed by locals from East Mountain (东山) and named Longfu Old Festival by the emperor. Because of its back storey, locals regard it as a "royal" festival (皇会).

Gu Beikou pass

Guangfu Town 广府镇

The Birthplace of Tai Chi

Guangfu is well-known as a classic ancient city, a bewitching waterside town, and as the birthplace of Tai Chi.

Guangfu Town, Yongnian County, Handan City, Hebei Province
河北省邯郸市永年县广府镇
Nearest city: Handan
Handan International Airport offers routes to Beijing and other major cities.
Trains to and from Beijing West Station take about 4-6 hours.
The simplest way to reach Guangfu Town is to take a taxi from downtown Handan (30 minutes).

Fang Guancheng (方观承), the head official of Zhili Province in the Qing Dynasty, once vividly portrayed Guangfu Town in a poem: "The broad and boundless paddy fields are dotted with glittering pools. Swaying reeds carry the intoxicating lotus fragrance in the breeze. Quliang Town (曲梁城，Guangfu's former name) is immersed in a sea of aromas, the Churi Tower (初日楼) lies at its far-reaching waters". (稻引千畦苇岸通，行来襟袖满荷风。曲梁城 (今广府古城)下香如海，初日楼边水近东).

Thirty kilometres northeast of Handan (邯郸市), Guangfu is a town that dates back 2,000 years. Dou Jiande (窦建德, a leader of the peasant uprising against the Sui Dynasty) renovated the ancient city from the very end of the Sui Dynasty to the beginning of Tang Dynasty. In the Jiajing period (1542) in the Ming Dynasty, the city walls, originally made of mud, were upgraded to brick. Outside the original four gates some defensive entrances (瓮城) were built. The ancient city, with four streets, eight lanes, and 72 corners, had quite an intricate layout. Inside the city walls, the old houses

The east entrance of ancient Guangfu

were all built with grey-green bricks and tiles.

The ancient Guangfu City, also named Guangpingfu City (广平府城), sits on the banks of the Yongnian Lake (永年洼淀) with an area of more than 20 square kilometres. The existing archaic city walls are 10 metres high and 8 metres thick. Gate towers were built at the four entries, there are turrets in the four corners and 876 arrow holes. The most distinguishing features of the city were once the barbicans built near the four entries, and the strongly fortified tunnels. The gate towers and turrets have been destroyed, but the city walls and the moat have survived.

The ancient Guangfu flourished as flocks of merchants and traders settled here. There were numerous official residences and temples and more than 30 streets and lanes formed an intricate layout. In recent years, an old secret tunnel called Dou Jiande's Military Transport Tunnel (窦建德运兵道) was been discovered in the city. It is said that during the war between Dou Jiande and Li Shimin (李世民, who was later the second emperor of the Tang Dynasty) as they contended for the imperial throne, Dou began to dig a 15-kilometre tunnel from the inner city to the outskirts of town. To confuse Li about the real number of his troops, Dou ordered the soldiers to make round trips through the tunnel, making it appear as if he had more forces than he actually did.

Another historical spot in the city is Hongji Bridge (弘济桥), which was constructed during the Song and Yuan dynasties and shares the same scale and structure as Zhaozhou Bridge

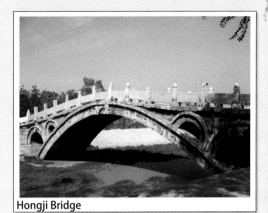
Hongji Bridge

(赵州桥, a famous ancient bridge in China). Remaining undamaged and magnificent, Hongji Bridge is a national heritage site. Recently, fossils from the Ordovician Period, including trilobites, have been found in the slates of the bridge.

Yongnian Lake is the third-largest swamp in northern China, only smaller than Baiyangdian Lake (白洋淀) and Hengshui Lake (衡水湖). The lake is about half a square kilometres, though it seems vast and boundless. It is deep, making it convenient for water transportation. However, the waterways on the lake are so intricate and the reeds so tall that it is quite easy to get lost for those unfamiliar with the lake. Overlooked from the sky, the lake is a labyrinth of criss-crossing waterways and reeds.

Guangfu is the birthplace of the Tai Chi created by Yang Luchan and Wu Yuxiang. The former residences of both Yang (杨露禅) Wu (武禹襄) are well-preserved and undamaged. Wu's former residence (武禹襄故居) is typical of what a wealthy home would have looked like, with an area of 9,000 square metres and three courtyards. The main construction of the residence remains undamaged and is a provincial heritage site.

Tai Chi

The two main branches of Tai Chi differ from each other in movements and style, with Yang's Tai Chi employing more dramatic movements and Wu's being exquisite and compact. They are both well-known for their principles of the hidden strength in being gentle and elegant integration of movement.

Tianchang Town 天长镇

A Song Dynasty Mountain Town

Tianchang Town was designated as a county seat in the Song Dynasty. The town has a gate on all sides but the north and each is equipped with a barbican and 19 crossbow towers, making the town easy to hold and hard to attack.

Ancient China: Towns

Tianchang Town, JingjingCounty, Shijiazhuang City, Hebei Province
河北省石家庄市井陉县天长镇
Nearest city: Shijiazhuang
Shijiazhuang is only a 2-hour train journey from Beijing West Station. Hebei Zhengding International Airport is served by a wide variety of domestic routes.
From Shijiazhuang Xiwang Long-distance Bus Staiton (石家庄西王长途汽车站, a 20-minute taxi ride from Shijiazhuang Train Station) there are regular buses to Jingjing County. From there transfer to a minibus to Tianchang Town (about 30 minutes).

Tianchang Town dates back to the Han Dynasty. There are two national heritage sites: the Jingxing Ancient Porcelain Kiln Site (井陉古瓷窑遗址) and the Jingxing Ancient Courtier Route (井陉古驿道). With more than 1,300 years of history, the Jingxing Kiln (井陉窑遗址) located in the Jingxing Mining Area is a fire with many functions.

The former county government office of the Ming and Qing dynasties (明清县衙) is located on the northeast side of Dajie Road (大街路), which is the centre of Tianchan. The main entrance of the official mansion is a stone arch with a gable-roof loft and a screen wall right behind it. There are two tent-roof bells and drum towers of five rooms' width on the two sides. The main hall, of five rooms' width, is covered by a multi-gabled roof. The rear chambers were the officials' living quarters.

The Confucius Temple (孔庙) is situated to the west of the Old County Government Office. From south to north, the main buildings of the temple are Lingxing Gate (棂星门), Zhuangyuan Bridge

The City God's Temple

(状元桥), Master Hall (万进宗师坊), Halberd Gate (戟门), Confucius Hall (圣殿), and the Ancestral Hall of Confucius (宗圣祠). Originally built in 1770 during the Emperor Qianlong's reign, the Jieshan Academy on the north part of Dongmennei Road is elegant with a sense of ancient beauty.

The distinctive Grand Chengguan Bridge over the Mian River was originally built as a 12-arch bridge in the 45th year of Qianlong's reign (1780). However, in 1790 and 1801, the eastern half of the bridge was successively destroyed by floods. In the Republic of China era in 1928, the eastern half was renovated after the Jin-Feng War.

The ancient dwellings in Tianchang are mainly quadrangles featuring blue bricks and grey tiles. Long lanes are lined with architecture of various styles, including tingtang quadrangles (containing large halls), liansuo quadrangles (connected by small alleys), taojin quadrangles (encompassing smaller quadrangles inside),

The Goddess of Mercy Pavilion on the old city walls

sanjie quadrangles (divided into three parts). A picturesque landscape is interwoven by scenic spots such as the Xiasi Tower (下寺塔) of the Jin Dynasty, whose "Reflection in the River" is widely known.

The Jingxing courtier route crosses Jingxing County, connecting Luquan City (鹿泉市) on its east and Guguan (固关) of Pingding County (平定县) on its west. It is a strategic passage between the former Zhili Province and Shanxi Province and has been a place of vital military significance since ancient times. There are still some remaining road tracks in the mountains and fields. In some parts of the region, the remains of courier stations and inns can still be found.

Residence

Groove On

Tianchang is also the hometown of the folk dance lahua. A type of yangko dance, lahua's main movements include shaking shoulders, rotating wrists, twisting arms, knee lifts, and leg stretching, which form a distinctive art form, coupling hardness and softness as well as ruggedness and exquisiteness.

Qikou Town 碛口镇

Harbour Town On the Yellow River

Qikou sits beside the Yellow River and the "qi" (碛) from "Qikou" refers to the shoals of the Yellow River. The river roars thunderously where it meets the stones of the shoal and the turbulent waves spit in every direction.

Ancient China: Towns

Qikou Town, Linxian County, Lishi City, Shanxi Province
山西省离石市临县碛口镇
Nearest city: Taiyuan
Taiyuan Wusu International Airport has good connections with major cities. A high-speed train from Beijing can now reach Taiyuan Station in less than 3 hours.
From Taiyuan Railway Station(太原火车站), there is a high-speed rail line link to Lü liang City (吕梁, two hours). After arriving at Lü liang, take a taxi to Lishi West Bus station (离石西客运站, a 30-minute taxi ride from the railway station). The station has several services a day heading to Qikou Town (碛口镇). The ride takes about one hour.

Qikou became prosperous during the Qianlong reign of the Qing Dynasty (1735-1795) and for a long time was the busiest commercial town in northern China.

500 metres southwest of Qikou Ancient Street (碛口古街), Datong Moraine (大同碛) is located where the Qiushui River (湫水河) runs into the Yellow River. The breadth of the river is suddenly reduced to 100 metres, then the water runs 3,000 metres to a fall of 10 metres, creating strong currents, big waves, and thunderous roars.

The old streets here were built in the Ming and Qing dynasties. The main street along Crouching Tiger Mountain (卧虎山) starts in the east, winds west along the Qiushui River, then turns north against the Yellow River. The ancient back alley is only 200 metres, but has 18 turns. The streets are paved with stone and the stores all have flat-panel doors. Because the land is low and there used to be frequent flooding, the roadside houses all have high pedestals, called gaogetai (高圪台). South of the main street are 2nd (二道街) and 3rd streets (三道街). Going south the streets become shorter and shorter, forming a trapezoidal pattern.

Going up a little along the Qiushui River (湫水河) to the back of the town sits the little Xiwan Village (西湾村), with mountains on three sides and river on the fourth. "Xiwan" means "west turn", and was so named

The stage of Heilong Temple

Qikou, a harbour town by Luliang Mountain on the east bank of the Yellow River

because it is at the turn of the Qiushui River.

Xiwan villagers all have the last name Chen. The village benefited from the vibrant economy of Ming and Qing era Qikou. The whole town belonged to the tycoon Chen family, and was nicknamed the "Chen family yard". The village holds more than 40 houses connected by five stone streets representing metal, wood, water, fire, and earth — the five elements of traditional Daoist philosophy. The high walls turn the village into a huge castle-like enclosure. There are only three gates to the south, which represent heaven, earth, and man, itself an architectural embodiment of the Daoist ideas of harmony between man and nature.

Heilong Temple (黑龙庙) was built in the Ming Dynasty. Located on Crouching Tiger Mountain of Qikou, the temple is mainly made up of the mountain gate (山门), main hall (正殿) and the music building (乐楼). The temple is near the mountain and beside the river, standing on rocky cliffs. The music building was built with superb craftsmanship and you can hear the music from 5,000 metres away without any amplification. From the temple's vantage point,

you can see the Yellow River right under your feet.

On every first day of the first and seventh month of the lunar calendar (around February and August), the villagers hold the Heilong Temple Fair, which attracts visitors from Shaanxi, Shanxi, and Sichuan provinces. There are performances rich with Loess Plateau heritage, including theatrical shows, local operas such as Lion Biting the Embroidered Ball (狮子啃绣球), Qikou waist drum shows (碛口腰鼓), northern Shaanxi shadow plays, paper cutting, instrument shows, and vocal performances.

Cave Houses

In the cave houses (窑洞) of Qikou Town, are earth kangs (土炕), and quilts and mattresses (被褥) with local Loess Plateau color. You can taste buckwheat jelly (碗砣荞麦粉), flour fish (面鱼), Yellow River Beach jujube (黄河滩枣) and Yellow River Damu jujube (黄河大姆枣), or simply enjoy the views of the Yellow River and listen to camel bells ringing in the valley.

Niangzi Pass Town 娘子关镇

The Great Wall's Women's Pass

Niangzi is the eastern gate of Shanxi Province and a key military area between Shanxi and Hebei provinces. The undulating mountains, hundreds of springs, majestic pass, and winding Great Wall are famous attractions.

Niangziguan Town, Pingding County, Yangquan City, Shanxi Province
山西省阳泉市平定县娘子关镇
Nearest city: Taiyuan
Taiyuan Wusu International Airport has good connections with major cities. A high-speed train from Beijing can now reach Taiyuan Station in less than 3 hours.
From Taiyuan Jiannan Bus Station (太原建南汽车站), a 10- to 15-minute ride from Taiyuan Station (太原站), take a bus to Yangquan Long-distance Bus Station (阳泉长途汽车站, about 90 minutes). Minibuses depart regularly from Yangquan for Niangziguan Town (one hour).

Niangzi Pass is the ninth pass of the Great Wall. "Niangzi" means "woman", and the pass was so named because Princess Tangping once stationed troops here. Located on a cliff with the Mian Mountain (绵山) at its back, the pass town occupies a commanding position. The Tao River (桃河) runs down and around the town from southwest to northeast. The east and south pass gate and 650-metre-long wall still remains.

There are two brick gates on either side of the pass, with a residential area in the middle, a platform for reviewing troops and observing enemies, and a stable gate tower in the inner city. The Great Wall on both sides of the pass town clings to the mountain, forming a natural barrier between Shanxi and Hebei provinces.

In the town there are ancient buildings, including the God of War Temple (关帝庙) and Zhenwu Tower (真武阁). It is said when Dong Zhuo (a powerful official and warlord of the late Eastern Han Dynasty) led troops to

Niangzi Pass

The Great Wall's ninth pass

里行不前，但觉飞湍醒毛发).

The stone grinders and springs of the "water dwellers" (水上人家) are unique to the Niangzi Pass. The houses and walls here are built with grey stones from the nearby mountains. The folk houses are old and simple, and double as places of business. The local people make grinders out of stones and wheels out of wood. Part of their culture is to sing beautiful folk songs in the stone houses and mills. According to historical records, Niangzi was already a key commercial town in the Tang and Song dynasties and was famous for its water mills and inns in the Republic of China period.

Xiadongzhai Village (下董寨村), he saw the cliffs and mountains and built Dongzhuo Castle and stationed troops here. After that, the pass came into being.

The Niangzi Pass Waterfall (娘子关瀑布) is located under the Dunu Temple (妒女祠) 300 metres away from the east gate of the town. There are numerous springs in the valley of the hills and the waterfall is composed of several streams which pour down along a 50-metre cliff like a sheet of white silk. Qiao Yu, a Ming Dynasty official, wrote Waterfall Spring Poem: "I look back at the Mian Mountain, and have come several times to see the hanging spring. The water under the waterfall connects to the sea, and its mist covers the high mountain". (回头形势接绵山，为看悬泉数往还。石乳下通沧海底，浪花高叠翠峰闲。)

The great Jin Dynasty poet Yuan Haowen wrote in Visiting the Hanging Spring, "Poets like mountains and water, and they go to see ice and snow in October. The spring hangs at thousands of metres, and my hairs are wetted by the its spray". (诗人爱山爱澈骨，十月重来犯冰雪。悬流百

River God

Two weeks after the Chinese New Year (usually in February), there are performances of traditional arts in the villages of Niangzi. Most of the performances are about ancient wars and feature acrobatic fighting and old weapons. The villagers carry long spears, broadswords, steel whips, swords, and war flags in the streets and perform whenever the drum is banged. Setting off the Niangzi river lantern (娘子关镇河灯) is another tradition. Every sixth day of the sixth month of the lunar calendar (around July) is the time to honor the river god. On that day, villagers put lanterns on the river and pray for blessings from the river god. The lanterns floating down and lighting up the river at night makes for a beautiful water village scene.

Jingsheng Town 静升镇

The Ancient Hill Town

Jingsheng is an ancient hill town that holds onto an array of vivid traditional culture, where people's peaceful daily life is embellished by folk art.

Jingsheng Town, Lingshi County, Jinzhong City, Shanxi Province
山西省晋中市灵石县静升镇
Nearest city: Taiyuan
Taiyuan Wusu International Airport has good connections with major cities. A high-speed train from Beijing can reach Taiyuan Station in less than 3 hours.
From Taiyuan Station take a train to Lingshi Station (灵石站, about two hours). Then continue by taxi to Jingsheng Town (30 minutes).

Jingsheng sits under the scenic Mian Mountain (绵山) and beside a river. A main street runs across town, and there are eight fortresses and 18 lanes scattered at the foot of the north side of the mountain. The town was first named Jingshan (旌善) and later changed to Jingsheng (静升), meaning "a quiet and peaceful place, prosperous and happy".

According to historical records, there were humans living in the area of present-day Jingsheng Town as far back as the Neolithic age and in the Shang Dynasty, a community called the Nei (内) was settled here. During the Qing Dynasty, Jingsheng developed rapidly and many temples and homes were built. The old Jingsheng remains well-preserved with a number of stores, pawn shops, wells, slate lanes, stages, and so on.

The Wang Residence (王家大院) is a series of courtyards built right down the mountain. The residence, which was renovated several times in the Qing Dynasty, was gradually expanded in its scale, and includes five lanes, five fortresses and five ancestral temples. Today, the Museum of Traditional Chinese Residences stands opposite the Wang Residence Museum (王氏博物馆), with a bridge linking them together. Both the complexes are built in the Loess Plateau (黄土高坡) castle style. The Wang Residence has numerous highlights in its layout and the

The Wang Residence in Jingsheng

different cultures of north and south China have been combined elegantly in the residence.

The Confucius Temple established in the Yuan Dynasty is another historical site of note in Jingsheng. The main building remains, and three annexes are well-preserved, including a screen wall carved with carp leaping through the dragon's gate (a symbol of good luck for students taking examinations), Kuixing Tower (魁星塔) and Wenbi Tower (文笔塔). In the seven metre screen wall carving, there are eight carp swimming and leaping in the waves energetically. Among them, one appears to have a combination of a fish body and dragon's head, indicating its success in jumping through the dragon's gate and turning into a dragon. The carved screen wall, named Nine Dragon Wall (九龙壁) by locals, was constructed several centuries earlier than the celebrated Nine Dragon walls in Datong and Beijing.

Wenbi Tower(文笔塔), with a height of 26 metres and a bottom circumference of 12.3 metres, has a square base made up of bluestone. The brick tower is said to be shaped like a calligrapher's brush pointing towards the blue sky. The brush is supposed to symbolize the numerous scholars of the Wang family.

In the middle of Jingsheng Village is Red Temple (红庙), which has a stage and gets its name from its red walls and gate. During the sixth month of the lunar calendar (mid to late July), the Red Temple holds its annual fair and locals swarm to Jingsheng's Main Street from the surrounding villages. During the fair, the attractions include opera performances, making candy floss (吹糖人), monkey tricks, and martial arts shows. The fair is the liveliest traditional event in Jingsheng.

Stilts

Colourful local folk activities include beigun (背棍, shouldering a person with a rod), taige (抬阁, several people lifting a tiny wooden platform holding two or three people performing a traditional opera), and gaoqiao (高跷, walking on stilts).

The Confucius Temple in Jingsheng

Chenlu Town 陈炉镇

Home of Celadon Porcelain

Chenlu Town is a good place to learn about Loess Plateau culture. During the Sino-Japanese War, the Red Army's second battalion also wrote a glorious page of history here.

Chenlu Town, Yintai Dirstrict, Tongchuan City, Shanxi Province
陕西省铜川市印台区陈炉镇
Nearest City: Xian
Xian Xianyang International Airport is the largest airport in northwest China. Xian Railway Station offers more than 100 services daily.
From the North Bus Station (城北客运站) located near Xian Railway Station (西安火车站) there are regular buses to Tongchuan City (铜川市, one hour). Then transfer to a minibus to Chenlu Town (one hour).

On a mountaintop 15,000 meters southeast of Tongchuan City of Shaanxi Province lies the small town of Chenlu. Chenlu means "display furnaces", and the name came from the town's famed kilns. The town has 1,400 years of history of firing pottery and porcelain. It has the only remaining "millennium furnace" and it is the biggest manufacturing base of Yao Porcelain (耀瓷).

Walking into the town, you can see the legacy of the Ming and Qing porcelain-making industry. Raw materials are dug up and transported from the mountain, where they are ground up and put into a mud pool. The wet clay is then shaped by hand on a potter's wheel, a process that results in mountains of pottery and porcelain. The potters' houses are

Jiangnu Temple

The walls are built with jars

surrounded by white walls and green trees.

The ascending town of Chenlu is a beautiful picture of red and white at sunset. Locals used rejected pottery to build kilns, walls, roads and to strengthen revetments, so the town is full of "jar walls" (罐罐墙) that stand between the furnaces, courtyards and roads. Some have painted the walls white, which makes them dazzle under the sun.

Chenlu porcelain is simple but the unique designs have great artistic value. Cutting, painting, carving, and printing patterns are widely used skills. The sharp yet fluid patterns look exquisite on the glittering blue-glazed porcelain. The people of Chenlu are meticulous in their craft and have passed down their skills from generation to generation. Blue is not the only colour of porcelain available in the town, there is also black, tea foam, black and white, white, and white and blue. The north Wei River folk art style is simple, fresh, and enduringly popular. The popular blue flower decorations are used to create landscapes and birds and flowers.

The porcelain business brought prosperity to Chenlu, described as "a place filled with ancient temples and beautiful jar houses". Even the paths of the ancient town are paved with ceramics, which look like oil paintings and are described by locals as "art underfoot". The dense ceramic dwellings, caves and jar walls on the mountain make for a beautiful scene. The nearby workshops and temples, including Kiln God Temple (社窑神庙), Cool Temple (清凉寺), King of Medicine Temple (药王庙), Bao Mountain Buddhist Temple (宝山禅林), and Lord Guan Temple (关帝庙), add Confucian, Daoist, and Buddhist color to the picturesque ancient town.

Jiangnu Temple

Tongchuan Jiangnu Temple (姜女祠) is 1.5 kilometres away from the Tongchuan City. You can take the No. 1 or No. 7 bus and get off at the Youku station (油库). The new gate (山门), pavilion (祭亭) and statue of Meng Jiangnu (孟姜女雕像) in Jiangnu Temple are worth visiting.

Qingcheng Town 青城镇

1,000-year-old Yellow River Town

Qingcheng was a transportation and commercial hub on the ancient Silk Road, as well a military fortress during the Tang, Song, Yuan and Ming dynasties. In the town, you can visit old Ming and Qing folk houses, enjoy beautiful Xi Xianng Diao music, and watch ram fighting.

Qingcheng Town, Yuzhong County, Lanzhou City, Gansu Province
甘肃省兰州市榆中县青城镇
Nearest city: Lanzhou
Direct routes from major Chinese cities serve Lanzhou Zhongchuan Airport, while Lanzhou Station is a major regional rail hub.。
Go from Lanzhou Bus Station (兰州汽车站), located in Lanzhou Station (兰州站), to Baiyin City (白银市) about a one-hour trip. Then get a cab or charter bus to Qingcheng, which will take about 30 minutes.

Formerly called Yitiaocheng, Qingcheng is situated beside the Yellow River, between the Grand and Wujin gorges and 60 kilometres northeast of Lanzhou.

Qingcheng was built when Di Qing was appointed prefecture governor of the Qin state during the Renzong reign of the Song Dynasty (1010-1063). The town became a trading center for hookahs, which encouraged the formation of a cosmopolitan, multicultural society. The remaining more than 50 old houses in Qingcheng were built in the Qing dynasty and have both Shanxi and Beijing courtyard characteristics. From their front gates to their screen walls, central to wing rooms, eaves to doors to windows, you can find exquisite decorations everywhere.

Qingcheng has a long history, throughout which generations of scholars came here, leaving a precious cultural heritage. Qingcheng Academy (青城书院), built in the Daoguang reign of the Qing Dynasty (1831) nurtured many

Climbing Up Benches

"Climbing up benches" is one of the most unique local activities — the benches form a 10–20 metre "mountain", which performers climb without any safety gear. They stand at the top motionless after reaching their goal.

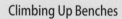

Gao Family Temple

Degree Candidate in the Imperial Examination", given to Gao Hongru by the Emperor Xianfeng.

Qingchenghuang Temple (青城隍庙) used to be the council chamber of the Qin governor Di Qing, and thus is also known as the Di Qing Residence. First built in the Baoyuan period of the Song Dynasty (1038-1040), it was turned into a garrison command center in the Wanli period of the Ming (1597). In 1724, during the Yongzheng reign of the Qing, the buildings were reorganized to become Chenghuang Temple. The main hall is well-preserved, and the gate tower and theatre were repaired recently.

The Luo Family Yard (罗家大院) is a grand quadrangle dwelling with unique special touches. It is a classical folk culture museum with Ming and Qing architectural styles. There are hookah factories, water jars, and stone tables in the yard, while in the back garden there is a thriving lotus pond.

talents, and was one of the six biggest academies in Lanzhou.

First built in the Qianlong reign (1785), the Gao Family Temple (高氏祠堂) covers a total area of 2,000 square metres. The building alone is 400 square metres. The temple is a quadrangle dwelling, with two tablets hanging inside. The first reads, "Literary and Military Virtues"and was bestowed to Gao Minggui by the Emperor Daoguang himself. The second says, "Third

On the east shore of Qingcheng, there are lotus ponds, a pavilion, a plank path, a wooden bridge, and a paddy field covering an area of more than 100,000 square metres. In the summer, the lotuses give off a delicate fragrance. Fishing and farming in the pond have become the area's main source of income.

Qingcheng Academy

Liancheng Town 连城镇

A Centre of Tibetan Buddhism

The ancient town of Liancheng sits in the mountains beside the Datong River. It has an agreeable climate, green trees, and combines culture from north of the Great Wall and south of the Yangtze River.

Ancient China: Towns

Liancheng Town, Yongdeng County, Lanzhou City, Gansu Province
甘肃省兰州市永登县连城镇
Nearest city: Lanzhou
Direct routes from major Chinese cities serve Lanzhou Zhongchuan Airport, while Lanzhou Station is a major regional rail hub.
From Lanzhou Bus Station(兰州汽车站), adjacent to Lanzhou Rail Station (兰州站), there are regular buses to Liancheng Town (about 90 minutes and 12 yuan).

Liancheng is located in the hinterland of the Datong River, 150 kilometres northwest of Lanzhou.

Since ancient times, Liancheng had been a key town connecting to the northwest to the rest of China. There were settlers here as far back as the Neolithic era and huge caches of delicate ancient pottery have been unearthed. The Ma Family Kiln's "Big Painted Jar" (马家窑大彩瓮) is 62 centimetres tall and has a circumference at its widest point of 148 centimetres. It is the biggest painted pottery relic ever found, and it is now preserved at the Yongdeng County Museum.

The old folk houses of Liancheng are generally small quadrangle dwellings with a courtyard, a main room, wing rooms, and a gate. There are several housing types, which are distinguished by their quantity of timber and decoration. In a quadrangle, the main room and gate are more important than the wing rooms.

First built in the early Ming Dynasty, the Residence of former local ruler Lu Tusi (鲁土司衙门) is one of the

Exquisite painted statues of the Gada Temple

Gada Temple

best-preserved ancient palatial Tusi buildings on the border of Gansu and Qinghai provinces. It is a simple and elegant official architectural complex, with an Ancestor Hall (祖先堂), Shentang Courtyard (神堂院), Yanxi Hall (燕喜堂), and many other buildings inside. The residence's grounds hold Miaoyin Temple (妙因寺), which uses both Han and Tibetan styles, and integrates Confucian, Daoist, and Buddhist culture. It reflects the town's multiculturalism and is the biggest Tusi temple, with the biggest and best murals. The glazed-tile temples (琉璃瓦寺) are radiant and are a unique feature of the residence. The Lu Tusi Garden (鲁土司花园) is well-designed and is one of the few remaining ancient gardens in northwest China.

Built in the Jiajing reign of the Ming Dynasty (1555), Thunder Temple (雷坛) is located on the northwest side of the Lu Tusi Residence, 80 metres away from the back wall of the residence. It was built for the Daoist gods of thunder, which are important in the Dragon Gate school of thought (道教龙门派雷部尊神). The remaining side and main halls of the temple are fine structures and the statues and murals inside are well-preserved. The buildings and garden of the Thunder Temple are designed to form the Chinese character for thunder (雷). The main hall has a gable-and-hip roof with a single eave (单檐歇山顶). There are several small painted statues

on the upper side of the door lintel. All are standing on auspicious clouds, with fluttering gowns and solemn looks. There are paintings of war generals of the Thunder Division — Shen Pang, Liu Hegou, and Bi Si — in the front of the hall. The mural, with its smooth lines, bright colors, and vivid images, is considered one of the best religious architectural paintings from the Ming Dynasty.

Liancheng's cultural heritage also includes Tang and Song dynasty city ruins (古城址) and cliff inscriptions (摩崖石刻), and the famous Tibetan Buddhist temples Xianjiao Temple (显教寺) and Gada Temple (尕达寺).

Fair Boss

From the early Ming Dynasty to the Republic of China period, a Lu Tusi (鲁土司, a government title) ruled the region for more than five centuries. In those years, overseeing festivals, temple fairs, and other cultural activities were the main duties of the Lu Tusi. The Great Bodhisattva Temple Fair (大菩萨庙会) in Niuzhan Village, held on the fourth day of the eighth month of the lunar calendar (mid August), the Buddha Bathing Festival (四月八浴佛节) at Gada Temple, and Tiaochan (跳禅) at Miaoyin Temple have become large-scale events.

Dajing Town 大靖镇

An Important Silk Road Town

Dajing Town has been settled for 4,000 years. The town has long been popular with merchants and was an important town on the Silk Road and Hosi Corridor. It is one of the four large ancient town of Gansu province.

Dajing Town, Gulang County, Weiwu City, Gansu Province
甘肃省武威市古浪县大靖镇
Nearest city: Lanzhou
Direct routes from major Chinese cities serve Lanzhou Zhongchuan Airport, while Lanzhou Station is a major regional rail hub. From Lanzhou Bus Station (兰州汽车站), adjacent to Lanzhou Rail Station(兰州站), there is one bus each day to Dajing Town, departing at 13.40. The journey takes about two hours.

Beside the eastern part of Chilien Mountain to the south, the mighty Dajing Gorge (大靖峡) features the majestic Danxia landform. To its north is the southern edge of the Tenger Desert (腾格里沙漠) which is vast and dotted with oases. The Changlin Mountains (昌灵山), with their near-virgin forests, are to the east.

Dajing has been a transportation hub of the east since ancient times. It was once named Palipali (Mongolian for "market"). In the Wanli reign of the Ming (1599), senior officer Tian Le (田乐) gathered more than 10,000 soldiers to beat Ah Chitu (阿赤兔) and recover the territory. The name Dajing means "great peace".

During the town's golden age, its dense concentration of residences, businesses, shops, temples, and palaces attracted an endless stream of merchants. Surviving historical relics, such as Fortune Tower (财神阁), the Ma Family Temple (马家祠堂), Mamiao Assembly Hall (马庙会馆), and Green Mountain Temple (青山寺) testify to this past. Canals and ditches crisscross through the town and forests sit between irrigated areas of the Dajing Gorge reservoir and the Yellow River's Jingdian.

Fortune Tower, also known as Drum Tower, is located in the centre of town. It was built in the Qing Dynasty's Kangxi reign (1718) and rebuilt in 1987. From the top of the three-storey tower, you can see the whole town. Built with 16 pillars, a height of 21 metres and perimeter of 30 metres, it is three storeys tall. The brick base was constructed when the tower was rebuilt, and it has a crossed arch gate from which you can emerge onto the streets. The second and the third storeys are the original wooden buildings, with a single eave on the top. Between the middle pillars, there are three-layer dougongs (dougongs are a joint between a pillar and a beam

Green Mountain Temple

used for support and decoration). There is a one-layer dougong between other pillars, with a layer on every pillar. Carvings of tangled tree branches are on two sides of the pillars and there are flat boards below the eaves. The ridges are tilted, with two smaller ridges from south to north in the middle and another ridge from east to west. The inside architecture is done in a canopy style with a pointed top. A gate is set on the third storey, as well as a statue of the Fortune God.

The Great Wall runs through the outskirts of Dajing. In the last years of the Ming Dynasty, Emperor Zhu Yuanzhang put a high priority on guarding the border, and the famed Dajing Batalion (大靖营) was born. Dajing is actually near two parts of the Great Wall — the "old wall" 55 kilometres south of the town and the "new wall" 1 kilometre to the north. The remaining mud wall of the "new wall" still has a width of more than 1 metre. Climb onto the wall and walk east and you will see a huge beacon tower in the distance. The tower is over 10 metres tall and constructed by earth. Standing straight on the isolated Gobi sands, it seems quite strange. Under the tower, there is a door just big enough for one person to fit through. There is no longer anything inside the door — it used to mark a strategic pass in the Dajing Batalion and was the only way to travel between the Hosi Corridor and Tenger Desert.

On the inner side of the foot of the mountain, there is the large Green Mountain Temple青山寺I. It was built during the North and South Dynasty, but later destroyed. In the 1990s, a large palace was rebuilt on the former site with a wing room and a refectory. Green Mountain is a meeting point for the Han, Zang, and Menggu religious schools of thought.

Making sacrifices to the Fire God (社火) is popular among townspeople — there is even a special committee set up to supervise the offerings. In the past, offerings were made over an eight-day period shortly after Chinese New Year (around mid February). A team would be formed to worship the gods of fire and earth. The start of the worship period is called "raising the body" (出身子), the end called "taking off the body" (卸身子).

The government office of Lutusi

Gannan New Town 甘南新城镇

The Town Shaped Like A Dragon

New Town is surrounded by mountains and has beautiful natural scenery. Cultural relics add to the beauty, such as an old fortified Ming Dynasty city, Thunder Temple and the Li Family Tomb. Large-scale cultural activities like the Dragon Boat Festival bring an excitement to the town.

Xincheng Town, Lintan County, Gannan Tibetan Autonomous Region, Gansu Province
甘肃省临潭县新城镇
Nearest city: Lanzhou
Direct routes from major Chinese cities serve Lanzhou Zhongchuan Airport, while Lanzhou Station is a major regional rail hub.
Lanzhou Bus Station (兰州汽车站), adjacent to Lanzhou Railway Station (兰州站), has direct buses to Xincheng Town (33 yuan and three hours.) Buses heading for Zhuni County (卓尼县) also stop at Xincheng Town.

New Town was called Honghe City and Taozhou City in ancient times. It was a political, economic, cultural, and military centre in the Qin and Han dynasties. It is the best-preserved fortified city in northwest China and is supposedly shaped like a huge coiled dragon. People from many different cultural backgrounds, including the Han, Hui, and Zang, have lived here and left their cultural mark. New Town is a medicinal herbs centre and most families even plant their own herbs, including the medicinal Xingzi (杏子).

The old Taozhou Frontier Wall built in the middle of the Ming Dynasty can be found in New Town. The wall was built

New Town — a huge coiled dragon

along the mountains, making it a spectacular sight. Beacon towers are positioned along the wall. There are also troops quarters at every big gate, called menyin gates (门音门).

After being battered down by history, the fortified walls are now nothing more than ruins. The walls were originally built for military defence, but also came to define an economic area over the years.

The Golden Palace of King Da (挞王金銮殿) was built in the Yuan Dynasty. It was originally the palace for Yuan Hu Bilie in Dali, Yunnan, when he fought in the south. Located in the south of Taozhou City and built in the Ming Dynasty, it is surrounded by a 9 kilometres of walls and mountains. Opposite the beacon towers, it is a historical relic with 800 years of history. It was also used by the Red Army in the 20th century.

In August of 1936, Communist military leader Zhu De (朱德) led two battalions of the Red Army occupying Lintan (临潭) on their Long March. They organised the people of Lintan (临潭) for the cause and on September 27 a meeting of the Communist Party's northwest central committee made the fateful decision to commence a push

Taozhou's folk culture festival

northward, which enabled Zhu De's forces to join the central Red Army.

Behind the site of the former military headquarters, there is a place for the public to pay tribute to fallen soldiers, called Huang Temple (隍庙). The four remaining main buildings, the Central North Great Palace, the East and West Palace, the Gate Tower, and the East and West Corridor, display typical Chinese architecture — deep corridors, tilted arches and colourful paintings of Fuwa.

The annual Dragon Boat Festival lasts for three days in Taozhou City. It is the biggest and most important temple celebration in Lintan County. The highlight of the festival is an exciting parade, which has a history of 500 years. There are also Shehuo performances, singing Taozhou flowers, folk handcraft exhibitions, and talks on economic issues.

Taozhou Flower

The Taozhou flower activity is unique to Xincheng. The flowers are spread widely throughout the town. The couplet on the gate of Huang Temple reads, "People are great and the spirit of Taozhou will be passed down for thousands of years; the heroes are eternal and the Dragon Boat Festival will be celebrated by thousands of people".

Longcheng Town 陇城镇

Home of Nüwa

Fuxi and Nüwa are the legendary ancestors of humanity, according to Chinese traditions, and worshiping Nüwa has a long history. Longcheng claims to be the hometown of the pair.

Longcheng Town, Qin'an County, Tianshui City, Gansu Province
甘肃省天水市秦安县陇城镇
Nearest city: Lanzhou
Direct routes from major Chinese cities serve Lanzhou Zhongchuan Airport, while Lanzhou Station is a major regional rail hub.
From Lanzhou Railway Station (兰州火车站) take a train to Tianshui Railway Station (天水火车站). In Tianshui, walk to nearby Tianshui Maiji Bus Station (天水麦吉汽车) and take a bus to Qin'an County (40 minutes and 6 yuan). At Qin'an, transfer to a bus to Longcheng Town (about one hour).

The Longcheng area has been populated by farmers for 7,800 years. It is said that Nüwa, the mythical ancestor of all humankind in Chinese tradition, was born in Longcheng. According to records, in 106 BC, Emperor Han Yuan of the Han Dynasty ordered that an emissary department be established here (at the time, Longcheng was known as Dragon Town).

Longcheng has had different identities throughout time. It was a county in the Jin, Northern Wei, and Tang dynasties, a walled village in the Song, and the site of an imperial inspection office in the Ming. It was even the capital of the Northern Wei and Northern Zhou dynasties, but was destroyed by the Tibetans in the Tang Dynasty, so relics of the old capital no longer exist. The layout of modern-day Longcheng dates back to the Song Dynasty, when it was rebuilt by Emperor Zhenglong. It is also known as Eight Diagrams Town due to its shape and the town is surrounded by a moat and a city wall.

The town was a commercial hub on the ancient Silk Road. During the Ming and Qing dynasties (1368-1912), trading activity was intense. The Shanxi Assembly Hall was built to house businesspeople and travellers from nearby Shanxi. The architecture on Longcheng Street (陇城街) was richest in the Ming and Qing dynasties. Duxian Archway (都宪牌坊) was built on Longcheng West Street (陇城西街) in the Ming. On the upper street, a Qing imperial inspection office was built with an archway inscribed with "Hometown of Nüwa" (娲皇故里). Most of the other archways, pavilions, and ancient shops have sadly been destroyed. The Ming and Qing architecture still standing in the town includes 40 shops, distributed on both sides of the short old street.

Longcheng was part of the ancient Xi'an Customs Pass and the most important path to Gansu Province, making it a strategic military pass that kingdoms fought over through many

Kuixing building on the Xifan Temple grounds

dynasties. The famed Weichu Jieting Battle occurred here during the Three Kingdoms period when Zhu Geliang asked Assistant General Wang Ping to stay and defend Jieting. Ma disobeyed Zhuge's orders and was defeated by Zhang Shi, a Wei Dynast general. After the loss, Zhu Geliang ordered Ma be beheaded. He also demoted himself three ranks. It was this battle that earned Jieting its place in history.

In 1977, the government of Qin'an County set up a stele in Longcheng to commemorate the story of Jieting.

There is a Nüwa Ancestral Hall on the north side of Qin'an County. Many sites in the area bear the family name "Feng" (phoenix) and Nüwa is said to have been born in Feng Gou (风沟 (Feng Valley). On the cliff of Feng Gou, there is still a deep hole named Nüwa Cave (女娲洞). Though the mouth of the cave is big and broad, it contracts into a size of a body at a depth of 10 metres. The cave is connected to Zhengjia Gou (郑家沟), and is about 1.5 kilometres long. Visitors don't typically go further than 10 metres into the cave, as there is a lack of oxygen past that. Outside the north gate of the town, there is a big well named Dragon Spring (龙泉), which is said to be the spring that Nüwa used to make humans out of clay. Near the south gate of town, there is the splendid Nüwa Temple (女娲庙) with a stone stele gate that reads "Home of Nüwa".

Xifan Temple (西番寺) is also known as Carefree Temple (无忧寺). When the first Qin emperor consolidated six kingdoms to unify China, he built Carefree Temple on Jimai Cliff (积麦崖). In the Tang Dynasty, Buddhism flourished in China and the town

received an order from the emperor to rebuild the temple and rename it Xifan Temple.

Today's Xifan Temple is a reconstruction from 1987. It is a replica of the layout from the Guangxu Emperor period. Though it is not the original building, the temple is still beautiful and worth a visit.

Dragon Spring

Nüwa Festival

Every third month of the lunar calendar (usually April), locals gather at Nüwa Ancestral Hall to pay tribute, continuing a tradition that has lasted for thousands of years. Since 2006, the Qin'an County government has also organised official activities to honour Nüwa. Music, gun salutes, performances, drum dances, lion boat races (狮子船), and martial arts shows are all available for visitors to enjoy.

Niuzhuang Town 牛庄镇

An Ancient Port

Most Chinese people know about Niuzhuang because of the town's savoury Niuzhuang pie, but the true significance of the town comes from its long history.

Ancient China: Towns

Niuzhuang Town, Haicheng City, Liaoning Province
辽宁省海城市牛庄镇
Nearest city: Shenyang
Shenyang Taixian International Airport offers direct flight connections to cities such as Beijing, Shanghai, Xian, and Harbin, as well as South Korea and Japan. Generally speaking, trains from Beijing, Shanghai and other major cities arrive at North Shenyang Railway Station, while trains from destinations within Liaoning province pull into Shenyang South Station.
From Shenyang Railway Bus Terminal Station (沈阳汽车枢纽站), adjacent to Shenyang Railway Station (沈阳站), there are regular services to Haicheng City (海城市, about 90 minutes). At Haicheng transfer to a minibus to Niuzhuang town (20 minutes).

Niuzhuang is located about 20 kilometres to the west of Haishi City. Since ancient times, it has been an economic and cultural hub due to its prime location and rich land.

There are several theories of the origin of Niuzhuang's name. Town records say that an officer named Jingde once set down an iron bull on the southeast corner of town for protection, naming the town Niuzhuang, which means "Bull Village". Another tale tells a different story. Niuzhuang once had a large port, and when the tide of the Taizi River (太子河) rose, boats could reach East Peace Bridge (东太平桥). The vessels would moor on the bank, which was covered with lights and from a distance looked like a village by the river. Since boats are called "niuzi" in the local dialect, the village was named Niuzhuang.

A courier post was established in Niuzhuang during the reign of Emperor Wanli of the Ming Dynasty (1573-1620) and the city wall was built in the late Jin Dynasty (1623). The moat was rebuilt in the Qing. There are three city gates — Desheng Gate (德胜门) on the east, Wairang Gate (外攘门) on the west and Fusheng Gate (福胜门) to the north. The town's ancient wall has long since crumbled but some of its foundation is still visible.

Xiaoji Temple Wharf (枭姬庙码头) on the Taizi River (太子河) was the oldest port in Niuzhuang, and though it is buried in the dust, it was the reason for the town's prosperity. After being built, the wharf attracted more and more

Temple of Avalokitesvara

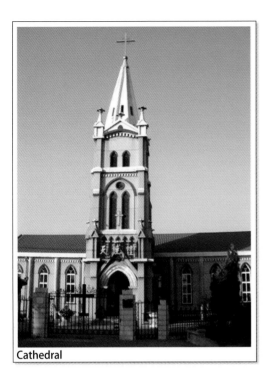
Cathedral

building the bridge was an elderly man with white hair and thick eyebrows. He spent days on end striking a single stone into a certain shape — not square, not circle, not long, and not flat. When he finished the stone, he left town before their bridge's completion. When the bridge was almost finished, construction came to a halt when a hole appeared that no stone could fit. When the builders finally tried the stone the old man had carefully carved, it fit perfectly. The townspeople compared the elderly man to the ancient engineer Luban, who came to help the construction of the bridge to ensure the peace of the town. Therefore, the bridge is named Peaceful Stone Bridge.

There are three God of War temples (关帝庙) in Niuzhuang, which are all devoted to Lord Guan of the Three Kingdoms era. The temple in the west is called Little Master Temple (小老爷庙). The north temple is called Shanxi Assembly Hall. The most interesting of the three is in front of the east gate. It is a five-storey building and has an opera stage. This temple is the biggest Lord Guan temple within three provinces. In front of the temple are vivid statues of two strong stone lions. The design and outlook of the lions are very lifelike. The statue of Lord Guan in the main hall is covered with a green robe and his face is red. He is sitting sideways, with his left hand holding his beard. His face is full of life and strength. Near the back door behind the statue, there is a Buddha in a red robe sitting and facing the back hall — a guardian for protecting the spirit of Buddhism. The back hall is used as a study room.

boats until it was too much for it to handle. The British consulate built a new port in Yingkou, causing Niuzhuang to fall into decline. The town was home to many beautiful sites of antiquity, though only the Peaceful Stone Bridge (太平石桥) remains in its original form. There is a French cathedral (法国教堂) and a mosque (清真古寺) that are reconstructions.

The well-preserved Peaceful Stone Bridge is located over the moat outside the east gate of the town. On the south side of the bridge, a stone is inscribed with the Chinese name of the bridge and the year it was built (道光己酉年菊月谷旦, during the reign of the Daoguang Emperor of the Qing Dynasty). Sculptures of lions, monkeys, pomegranates , and peaches can be found on both sides of the structure. The bridge actually sits on the soft mud of the river but amazingly it is still stable, even after being rocked by a magnitude 7.3 earthquake in 1975. In October 1990, the local government collected money to completely repair the bridge.

There is a story to the bridge. Business was prosperous near the area where the bridge was to be constructed. One of the stonemasons

Lord Guan Temple

One interesting part of the Lord Guan Temple is its big opera building out front. It has heavy eaves and high columns. There is ample space at the back of the stage. It is said that it was built by engineers from Shanxi and it was based on the design of a temple in the Yugang grottos of Datong. Niuzhuang residents light lanterns on the river every summer, creating quite a sight.

Yonglin Town 永陵镇

The Manchu Heartland

Yongling, located in the middle of the Xinbin Manchu Autonomous County in northeast Liaoning Province, was the birthplace of the Qing Dynasty and a cultural heartland for the Manchu people.

Ancient China: Towns

Yongning Town, Xinbin Man Nationality Autonomous County, Fushun City, Liaoning Province
辽宁省抚顺市新宾满族自治县永陵镇
Nearest city: Shenyang
Shenyang Taixian International Airport offers direct flight connections to cities such as Beijing, Shanghai, Xian, and Harbin, as well as South Korea and Japan. Generally speaking, trains from Beijing, Shanghai and other major cities arrive at North Shenyang Railway Station, while trains from destinations within Liaoning province pull into Shenyang South Station.
From Shenyang Sation (沈阳站) take a train to Fushun North Station (抚顺北站, about 45minutes). Proceed to Fushun Long-distance Bus Station (抚顺长途客运站) near Fushun North Station), then transfer to a bus heading to Xinbin Man Nationality Autonomous County (新宾满族自治县). Get off at Yongning Town (about 90 minutes).

The Corridor of Manchu History in Yongling

Qingyong Mausoleum (清永陵) is located at the foot of Qilian Mountain in the northwest part of Yongling, where the tombs of the ancestors of the first Qing emperor, Nurhachi, are located, as are tombs of other Qing Dynasty ancestors. The mausoleum was built in 1598, during the reign of Emperor Wanli of the Ming..

The front yard is on the south side of the mausoleum with a red gate in the middle. After entering the yard, you will see rooms on three sides, which all have a mountain-like tile roofs and windows of colored glaze. The ridges of the roof are set with sculptures of animals. Within the gate, four steles are lined up and inscribed with the names of four early Qing emperors — Mengtemu (肇祖原皇帝) Fuman (兴祖直皇帝), Juechang'an (景祖翼皇帝), and Takeshi (显祖宣皇帝). Other inscriptions are also visible in Manchurian, Mongolian, and Han.

On the north side of the steles is a square (方城). To the north of the square is Qiyun Palace (启运殿), build in the ancient Xishan architecture style. The ridge of the palace has similar sculptures to those found on the ridge of the gate — eight dragons playing with balls, the Chinese characters for sun and moon, and carvings of six animals. There are three roads in front of the palace. The centre lane is Royal Road (御路). The palace name is carved into the beams of the building. Inside the hall, you will find the Treasure Seat (宝座) and the Stele of God (神牌). The east and west part of the palace have three halls. The front of the west section is Fenbo Pavilion (焚帛亭).

Bao City (宝城) is behind Qiyun Palace (启运殿), surrounded by a half-circle city wall and a two-storey clay platform. One of Emperor Nurhachi's uncles is buried on the first floor of the wall, while his ancestors Lidun and Tachapiangu are on the left and right, respectively. The centre of the second floor is the burial place for Nurhachi's great-grandfather Fuman. On the east is his grandfather Juechang'an and on the left his father, Takeshi. To the northeast of Fuman is the tomb of the sixth Qing Emperor Mengtemu.

"Hetuala" is a Manchurian word meaning "small flat mountain". Hetuala (赫图阿拉) was the first capital of the Houjin Dynasty, and it was also the last mountain capital in the history of China. It was once a centre for politics, trade, military, culture, and diplomacy. The city is considered the birthplace of the Qing Dynasty and the Manchurian heartland. Sadly, in the Sino-Russian War, the city was destroyed completely. Everything standing today is a reconstruction.

Hetuala consists of an inner and outer city. The city walls are made of clay, stone, and wood. The remains of the main buildings in the inner city include four old government offices, a God of War (关帝庙) the Manchu Residence (满族民居) and the Zhaozhong (昭忠祠) and Liugong (刘公祠) ancestral halls. The 500-year-old King Han Well (汗王井) is a rare Ming-era wooden spring well.

The old mud roads in the city have been replaced by black stones. King Han Palace is where Nurhachi handled political affairs. In 1619, he led the empire into the Sawuer War (萨尔浒之战), which would decide the fate of the Late Jin, which was consolidated into the Qing.

Manchu Old Street (满族老街) is situated in the southeast part of outer Hetuala, and was a trading centre for businesspeople from nearly Nuzhen and Jianzhou in the Late Jin. The street is now a commercial hub bustling with tourists and locals.

Corridor of History

Built in 2002, the Corridor of Manchu History (满族历史文化长廊), located in Hetuala's gardens, is about 560 metres long. The wall paintings in the corridor illustrate the history of the Manchu people and the Qing Dynasty.

Mausoleum outside of Yongling — Yiqing Yongling

Yehe Town 叶赫镇

Hometown of Queens

The Turn Lake area is home to a large number of people of the Manchu ethnic group. Queen Xiaocigao Nala, wife of the first Qing emperor, was born here. So was Empress Dowager Cixi of the late Qing, earning Yehe the moniker "Hometown of Queens".

Yehe Town, Tiedong District, Linshu County, Siping City, Jilin Province
吉林省四平市梨树县铁东区叶赫镇
Nearest city: Changchun
Changchun Longjia International Airport offers direct connections to major cities across China. Changchun Station and Jilin Station offer a wide variety of land routes.
Take a train from Changchun Station (长春站) to Siping Railway Sation (四平站, one hour). Transfer to Siping Bus Station (四平客运总站) near Siping Train Station for buses to Yehen.

Located near to the border of Jilin and Liaoning provinces, Yehe covers an area of 68 square kilometres. In the Manchu's native language, "Yehe" refers to the armour presented to outstanding officials by the emperor. Yehe's natural scenery consists of mountains rising and plummeting into ravines and gullies

At the end of 2008, a group of Bronze Age sites were uncovered in Yehe, spread over an area of around 100,000 square metres. There are six sites in all, which feature ancient tombs and stone coffins. They are relics of the Spring and Autumn and Warring States periods of 3,000 years ago.

For tourists, Yehe is divided into two parts – the Ancient Castle Cultural Area (古城文化区) and Turn Lake Resort (湖风景游艺渡假区). The castle, situated to the east of the lake, was built in the Manchu style and is tucked away among

Yehe Town

mountains. Each defensive wall is unique. One is wood, one mud, yet another stone. A moat runs along the outside of the castle. Inside, there is a simple octagonal tower, which has remained intact from the Qing Dynasty. The tower's Dianjiang Platform (where commanders were appointed to their offices) and the War Flame Platform are the most interesting parts of the structure. There are also tall divining rods, rings of waist bells, and other mysterious artefacts. Within the cultural area, attractions include ancient post stops, Jialan Temple (伽蓝寺), Goddess Temple (娘娘庙), a set of dual towers, and the King of Worms Temple (虫王庙). Jialan Temple is now an exhibition hall of ethnic minority culture, making it a favourite for archaeology and history buffs and scholars. Located on a secluded mountain to the north of the Turn Lake, the temple's incense smoke hangs fragrantly in the air and bells ring over the area.

Turn Lake Resort is a mix of natural and cultural delights. A man-made reservoir, the lake itself covers an area of 33,000 square metres and is surrounded by mountains. It is shaped like an S and was not totally completed until 1981. The two mountains that lie to the east and west of the lake supposedly resemble to a pair of meditating turtles. There is an amusement park at the top of the mountain. Surrounded by water on three sides, the park enjoys great views. The newly built Yehenala Tower (叶赫那拉城) on Turn Lake's eastern mountain showcases the folk customs of the Nuzhen ethnic group. The structure includes spectacular arrow-shooting watchtowers and quadrangle dwellings.

Visitors can participate in a range of fun activities on the flat and broad sloping field of Yehe. Horseback riding lessons are available from Manchu instructors. More experienced riders can rent a horse and venture out on their own. The ride along the lake is easy and safe. If you come in the winter, you may get the chance to ski mountain slopes or be pulled around by a dog or horse sleigh. The lake also makes for a natural ice rink. It is open 24 hours a day and even plays a pre-recorded skating lesson on loop in case beginners stumble onto the ice.

The Manchu Fantasy Park teaches visitors about Manchu customs. There is traditional clothing on display, shadow boxing shows, roly-poly competitions, and other games. Bull riding, fireworks, storytelling, and dance events also spring up throughout the year.

Antlers

Siping is famous for its high-quality deer antlers. Deer blood and reproductive organs are considered precious medicinal ingredients and are widely available in Yehe. Fatty meat with intestines (肠余白肉) is a popular local Manchu dish. The dish was traditionally eaten at ceremonies to pay tribute to gods or homage to ancestors.

Wulajie Town 乌拉街镇

Birthplace of the Manchus

As the capital of Wula Kingdom, Wulajie Town is also an ancestral home for the Manchu ethnic group. Though it has long been overtaken by the provincial capital Jilin in size and influence, this history remains in sayings such as "as big as Wulajie" or "as small as Jilin".

Wulajie Town, Longtan District, Jinlin City, Jilin Province
吉林省吉林市龙潭区乌拉街镇
Nearest city: Changchun
Changchun Longjia International Airport offers direct connections to major cities across China. Changchun Station and Jilin Station offer a wide variety of land routes.
From Jilin Bus Station (吉林市客运总站), near Jilin Railway Station (吉林火车站), there are direct buses to Wulajie Town, (5 yuan and 40 minutes).

Situated upstream at the start of the alluvial plain formed by the Songhua River (松花江), Wulajie Wula Street) Town is 30 kilometres from the centre of Jilin. With Longtan Mountain in the south and Fenghuang Pavilion in the north, the Songhua river to the west and Changbai Mountain in the east, Wula Street is blessed with rich mineral and agricultural resources.

Wula is the Mandarin pronunciation of a Manchu expression meaning "along the river". It was called Bulatewula under Han rule. After the establishment of the Ming Dynasty, the emperor stationed an army in Wula Street to assert his political power. In the middle of the Ming, the Haixi Nuzhen ethnic group began gaining power, so the Wula tribe overtook other tribes in the region and established its own kingdom, with Wula Street as the capital. The kingdom almost immediately found itself embroiled in a continuous battle with Nuerhachi, leader of the Jianzhou Nuzhen. In 1613, Nuerhachi finally defeated Wula Kingdom. He established himself as the Shunzhi Emperor of the Qing Dynasty and claimed a large area around Wula Street to be the "sacred birthplace of the Qing Dynasty".

Several of ancient Wulajie's old buildings are still standing today, including the Kui (魁府), Sa (萨府), and Hou houses (后府), as well as the White Flower Dianjiang Platform (白花点将台). Kui House is a quadrangle dwelling from the Qing Dynasty and is relatively well preserved. It

Manchu buildings

White Flower Dianjiang Platform

is located in the centre of town to the west of the old local government building. The General Yamen, is modelled after the Vice Dutong Yamen. The General Yamen was a special organization under the Qing that was in charge of overseeing local tribes' animal offerings to the emperor. Together with Suzhou, Nanjing, and Hangzhou, the Yamen in Wula is considered to have been one of the centres of imperial tributes.

Not far from Wula is a castle with a history of more than 1,200 years. Wula Ancient Castle (乌拉古城) used to consist of an outer, middle, and inner wall, but now things have changed. The outer wall is no longer standing. The middle wall — which previously encircled Hongniluo Town — is recognizable and the inner wall is basically complete. The White Flower Dianjiang Platform is a high stage built up with mud. The main buildings on the grounds include Sanxiao Palace, the Yuantong Building and the Lexian Pavilion. The earthen stage somehow has a considerable amount of charm, especially after reading about the legend of the White Flower Princess .

Winter wonderland

Manchu Wedding

The Manchus of Wula are still mindful of their unique customs, especially wedding traditions. Days before the wedding, the woman's family sends their daughter and her dowry with clothes to her future husband's home while the man visits his future wife's family to express his appreciation and gratitude for her hand in marriage. The bride wears cotton clothing at the wedding ceremony and shoots three arrows at her sedan chair with a bow made by the groom.

中　原　古　镇
C e n t r a l
Plains Towns
Iron and bamboo

Zhuxian Town 朱仙镇

Hometown of Wooden New Year Paintings

Throughout history, Zhuxian has been one of the most famous ancient towns in China. The victory here of Yue Fei, a national hero of the South Song Dynasty, put the town on the map and a temple to Yue Fei still stands today.

Zhuxian Town, Kaifeng County, Henan Province
河南省开封县朱仙镇
Nearest city: Zhenzhou
Zhengzhou is a major railway hub and Zhengzhou Xinzheng International Airport is also one of the country's gateway airports.
From Zhengzhou South Bus Station (郑州客运南站, a 15-minute taxi ride from Zhengzhou Railway Station), there are shuttle buses to Zhuxian Town (9:00 and 15:00). The ride takes about an hour.

Zhuxian is located 23 kilometres southwest of Kaifeng. The town was named after Zhu Hai, a butcher-turned-military strategist from the Warring States Period. It is said that Zhu used to live in "Celestial Village" in north Zhuxian Town. People called him Celestial Zhu and named the town after him.

Since the Tang Dynasty, the town has always been known as a road and water transportation hub and an important market town. It reached its apogee in the late Ming and early Qing.

Zhuxian has not only been an important commercial town, but is also the site of a famous ancient battle. The Yue Fei Temple was built in the Chenhua reign, during the Ming Dynasty. Located in northwest of the town, it covers 12,320 square metres and has three yards. The temple is considered one of the four most significant Yue Fei Temples in China. In Zhuxian, Yue Fei fought off the Jin army and won a famous victory, astonishing royal administrators. After the founding of the PRC in 1949, many parts of the Yue Fei Temple have

Mosque

Ming Dynasty mosque

been restored, including the mountain gate, and statues of "five evils kneeling". Inside the temple, in the main hall in the front yard, Yue Fei's statue is flanked by representations of four of his beloved generals, Yue Yun (岳云), Di Lei (狄雷), He Yuanqin (何元庆), and Yan Chengfan (严成方). They reportedly brandished eight hammers as they fought the Jin army, leaving the legend of "eight hammers' havoc in Zhuxian Town". In the back yard stand statues of Yue Fei and his wife; in the east and west rooms are of his son and daughter-in-law, as well as a number tablets commemorating his victories.

Zhuxian has been home to temples throughout its history. It is said that all the gods in heaven had temples in Zhuxian, earning it the title of "town of 72 temples" and "Gods' gathering town". There is a mosque on Tiger Cave Street (老虎洞) in the southeast of Zhuxian. The mosque was built in the Ming, and repaired during the Qing. It is the largest existing Islamic mosque in Kaifeng. The mosque's single-eave mountaintop roof is mounted with glazed green tiles. Visitors like touching the back and front columns supporting the mountain gate, as they are exquisitely carved with images of plants and small creatures. In the magnificent Main Worship Hall hangs an inscription from the emperor.

The Jialu River (贾鲁河) which runs through Zhuxian, is called the East Capital Grain Canal (东京运粮河) by local residents. The large stone bridge and double-board bridge that cross over the river connect the whole town and are set majestically against the ancient-style old residences.

Zhuxian's wooden New Year paintings are among the most famous in China. The local style has special characteristics: the lines are rough, alternating thick with thin. The features are exaggerated, with large heads and small bodies. Also, the painting structure is full and symmetrical. The most common subjects of Zhuxian New Year paintings

Yue Fei Temple in Zhuxian Town

are gate gods, usually loyal officials, freedom fighters and heroes in operas.

Zhuxian wooden New Year paintings got their start in the Tang Dynasty, and blossomed during the Ming and Qing dynasties. Russian Emperor Alexander III collected a "four-beauty picture" from Zhuxian. The Lord Guan Temple east of Yue Fei Temple is the current production centre for Zhuxian New Year paintings. The large stone lions that stand in front of its gate are solemn, grand, and eye-catching. Walking inside the temple is like entering a palace of art, full of impressive gate paintings, stove paintings, scrolls, screens, tablets, and more. They are mostly concerned with popular themes from historic plays, myths, folklore and more. The most famous include Changban Slope (长坂坡); Painted-face change for jade belt (铜锤换御带); Hit the mountain (撞山); Battle of Yue Fei & Jin Wushu (the fourth son of Emperor Taizu of Jin岳飞大破金兀术); and Worship Tower. (祭塔).

Stone lions in Zhuxian Town

Lord Guan Temple

Art Mart

There are several wooden New Year painting stores around the entrances of Zhuxian. The most famous stores include Tiancheng (天成) Old Store and Zhuxian Town New Year Painting House (朱仙镇木版画年社). Paintings are about RMB5 each.

Guxing Town 古荥镇

The Han Dynasty Steel Town

Guxing Town, known as Xingyan in historical times, has a deep cultural heritage. The town's walls were built in the In 6th and 7th centuries BC, and Guxing was a centre of politics, economics, culture, and transportation.

Guxing Town, Huiji District, Zhengzhou City, Henan Province
河南省郑州市惠济区古荥镇
Nearest city: Zhengzhou
Zhengzhou is a major railway hub and Zhengzhou Xinzheng International Airport is also one of the country's gateway airports.
Take a taxi from downtown Zhengzhou to Guxing Town (costs about 50 yuan and takes 40 minutes). Admission to the Yellow River Scenic Area costs 25 yuan and it is another 20 yuan for a 40-minute boat ride that offers great views of the mountain and river.

The West Mountain Ruins (西山遗址), discovered in 1983, are located in the Sun Family Village (孙庄村) area of Guxing, with a total area of 31,000 square metres. The finding at this site of earthen walls from the late Yangshao period has been very important to the study of city development in ancient China.

Guxing — earlier known as Xingyang ancient town — was built in the Warring States Period. Most of its rectangular dirt walls have survived. The northern city walls extend east to Fishing Pavilion Village (钓鱼台村), where they connect to the ancient village's walls. The east walls have been washed away by floods from the Ji River, and only the northeast and southeast corners remain. There are three gaps in the west walls, which were once gates.

The old city palace is 2,200 metres long south to north and 1,500 metres wide east to west.

Guxing's still-standing 120,000-square-metre ironworks (冶铁遗址) are a relic of Han Dynasty smelting and iron manufacturing. The site is the largest remaining iron smelting base in Henan Province. There are two blast-furnaces for iron. The hearth walls and bases are both rammed with dark brown refractory dirt; there are remains of wooden shelves for smelting in the front and sides of the hearths. The No. 1 hearth is the largest among all the known Han iron hearths, standing nearly six metres high. Near the hearth are sets of casting moulds and iron equipment that have been turned up by excavations. Also uncovered have been 14 ceramic cellars and other relics related to smelting.

First built in the seventh year of the Tianbao reign of the Tang dynasty (748), the Jigong Temple (纪公庙) is located in Jigong Temple Village. The temple was built for Jixin (纪信), a general of Liu Bang's (刘邦, the first emperor and founder of

Jigong Temple

Yellow River View

the Han Dynasty). While the original temple no longer exists, a temple built in the Tang Dynasty and more than 30 tablets with inscriptions remain.

The City God Temple (城隍庙) is located on Commercial Store Road in Guxing, and is the largest and most well-preserved ancient building complex in Henan. It was built in the early Ming Dynasty, and repaired in the Hongzhi reign of the Ming dynasty. In addition to the main hall, the temple has mountain gates, musical towers, and bedchambers. All of its buildings are covered with glazed tiles and have compactly structured upturned eaves. The musical towers are 15 metres tall. The central column in the main hall is decorated with vivid carvings of dragons and flying phoenixes, set off by lotuses and lions. The hall also boasts carvings of popular myths, as well as green pines and cedar, birds, and animals.

On the 18th day of the third month in the lunar calendar (usually during the end of March), Guxing City God Temple hosts a temple fair. All kinds of folk arts, crafts, and foods are on display for the lively fair.

The Yellow River tourism zone is located 30 kilometres northwest of the temple area, with the mighty river to its north, and Yue Mountain to the south. Ascend the mountain to the north for superb views of the Yellow River flowing to the east. To the south of the tourist zone are classic pavilions built along the mountain. Other main landscapes in the tourism zone are Yue Mountain Temple (岳山寺), Camel Ridge (骆驼岭), Two Han Emperors City (汉霸二王城), and Stone Status of Emperor Yan and Huang (炎黄二帝石塑), among others.

Yellow River Landscape Crane Tower

Fake China

The northern suburb of Zhengzhou, south of the Mang Mountain (邙山), houses a modern theme park (文化公园). It boasts a simulated 3.7-kilometre Yellow River, split into a cultural zone and hi-tech entertainment zone. The former consists of 19 scenic leisure spots, including replicas of China's most well-recognised tourist spots.

Shenhou Town 神垕镇

The Capital of Jun Porcelain

Shenhou Town is known widely for its porcelain production. The coal from the mountains to the south, the glaze from those to the west, and clay from the east come together to make Jun porcelain, one China's five famous porcelain types.

Shenhou Town, Yuzhou City, Xuchang City, Henan Province
河南省许昌市神垕镇
Nearest city : Zhengzhou
Zhengzhou is a major railway hub and Zhengzhou Xinzheng International Airport is also one of the country's gateway airports.
The Zhengzhou Long-Distance Bus Station (郑州长途汽车总站Tel:0371-8728294, adjacent to Zhengzhou Railway Station) has many shuttle buses to Yuzhou City (禹州市about 90 minutes and 21 yuan). There, transfer to a minibus at Yuzhou Bus Station (禹州汽车站) to Shenhou Town (buses leave every eight minutes, ride time is about an hour).

Shenhou, also called Shenhou Dian, became a town in the Ming Dynasty. But humans lived here far earlier, in the Xia and Shang dynasties, farming and making ceramics. When Jun porcelain was invented during the Tang Dynasty, Shenhou gradually become one of the ceramics centres of northern China. In the Ming and Qing dynasties a popular folk song said: "Entering Shenhou Mountain...smoke and fire cover the sky, consumers and merchants are everywhere, they do a thriving business".

Shenhou Old Street (神垕老街) is located at the town's centre. Its highlights include Red-Stone Bridge and Guanyu Temple. Xiao River (肖河) crosses through the Old Street from west to east. The Zouyu Bridge (驺虞桥) connects the east and west. The Old Street strings together four former villages, known uninterestingly as the north, east, south, and west villages. There are many village gates on the Old Street, built high and firm to defend against intruders. All villages in Shenhou have elegant names, including "Look High" (望嵩), "Heaven Blesses" (天保) and more.

The buildings along both sides of the Old Street are well-preserved, and architecturally diverse. The major buildings are religious, residential, or used for special markets or stores. The major religious buildings include Sir Boling Temple (伯灵翁庙), Guanyu Temple (关帝庙, dedicated to a famous warrior in the Three Kingdoms era), Wen Temple(文庙), and "White Cloth Hall" (白衣堂). The major Ming and Qing residences are the Xi Family Courtyard (郗家院), Bai Family Courtyard (白家院), Wen Family Courtyard (温家院), Huo Family Courtyard (霍家院), Wang Family Courtyard (王家院), and Xin Family Courtyard (辛家院). The Founder Temple (祖师庙) is located on top of Qianming Mountain (乾明山), north of Tianbao Village.

Seven Li Long Street

Jun porcelain was one of the first ceramic copper red glazes, and its production technique was summarised as "one colour enters the oven, various colour come out", while its value was summarised as "a piece of Jun porcelain is worth more than a pot of money".

There are 58 Jun porcelain manufacturers in the town today. Large-scale firms include the Kong Family Jun Kiln, Rongchang Jun Kiln, Miao Nation Jun Kiln, and Golden Jun Kiln.

The Jun porcelain tradition, dating from the Tang Dynasty, has made Shenhou famous. Many classical legends have contributed to the colour of the ancient town: the first Han Emperor hunted in the nearby Great Liu Mountain; the Han emperor Guangwu experienced a miracle here; Han general Deng Yu stationed troops in Shenhou and fought off enemies.

Built in 2001, Shenhou's antique market covers 7.48 hectares. The antique market offers bronze, jade, stone, wood, jewellery, calligraphy, and paintings, boasting thousands of antiques.

Walking on Stilts

Shenhou folk arts include "walking on stilts" (踩 高跷), land boats, dragon lanterns, and lion dances. On holidays, local businesses raise money to hire Henan opera troops that perform.

Shedian Town 赊店镇

Rebel's Town on the Old Tea Road

The past glory of Shedian town can largely be attributed to the endeavours made by its tea and salt merchants during the Qin and Jin dynasties.

Shedian Town, Sheqi County, Nanyang City, Henan Province
河南省南阳市社旗县赊店镇
Nearest City: Luoyang
Luoyang Airport has flights to cities across China while Luoyang Longmen Station offers routes to Beijing, Xi'an and Zhengzhou.
Take a train from Luoyang Railway Station (洛阳) to Nanyang Railway Station (南阳火车站) (three hours). Then, walk five minutes to Nanyang Bus Station (南阳汽车站), where there are regular buses to Shedian Town (trip takes about an hour).

In the Qing Dynasty, when transport via water was highly developed in China, Shedian Town served as a post for those travelling both via waterways and land routes. Ships and horses carrying various items came from all over to the town, one of the four most well-known in Henan Province.

Shedian Town gets its name from a story harkening back to the late Western Han Dynasty, when Liu Xiu, from a family of Western Han loyalists, rose in rebellion in the Battle of Wancheng to defend the faltering empire. He was outnumbered and retreated with his followers to an ancient town, where he found an inn. A wild night of drinking mended and refreshed their bodies and spirits, and a new plan was settled.

The counterattack was ready, save for a flag, a crucial element of ancient battles. Liu stepped out of the inn and found its banner blowing in the cold wind, with the character "Liu" embroidered in the middle of the banner. Using the inn banner as his flag, he swept away his enemies on his road to the emperor's throne. After being enthroned as the first emperor of the Eastern Han Dynasty, Liu named the town Sheqidian — a combination of the characters "to borrow on credit", "flag", and "store" — and gave its liquor the name "Shedian", or "borrowed liquor".

In history, Shedian town was a transfer stop on the famous "Tea Road", and home to the famous "Guangsheng Escort Agency" (广盛镖局), which helped people send goods under the protection of armed escorts. The agency was one of the ten largest of its kind in China, and the largest in central China. In the Daoguang period of the Qing Dynasty, exchange shops (an early form of bank) such as Rishengchang (日升昌) and Weishengchang (蔚盛长) were set up in Shedian. Silver notes issued by the exchange shops could be freely converted into silver currency anywhere in China, addressing the concerns of merchants who had to travel with silver currency.

The armed escort services were dealt a heavy blow by the exchange shops, and Guangsheng was shut down in 1830. Guangsheng's building has since been reconstructed and become a major local attraction as a museum where visitors can learn about local history.

Sheqi Shanshaan Provincial Guild (社旗山陕会馆) is located in the middle of the market area of Shedian. Started in the Qianlong reign of the Qin Dynasty and completed in the Guangxu reign, the continuous construction of the guild took 136 years, spanning eight emperors. The guild was built with funds raised by merchants from Shanxi (山西) and Shaanxi provinces (陕西). Because Guan Yu, a famous general from the Three Kingdoms period, was enshrined by the merchants in the guild, the guild is also known as Lord Guan Temple (关帝庙).

The main structure is narrow in the front and wide in the back, with courtyards located in the front, middle and rear. The guild's structure offers architectural beauty of palaces, temples, commercial guilds, residential households, and gardens.

Built in the Jiaqing reign of the Qing Dynasty, the Xuanjian Theatre (悬鉴楼) is 24 metres high, with triple eaves and a Xieshan-style roof. The theatre employs a Goulianda construction (whereby two buildings are connected to each other lengthwise), with the Gate and wide Eaves Galleries (a corridor under the eaves on the ground floor) on its southern side, and a opera stage to the north. The theatre is regarded as one of the best surviving ancient opera theatres in China.

Daofang Courtyard (道坊院), also known as Yeyuan Palace (掖园宫) or Jieguan Hall (接官厅), is located at the northern end of the west courtyard in the northwest corner of the Shanshaan Provincial Guild. It was a place where Daoists who managed the guilds lived and where noblemen were received and it has a design that combines the advantages of northern quadrangle dwellings, southern architectural gardens, and residential households.

The most unique feature of the provincial guild is its decorative technique. Its coloured glaze, or Zhaobi, combines designs of auspicious plants, mythical creatures, couplets, and depictions of

Shedian's Ancient Street

characters endowed with positive meaning, such as 福 ("good fortune") and 寿 ("longevity").

The Sheqi Shanshaan guild houses over 40 valuable works of embroidery from the Qing Dynasty, five of which are recognised by the State Administration of Cultural Heritage as grade-1 cultural relics.

Porcelain Street

Opposite the guild is the 310-metre North and South Porcelain Street (瓷器街), the longest and best-preserved street in central China from the Ming and Qing dynasties. Once renowned nationwide for its porcelain, the ancient street is still lined with stores that bear banners from the 1960s and 1970s, usually wooden boards painted with Chinese wood oil and inscribed with Chinese characters written in yellow.

Chengji Town 程集镇

The Ming Dynasty Market Town

Defying the passage of time, the old streets of Chengji Town remain in an unadorned classic style. Although the old town is realtively obscure, its long story and quiet charm make it worth a visit.

Chengji Town, Jianli County, Jinzhou City, Hubei Province
湖北省荆州市监利县程集镇
Nearest city: Wuhan
Wuhan Tianhe International Airport is one of China's busiest airports. The new Wuhan Railway Station is used by Wuhan-Guangzhou high-speed trains, while the old Hangkou and Wuchang stations offer regular connections with various destinations across China.
From the Wuhan Fujiapo Long-Distance Bus Station (武汉傅家坡长途汽车站about a 30-minute drive from Wuhan Railway Station), take a direct bus to Jianli County (监利县, 2.5 hours). At Jianli Bus Station (监利汽车客运站), transfer to a minibus to Chengji Town (40 minutes).

Located in the northwest of Jianli County (监利县), Chengji was called Chengjiaji (程家集), or "Chengjia Fair Market" in ancient times. In the Spring and Autumn Period, the King of Chu (楚王) decided to establish grand temporary abodes called Jingtai (荆台) near what is now the town's Yaoji Street (姚集街). The Jingtai was first built as a platform for the king to observe celestial phenomena, oversee military affairs, and to be entertained. In the early Ming Dynasty, Chengji developed into a large market town on the northern bank of the Changjiang River.

Taking a walk 20 metres along the walls enclosing the current governmental buildings of Chengji and then through a lively market, you will find Chengji Old Street (程集老街). The street stretches for more than one kilometre from east to west and there are over 110 well-preserved old houses on both sides. The fronts of these houses were used as stores, while the yards in the middle served as sitting rooms or workshops. Various shops run by locals sell tofu, ironworks, cakes and many other sundries.

Doors and windows in these old houses have all been designed with checked wooden carvings. The residences also offer panoramic views of the old street. Most of the doors and frames are mostly made of wood, finished with Chinese wood oil (桐油) instead of paint. This helps to preserve the wood's original colour.

The old residences along the street were first constructed in the Song Dynasty, though they appear closer to the style of the Yuan dynasty. In the Ming Dynasty, the town began its rapid development, eventually reaching the peak of prosperity during the Qing. Most of the surviving old houses were built during the Ming years.

The Wei Bridge (魏桥), located on the Laochanghe River

(老长河) in Chengji's southeast, was built by the ancestral Wei family in the Hongwu Period of the Ming. It is built in an open and single-spandrel architectural style (敞肩单拱式). In 1935, the bridge was destroyed by floods, but it was rebuilt the next year.

Chengji has long been well-known for its associations with the Communist Revolution. From 1929 to 1932, revolutionaries like He Long (贺龙) and Zhou Yiqun (周逸群) set up a distribution centre here, supplying the nearby Xiang'exi Revolutionary Base (湘鄂西革命根据地).

Chengji is also known for its tolerance of various cultures and lifestyles. Residents here are drawn from at least five major districts, including Hubei, Hunan, Henan, Guangxi and Jiangxi. It is home to families with more than 50 surnames, significant for a small area in China.

Wenchang Ancient Palace

Union Town

Chengji Town's commercial traditions date far back, with well-preserved old workshops standing throughout. The town is recognised for its distinct "Trade Union" Culture (行帮文化), with merchants from throughout the country settling here and organising into groups according to their hometowns for convenience and mutual protection. Chengji also preserves several traditional activities including the making of dragon lanterns (挂龙灯) and lotus gathering boats (采莲船), as well as performing lion dances (玩狮子).

Typical indoor patio of the centuries-old houses along the old streets in Chengji

Smooth streets paved with slates

Zhicheng Town 枝城镇

Cement Capital

Once known as Danyang, Zhicheng is in the transitional region between the Exi Mountains and Jianghan Plain. Due to its geographical position, the town is known as "the throat of Hubei and Wuhan provinces, and the gate of western Hubei Province".

Zhicheng Town, Yidu City, Yichang City, Hubei Province
湖北省宜昌市宜都市枝城镇
Nearest city: Yichang
Take a train from Yichang East Railway Station to Zhicheng Railway Station (枝城站, one hour). The town is about a 15-minute walk from the railway station, or five minutes by motorcycle taxi.
Yichang Sanxia International Airport has services to major Chinese cities, while train services operate from Yichang Railway Station and Yichang East Railway Station .

Zhicheng has always been an important goods collecting and distributing centre between Guizhou, Hunan and Hubei provinces The Yangtze River connects the east and west, the north-south Jiaoliu Railway crosses through, Sanxia Airport is on the other side of the river, and the Yali, Yalai and Hongdong provincial highways intersect here. It is one of the nine largest national railway and water transportation junctions in the region and one of the four biggest national coal distribution centres.

Another old name for Zhicheng is Chengponao (城坡垴). It is home to Fuxing Mountain (复兴山) and Dragon King Terrace (龙王台) above, and Iron Lock Well (铁锁井) nearby. Each of these three places has their own legends. Legend says that Fuxing Mountain is the burial site of the King of Chu. It is said that the Japanese searched for the entrance of the tomb here when they invaded China, but left empty handed. The Ancient City of Danyang (古丹阳城) is said to have one gate each in the east, west, south, and north. There is a ruin called North Gate Jitou (北门矶头) to the north. The west and east gates are the only remains from ancient Danyang, with two columns on both ends of the old street, hinting at the town's long history.

Built in the 1970s, the Zhicheng Yangtze River Bridge (枝城长江大桥) joins with the Jiaozuo-Liuzhou Railway, connecting its south and north. The newly developed Zhicheng Port (枝城港) has helped the area gradually become a national water and land transportation junction. Some major national hydroelectricity projects like the Yangtze Gorges, Gezhouba Dam, Geheyan Hydropower Station, and Gaobazhou Hydropower Station have made it a centre of national hydropower development.

Huaxing Cement (华新水泥) is a famous local cement

company with a 100-year history. Its origins can be traced back to the Daye Hubei Cement Plant founded in 1907. The plant was established by Cheng Zufu of Fujian Qinghua Corporation. Cheng raised 300,000 taels of silver (over 15 million dollars today) and the plant completed construction and went into production in 1909. The establishment of the town's Huaxin Wet Process Cement Rotary Kiln was a milestone in the history of China's cement industry development. Because the corporation made a huge contribution to China's cement industry, the area is honoured as "the cradle of China's cement industry".

Huaxin successfully purchased 51% of Suzhou Jinmao Cement Corporation (苏州金猫水泥有限公司) in 2003.

The Louzi River Tangerine Plantation was built in March, 2008, covering an area of 133,333 square metres.

Jiaguo Mountain Village (架锅山村) is in the southwest of the Zhicheng Town. The town cultivates fruits such as orange, cherry, and plum. The fruit industry brings significant income to the farmers every season, and has paved a path to greater prosperity for the mountain village.

Jujube

Jiudaohe Village of Zhicheng Town is located in a mountain area. The village's soil and weather conditions make it good terrain for winter jujube (冬枣). The villagers bring in seedlings from Zhanhua, the hometown of Chinese winter jujube, to grow them.

Bird's-eye view of Zhicheng

Shangjin Town 上津镇

A Town that Constantly Changes Hands

Shangjin Town has a history of over 1,700 years. The town's many different species of willows are said to have been grown by visitors from all around China to express their homesickness.

Shangjin Town, Yunxi County, Shiyan City, Hubei Province
湖北省十堰市郧西县上津镇
Nearest city: Wuhan
Wuhan Tianhe International Airport is one of China's busiest airports. The new Wuhan Railway Station is used by Wuhan-Guangzhou high-speed trains, while the old Hangkou and Wuchang stations offer regular connections with various destinations across China.
Take a high-speed train from Hankou Station (汉口站) to Shiyan Railway Station (十堰站, about four hours). From Shiyan Rail Station, walk eight minutes to Sanyan Long-Distance Bus Station (三堰长途汽车站). There is one bus to Manchuan Town (漫川镇) at 8:20am which passes through Shangjin Town after two hours.

This ancient town sits in the northwest of Yunxi County, and borders Shanyang Town in Shanxi Province, with the Han River to the south and Qinling Mountains to the north. In the Spring and Autumn Warring States Period, the town was surrounded by the Qin State on three sides and Chu State on another. It was ruled by both, leading it to inspire the idiom "a town that constantly change hands". Located in the northwest of Hubei Province with Han River Basin to the south and the Qin Mountains to the north, Shangjin always been a political, economic and cultural hub, and a place where northern and southern cultures mixed.

Shangjin has a rich historical heritage, including Yangsi Temple (杨泗庙), Yuanzhen Daoist Temple (元贞观), and Chenghuang Temple (城隍庙). It has more than 10 assembly halls, and other attractions include the Ancient City Wall (古城墙), Ancient Theatrical Stage (古戏楼) Guqu Street (古趣街), and a Ming and Qing ancient architectural complex (明清古建筑群).

Shangjin architecture

Bamboo woven articles in the Tourism and Culture Festival

Shangjin was first built in the late Wei Dynasty of the Three Kingdoms Period, but was destroyed in the middle period of the Ming due to wars and natural disasters. Shangjin was re-established in the early Hongwu period of the Ming, and a city was built 200 metres north of the first town's ruins. Since then the city has been rebuilt at least twice, during the Ming and Qing dynasty periods.

The town was named "the Town of Willows" because it stands by mountain and river and is surrounded by willows. With the Jinqian River outside the town, the masts of the ships could once be seen just 10 steps away from the west gate, as the river was only 15 metres from the walls.

The records report famous battles throughout Chinese history.

After the foundation of the PRC in 1949, the ancient town lost its military value, but took responsibility for flood protection.

Fire Lion

Western Yun Fire Lion (郧西火狮子) is an old folk dance in Shangjin. It is said that a drought and plague hit the area during the Ming. An old doctor mentioned that sulphur could be used to prevent and cure the plague. Some folk artists learned about the remedy, and thought of combining the sulphur with the lion dance because at that time people believed dragons and lions were symbols of power. The artists did some experiments and finally they decided to use an iron helmet as the head of the lion, and spray gunpowder (with sulphur inside) while playing the lions to indicate that the disaster and illness had been eliminated. The Shangjin coloured lions turned into fire lions, and the lions' hair became red. The fire lion dance is still popular nowadays.

Shangjin ancient town

Liye Town 里耶镇
The Forgotten Qin Dynasty Town

The Qin Dynasty wells and Han Dynasty paths of Liye Town have witnessed a glorious history, and have a beautiful setting. Liye was once a "forgotten town". In 2002, an archeological discovery in an old well here amazed China and brought fame to the town.

Ancient China: Towns

Liye Town, Longshan County, Xiangxi Tujia and Miao Autonomous Prefecture, Hunan Province
湖南省湘西土家苗族自治州龙山县里耶镇
Nearest city: Huaihua
Huaihua is located in a mountainous area of southwest Hunan Province. Flights between Huaihua Zhijiang Airport and the provincial capital of Changsha take about an hour. The same journey takes about 6 hours by train.
Take a train from Huaihua Railway Station (怀化站) to Jishou Railway Station (吉首市, one hour), then walk 10 minutes to Jishou South Bus Station (吉首市汽车南站). There are regular direct buses to Liye Town (90 minutes).

Sitting in the hinterland of Wuling Mountain in Hunan Province, Liye is located within the Tujia and Miao Nationality autonomous district. "Liye" means "exploring this land" in the Tujia Language. The Tujia ancestors became farmers on this land, rather than fishermen. There were dwellers here as far back as 6,000 years ago, but the town was a poor place as it lacked convenient transport connections. During the Kangxi reign of the Qing Dynasty, streets and docks were built here and Liye was officially developed. The town became prosperous after a market came into being, and was known as "little Nanjing" for its rich culture, and thriving commercial activity.

The ancient town is on the north bank of the Youshui River (酉水). There are three docks on the upper, middle, and lower reaches of the river, and streets of ancient buildings leading in every direction. When the night falls, over 100 boats anchor by the bank, and their lights shine together with the twinkling light from the households, forming a memorable scene.

The north and west city walls of Liye Ancient City are well-preserved. The walls were built with cobblestones, and are 2 metres high, with 24-metre high pedestal. There is a 6-meter-wide, 3-meter-deep moat outside the wall, forming an impregnable defensive layout with both fortress and moat.

Liye's surviving Ancient Streets (里耶古街) were built in the early Qing Dynasty, with shops on both sides. The antique signs are tablets made of catalpa wood with black paint or screens made of nanmu, all decorated with embroidery. The signs are made of cloth or curtains with golden, green or red characters written on them. Every street is directly connected to the dock. Most of the roadside buildings are wood

Folk houses of Liye Ancient City

houses with two courtyards: a storefront and a residential area behind.

Wenchang Pavilion (文昌阁) was built in Yongzheng reign of the Qing Dynasty. It covers 2,666 square metres, and is for ceremonies to honour Confucius. The stately pavilion has red columns, green glazed tiles, and there are 18 wind-bells on the eaves which create a pure ringing sound in the wind.

Yalu Buddhist Convent (雅麓庵) is on Yalu Mountain behind Liye. The mountain is secluded, and full of singing birds and fragrant flowers. Hu Jinchun, a student of the imperial academy in the late Qing Dynasty, wrote a poem called Climbing the Yalu Mountain. It reads: "Climbing the mountain with friends in our spare time, and staying in a quiet small meditation room. I hear cuckoo cries from the remote woods".

The Grandma Temple (婆婆庙) next to Youshui River was built in memory of Madame Chongbani, the wife of an ancient Tujia leader. There is a 400-year-old tree in front of the temple. The exquisite temple has unique coloured stone sculptures and is the most well-preserved maternity worship spot of the Tujia nationality region.

Liye Ancient City street

Secret of the Well

In a 2002 archaeological excavation, over 36,000 wood and bamboo slips were unearthed from Liye's No.1 ancient well. The font of the characters uses an ancient clerical script. The contents are official records, touching on politics, the economy and culture. These materials added abundant information to our knowledge of Qin Dynasty history. Jiudging from the unearthed building materials, pottery shards, and bronze weapons, the town was a military fortress built by the Chu State in the Warring States Period.

Furong Town 芙蓉镇

Hibiscus Town

In China Furong Town is famous as the site of the much-loved film Hibiscus Town. Though the town has a long history, it was only discovered after the film's release. And so it is now best known as Hisbiscus Town.

Furong Town, Yongshun County, Xiangxi Tujia and Miao Autonomous Prefecture, Hunan Province
湖南省湘西土家苗族自治州永顺县芙蓉镇
Nearest city: Huaihua
Huaihua is located in a mountainous area of southwest Hunan Province. Flights between Huaihua Zhijiang Airport and the provincial capital of Changsha take about an hour. The same journey takes about 6 hours by train.
Take a train from Huaihua Railway Station to Mengdonghe Railway Station (猛洞河站, three hours). Furong Town is a 10-minute motorcycle taxi ride from the train station.

Located in a scenic area of the Mengdong River (猛洞河), the town is more than 2,000 years old, being known as Youyang during the Qing and Han dynasties. It was the ancient capital of King Tu, when it was named Xizhou (溪州) or Xia Xizhou (下溪州). Then King Tusi of the Peng Family set his capital here, so its name was changed into Wang Village(王村), or "King Village". For several hundred years it was a centre of politics, economics and culture, connected by the river to Sichuan Province upstream and Hubei downstream.

Five-mile Long Street (五里长街) begins at the port and its black-brick pavement stretches through the ancient town. The town's museum of folk culture is located on the street. Inside the museum, roughly 100 daily folk tools are exhibited, including the rolling cotton machine, carved beds and more, telling the rich history of the Tujia people. The three-storey building is precariously half on the shore and half on the water, supported by concrete columns. The columns extend straight to the bottom of the river and the hanging house stands steadily.

The tofu shop at No.113 was a location in the film Hibiscus Town. Each bowl of tofu is just 2 yuan, and the sour and spicy taste is distinctive. When night falls, many other snacks are available on the street: sweet and fresh grouper, and homemade icy glutinous rice wine from the Tujia people.

Xizhou Copper Pillar (溪洲铜柱) is regarded as spiritually important by the Tujia. It was originally located in the Hexagonal Pavilion (六角亭) , but now can only be seen in Wang Village Folk Culture and Customs Exhibit House (王村民俗风光馆). In 940, Wang Xifang (the King of Chu) and Pen Shichou (the provincial governor of Xizhou), after years of military conflicts with each other, finally shook hands and promised peace, and they marked a border. The 5,000 kilograms copper pillar was made especially for their reconciliation and the battles and the specification of agreement were inscribed on the pillar as evidence. The calligraphic inscription of the agreement is still an important document for studying the history of the Tujia.

Ox Horn Rock (牛角岩) is another site worth checking out. It is located in a unique stone forest filled with stones of different shapes that suggest stalagmites, mushrooms, beasts, women, warriors, and an ox horn.

Hibiscus Town

Wedding Song

Most people of Wang Village are Tujia, who call themselves "Bizika". Though their dressings have been "Hanicised", they still keep many of their own traditional customs. "Tan Hou Shai Pi" (覃后晒皮) is one of the most important Tujia festivals. It is celebrated on the 6th day of the 6th month of the lunar calendar (usually late June or early July), the day that King Tan, the leader of Tujia people in the early Ming dynasty, died. Another local custom is the "Wedding Song" (哭嫁): the bride has to cry for three days to show gratitude to her parents and siblings.

The hanging houses of Hibiscus Town

Jinggang Town 靖港镇

The Ancient Brothel

Jinggang was once reputed by locals to be a kind of "heaven on earth" that attracted people from near and far "Once boats or ships reach the port of the town", a local proverb says, "even a favourable wind can't make them leave".

Jinggang Town, Wangcheng County, Changsha City, Hunan Province
湖南省长沙市望城县靖港镇
Nearest city: Changsha
Changsha Huanghua International Airport is served by a large number of domestic routes. Changsha Railway Station has connections to most cities in China, including a high-speed rail link to Guangzhou that takes only 4 hours.
From Changsha Changzhutan Bus Station (长沙长株潭汽车站, opposite Changsha Railway Station), take a bus to Wangcheng Bus Station (望城汽车站) then transfer to a minibus to Jinggang Town (20 minutes).

Located at the northwest of Wangcheng County, Jinggang is on the western shore of the Xiang River (湘江). It is a fine natural port, with ample water traffic. Once the town was one of the four largest rice markets in Hunan Province, and also an important trading hub. In the middle of the Republic of China period the town — together with Jin City and Hong Jiang — was one of the three most prosperous towns of Hunan Province.

Jinggang reopened to tourists in May, 2009, after a complete makeover. The town has renovited sites such as the Hongtai Fang brothel and the reconstruction of other places is expected to start soon, including the Museum of Revolutionary History (革命历史红色博物馆), The Museum of Fishing Tools (古镇水乡渔具博物馆), and the Lu River Opera Room (芦江戏院).

Jinggang features rivers, temples, and ancient buildings.

Jinggang: A natural port

Residences in Jinggang

statues, and the shore of Xiang River.

Mashi Ancient Street (麻石老街) is about 1,000 metres long. Because the middle part of the street is partly connected to the river, it is also called "Half Side Street". The street is the best preserved ancient street in the Changsha area and most of the buildings on the street date from the Qing Dynasty. The classic scene of thousands of parked boats on the port of Jinggang can no longer be seen because the course of the Wei River changed its route due to flood protection measures carried out in the 1970s.

Bayin Hall (八音堂), originally known as Ningxiang Assembly Hall, is located on Baojian Street in Jinggang. It was built in 1861, and stands 4 metres high with a wooden opera platform in the middle. The hall is supported by two tetragonal columns made of granite, which divide the hall into two parts: the front and back halls. The front hall is now a tea house, and Yunyou Tea made from reed catkin water is a popular choice. The back hall is an ancient opera building, where folk artists perform local opera, play the Dihua drum, or act out shadow plays. All the performances are a great way to experience the local folk culture of Jinggang.

The area has also been the site of many battles. Zeng Guofan, the head of the Xiang army in the Qing Dynasty, fought off the Taiping Rebellion here.

Famous religious buildings include Yangsi Temple (杨泗庙）, Alalokitesvara Temple (观音庙), and Purple Cloud Palace (紫云宫）. Other places of interest in the town include the Ancient Opera Place of Lu River (芦江古戏院), and the Ancient Opera Platform near the water. The Lotus Natural Park of Ruyang Lake (汝洋湖荷花生态公园), located in the western suburbs of the town, is known for its "moonlight over the lotus pond".

There are squares on both the east and west gates of the town, forming its two entrances. The square on the west gate is a symbolic building consisting of a symbolic archway, Lu River Port, and more. The square on the east gate, near Xiang River, sits near the ancient Purple Cloud Palace built 400 years ago. The east square is a combination of gates, archways, green plants,

Brothel

The Hongtai Fang (宏泰坊) brothel was opened for business in the town in 1733. Today the brothel has been transformed into a museum. It is mainly constructed from woods and brick, and has three entrances, each with a courtyard. The carvings of the wood building are delicate, and the luxurious decoration suggests the town's former prosperity. Inside the building, the thousands of years of brothel culture in China are explained, including the origins, development and disappearance of the institution. This history is introduced by paintings, calligraphy, sculpture, clay art, and other exhibits. Hongtai Fang is associated with many stories or legends of the brave women who worked in the brothels in ancient times.

Yaoli Town 瑶里镇

China Town

Yaoli Town is located on the northeastern side of the internationally famous pottery town of Jingdezhen. During the Tang Dynasty, ceramics workshops were established here. Yaolli is also at the centre of three world cultural sites: Huangshan Mountain, Lu Mountain, and Xidi and Hong villages.

Yaoli Town, Fuliang County, Jingdezhen Town, Jiangxi Province
江西省景德镇市浮梁县瑶里镇
Nearest city: Jingdezhen
Jingdezhen Station on the Jianxi-Anhui railway line is connected to key centres such as Nanjing and Shanghai. There are also direct flights between Shanghai and Jingdezhen Airport (1 hour).
From Jingdezhen Airport (景德镇机场), take a taxi to Fuliang County Coach Station (浮梁汽车站, 10-15 minutes). Then, take a bus to Yaoli Town (one hour).

Along the river from east to west, residences are located at the north and south of Yaoli Town. On the main commercial street from the Ming and Qing era, you will see roughly 100 shops on both sides of the street. They remain well-preserved, especially the unique shops of the Ming. Dongbu Street (东埠街) which consists of an ancient street, bridge, and port.

The area containing the Relics of Kaolin Mine (高岭土矿遗址园区) is a great place for archaeologists studying ancient ceramics, or for a humble stroll along the 5-kilometre granite-paved ancient mountain road. The walk also allows you to admire the dragon-shaped Dragon Mouth Waterfall (龙口瀑布) or the thick camphor trees in Juxiu Pavilion (聚秀亭) .

Constructed in the middle of the Ming, the Chen Family Ancestral Hall, also known as Dunmu Hall, is located alongside the Yao River (瑶河) and sits in front of Lion Mountain (狮山) . The use of fengshui has given the hall its unique structure. Within the building, the carvings of bricks, stones or wood are various and rich, with delicate and vivid design.

Shi Gang Great View was built in the Qing Dynasty on Yao Mountain (瑶岭) , facing Lion Mountain (狮山) and also near the Yao. It is a residential house in the style of the Hui people, combining Chinese and western design. The windows and beams of the house have been decorated with over 100 vivid and delicate wood carvings, which were inspsired by the four great classical novels of China, as well as other stories. It is said that a sculpted bed that once was the trousseau of the family's daughter took one year for the carpenter to finish.

Yaoli town was also an important military base for the New Fourth Army during the Sino-Japanese War. The old residence of General Chenyi, and the old army station have been well preserved. Chenyi's former residence (陈毅旧居) now houses an exhibition that introduces the history of the New Fourth Army and the general's life. Meanwhile, Hongyi Ancestral Hall (宏毅词) is a branch of the Wu Family Ancestral Hall (吴家祠) and is a place where the clan's people pay tribute to their ancestors.

One more highlight of Yaoli is Wang Lake (汪湖). Walking into the thick forest around the lake, you can hardly see the sky. In front of the withered trees, flourishing woods grow, and inside this natural oxygen bar, even the most tired travellers will find their strength.

Yaoli is located in a mountain area, at an altitude of 600-900 metres. The forest coverage is about 94%, and fresh air permeates throughout. There is abundant rainfall and a good temperature for local agriculture, especially tea. The history of producing tea in Yaoli is long,

Yaoli villages by the river

and Fuliang (浮梁) is the most important of its tea-producing areas. Yaoli tea (瑶里茶) is one of the world's three teas grown at high altitude, and used to be the tea provided as tribute from Yaoli to the capital. In the modern era, the tea has also been served at state banquets at the Great Hall of the People in Beijing.

187

Central Plains

Yaoli Diet

Yaoli people are very particular about their diet, and most of the ingredients used in their cooking are natural. Specialties include boiled stone chick (清炖石鸡), turtle and mushroom (神龟偷菇), and bacon loach soup (腊肉泥鳅汤). Popular vegetable dishes, are duck foot (鸭脚板), longevity grass (长命草), and ma chilan (马齿苋). Popular snacks include pumpkin beans (南瓜豆), batata dates (红薯枣), bean pie (豆渣饼), or kudzu vine (葛根).

Shangqing Town 上清镇
The Daoist Town

Shangqing Town is endowed with a style exclusive to the southern reaches of the Yangtze River, with stilted houses and docks closely dotted along rivers like the teeth of a comb or scales of a fish. Along the river are women washing silk clothes, children playing in the water, and floating fishing boats.

Shangqing Town, Mount Longhu Scenic Spot, Yingtan City, Jiangxi Province 江西省鹰潭市龙虎山风景区上清镇
Nearest city: Shangrao
Shangrao Sanqingshan Airport offers services to a selection of major Chinese cities while Shangrao Train Station on the Jianxi-Anhui line is linked with large regional centres such as Shanghai.
From Shangrao Railway Station (上饶火车站), take a train to Yingtan Railway Station (鹰潭火车站, about one hour), then go to the long-distance bus station located in the west part of Yingtan Station. There are regular buses to Shangqing Town, which cost 5 yuan for a 30-minute ride.

Located in the southwest of Yingtan City in Jiangxi Province (江西省鹰潭市), Shangqing is known for its pleasant weather. The Luxi River (泸溪河), running across the town from east to northwest, was once was an important waterway for businessman from Fujian Province (福建). In the Tang Dynasty and the Five Dynasties period, the town was called Xiongshi Town (雄石镇). In the Song and Yuan dynasties it was given the name Shangqing.

As a birthplace of Daoist culture, Shangqing is the highlight of Dragon and Tiger Mountain in Yingtan City – the mountain is honoured as the cradle of Daoism. There are many places of historical interest in Shangqing. On the 2-kilometre Shangqing ancient street (上清古街) are sites like Liuhou Ancestral Temple (留候家庙), Tianyuande Drugstore (天源德药栈), and the Catholic Cathedral. In the east of the Town are Shangqing Palace and East Mountain Palace; in the northeast is Elephant Mountain Institute, one of the four largest institutes of its kind from the Southern Song Dynasty. On the other side of Luxi River is Guizhou Country (桂洲村), hometown of Xiayan (夏言), who served as prime minister of China in the Ming Dynasty.

Shangqing's ancient street is endowed with intangible natural beauty. Walking along the street up the Luxi River, houses to the

Shangqing Palace

Shangqing Palace

left are arranged in the shape of a stairway; every house protrudes out roughly 1 metre higher than the previous one, symbolising the prosperity of each family.

Sihan Daoist Masters' Mansion (嗣汉天师府) was once situated at the foot of Dragon and Tiger Mountain and later moved to Changqing Workshop (长庆坊) in the town's west. Consisting of a front and back hall, private residence, reading room, garden and Chengfa Ancestor Hall (成法宗坊), the mansion is laid out with crossing pathways and corridors, and layer-on-layer of halls and pavilions that resemble an imperial palace. Painted dragons decorate its pillars. Inside the mansion old trees shade the ground from the sun and make the house a quiet and beautiful retreat.

Located at the east end of the Gui River (贵溪), the Shangqing Palace was first constructed in the Eastern Han Dynasty. It is the site where Zhang Daoist Masters of each dynasty performed religious activities, and where followers of Daoism worshipped the prophet Lord Taishanglaojun (太上老君). Built in the Tang Dynasty, the Palace went through repairs and extensions during the Song, Yuan, Ming and Qing dynasties before its current grand scale was achieved.

In the east of Shangqing Palace, Dongyin Institute (东隐院) is a prestigious Daoist temple built during the Southern Song Dynasty on Dragon and Tiger Mountain, whose reputation was greatly boosted during the Yuan Dynasty when Zhang Liusun (张留孙), a Daoist from the temple, was treated with special courtesy by Hubilie (忽必烈), the founding emperor of the Yuan Dynasty.

Xianshui Cliffs

A genuine wonder, the site of hanging coffins is located on the steep walls of the Xianshui Cliffs (仙水岩). Jade coffins are hung in the caves and the Luxi River runs below. On the broad stretches of cliff walls, caves are scattered. From a boat on Luxi River, a vague scene of wooden stakes or planks comes into sight. The cave's treasures were discovered in the late 1970s by archaeological scholars from Jiangxi Province. It is still unknown how the hanging coffins were placed dozens of metres high above water in ancient times.

A view of Shangqing from behind ancient trees

Geyuan Town 葛源镇

The Source of Kudzu

Surrounded by verdant mountains and farmland, Geyuan Town is not prosperous or bustling, but with courtyards shaded by green bamboo, pools circled by nodding willows and a crystal river running slowly through the town, Geyuan has a natural beauty.

Geyuan Town, Hengfeng County, Shangrao City, Jiangxi Province
江西省上饶市横峰县葛源镇
Nearest city: Shangrao
Shangrao Sanqingshan Airport offers services to a selection of major Chinese cities while Shangrao Train Station on the Jianxi-Anhui line is linked with large regional centres such as Shanghai.
From Shangrao Bus Station (上饶汽车站, a 10-15 minute taxi drive from Shangrao Railway Station), there are regular buses heading to Geyuan Bus Station (葛源汽车站, about 90 minutes).

Geyuan Town is located at the juncture of three counties — Yeyang (弋阳), Dexing (德兴) and Shangyao (上饶) — in the northeast of Jiangxi Province.

It is called Geyuan for two reasons. The first character, "ge", depicts kudzu vines, which grow far and wide here. The second, "yuan", in Chinese means "source". Geyuan thus enjoys a reputation as the source of kudzu, and the origin of the kudzu root in China. Geyuan became a prosperous market in this mountainous area during the Song Dynasty when families like the Zheng, Cai, Ye, Luo and Wang moved here following the initial settlers, the Su and Feng families. During the official reign of the Jiaqing Emperor in the Ming Dynasty (1796-1820), Geyuan was defined under the administration of Xingan County (兴安县), also called Hengfeng County.

Known as the sixth-most important crop in China (falling behind the so-called "five grains"), kudzu, a plant used both in cuisine and medicine, offers farmers a short growth period, fast reproduction, easy crop planting, and resilience. Since as early as at the end of the Sui and beginning of the Tang, people in Geyuan have made kudzu into powder. It was supplied to the emperor as a tribute in the Ming and Qing. Today kudzu is made into different products such as kudzu powder, kudzu slices, kudzu tea, and kudzu juice.

Geyuan maintains its ancient charm as an old town in a mountainous area, with distinctive

Antithetical couplets about the revolution

government of Fujian, Zhejiang and Guangxi.

The former provincial office for the Soviet of Fujian, Zhejiang, and Guangxi (中共闽浙赣省委旧址) is situated at the end of North Mountain Kan Road (北山堪路) in Maple Forest Country. It is composed of provincial offices for the Red Army, such as the general bureau, treasury for the finance ministry and a residence for guards.

The military headquarters was established on Dec. 11, 1932 and moved from Geyuan to Maple Forest Country at the end of 1932. With a simple gate in front of the body, the headquarters is divided into front and rear buildings with 12 rooms.

The site of the Fifth Branch School of Workers' and Peasants' Red Army of China (中国工农红军学校第五分校旧址_, located at the Yang Ancestral Hall in Geyuan County, is 1,200 square kilometres and consists of a gate hall, residences, six rooms, and an exhibition room in the backyard.

Lenin Park (列宁公园), allegedly the first park established by the China Communist Party, was established by Fang Zhimin in 1931, located on the Ge River in Geyuan County. It is a unique tourist scenic spot due to its significance in Red Army history.

Lanes in Geyuan

cottages characterised by mud walls, tiled ceilings, cereal bases, verandas and patios. Historical sites include the Ancient Streets of the Ming and Qing dynasties, the site of the White Stone Institute, and Eternity Stage. The town's arch bridge, paved with granite, is equally impressive.

With a special geographic position, — the town is surrounded by mountains on all sides and a river runs near — Geyuan has been a cradle for many talented individuals, and also served as a base during the Communist Revolution. Over 70 years ago, as one of the six largest revolutionary bases in the country, Geyuan was the location of the provincial Communist Party committee and

Hangover Cure

Kudzu is highly nutritious, used both as a food and a medicine. According to traditional Chinese medicine, kudzu powder is good for reducing "excessive internal healing" and for general nourishment. The kudzu flower can also cure a hangover, traditions say. It makes for a good souvenir to take home to friends and relatives.

岭 南 古 镇
Lingnan Towns (South
of the FIve Ridges)
Watchtowers and dragons

Chikan town 赤坎镇

The European Street

Chikan is an ancient town that combines architectural and cultural elements from both China and the west. The dark hazel arcade towers stretch for miles, Roman pillars are wrapped in tender ivy, and sleek slate pathways juxtaposed with rusting Baroque pediments all radiate an exotic beauty of days past.

Chikan Town, Kaiping City, Guangdong Province
广东省开平市赤坎镇
Nearest city: Guangzhou
Guangzhou Baiyun International Airport is the second busiest in China, and Guangzhou's four railways stations are connected with cities across China through an ever-expanding number of high-speed railway lines.
Guangzhou Tianhe Bus Terminal Station (广州天河客运站) has regular buses to Kaiping Yici Bus Station (开平义祠汽车站), about 2 hours away. At Kaiping, transfer to a minibus to Jiji Town (金鸡镇). The bus will pass by Chikan Town 30 minutes into the trip.

Located in the central region of Kaiping City in Guangdong Province, Chikan Town was built during the Qing Dynasty on the northern bank of the Tan River(潭江), and was so named because of the red soil there ("chi" means "red" in Chinese, while "kan" means "riverbank"). It is recognized as the hometown of many famous Chinese people who moved abroad, and is home to the oldest watchtower in Kaiping (开平碉楼).

Chikan's mix of traditional Chinese and western culture is embodied by the unique "European Street"(欧陆风情街), which is lined by more than 600 arcade towers that stretch for 3 kilometres by the riverbank. Combining the features of western and Lingnan architecture, the arcade towers are suited to the rainy and hot climate of southern China. Concrete was added to the basic grey brick structures with traditional tiled gable roofs, forming the two-to-three-storey arcade towers. There are three corridors from bottom to top, each of which has rooms and parapet walls, elements unique to western architecture. With traditional Chinese designs decorating the walls, the arcade towers suggest features of the Roman Arcade, as well as Gothic, Baroque, Muslim, and traditional Chinese architecture.

Chikan watchtower

Chikan European Street

Chikan town also boasts abundant historical and cultural relics, such as the Red Chamber (红楼) on the northern bank of the east Tan River. Other landmarks include the Christian church, Catholic church, Aishan Hall (爱善堂), and the Public Wealth Memorial Pavilion (公福纪念亭), all of which speak to the prosperity of Chikan's educational and religious history.

The Situs Library (司徒氏图书馆) was built in 1923. It is a three-storey style building that boasts a fusion of east and west, and includes a courtyard that holds newspapers, magazines, a large variety of books, calligraphy, and paintings. The Guan Library (关族图书馆) sits on the riverbank to the west of the upper dam of Chikan, opposite its counterpart Situ Library, which lies east of the dam. A collection of 10,000 books was held in the Guan Library at its inception, including up-to-date newspapers and magazines from abroad.

Five kilometres north of the ancient town is Canadian Village, which is also known as the Yaohuafang Village (耀华坊). It was built by overseas Chinese from Canada, with ancient western villas, imposing watchtowers, and poetic pastoral landscapes. There are ten two-to-three-storey mansions of different styles in the village, such as Spring-like Mansion (春如楼) and the Four Heroes Mansion (四豪楼), all as which were funded by overseas Chinese from Canada.

Greet Dragon Hall (迎龙楼), the oldest watchtower in Kaiping, can be found in Sanmenli (三门里) of Luyang village (芦阳村), less than 500 metres north of Canadian Village. Greet Dragon Hall (迎龙楼) was built in the Qing Dynasty, and was gradually reconstructed into a three-storey traditional watchtower in the Kaiping style. The tower now stands 10 metres high. On the front of the ground floor there is an arch gate. Each floor is divided into a main hall and two wing-

The Guan Library

rooms on both its west and east sides.

Pockmarked with bullet holes, the five-storey Chikan South Tower (赤坎南楼) was built in 1913 in Tengwen Village (藤蚊村) with funds raised by overseas Chinese to defend the town-folk against bandits. The tower stands by the Tan River across from the North Tower, and on the transportation junction of Sanbu and Chishui, an important location. A single guard can ward off a troop of thousands. With searchlights set on its top, the South Tower serves as a beacon in peaceful time and a barrier pass during wars.

Chikan Film City

Keen-eyed film Chinese film producers and directors have been attracted by Chikan, with its neat and exotic arcade towers and unique European influence. In 2004, the Chikan Film City was completed at the upper port of the town. It represents the Xiguan, an area of Guangzhou, from the 1920s and 1930s, and is a perfect artificial landscape for tourists to experience the culture of that time.

Chikan South Tower

Chikan Film City

Shawan Town 沙湾镇

Town of the Flying View

Shawan town is an unusual small town with a rich significance as one of the birthplaces of Guangdong opera. "Shawan Flying View," and the "Shakeng Awakening Lion" are among the other highlights of the town's unique cultural heritage.

Ancient China: Towns

Shawan Town, Panyu District, Guangzhou City, Guangdong Province
广东省广州市番禺区沙湾镇
Nearest city: Guangzhou
Guangzhou Baiyun International Airport is the second busiest in China, and Guangzhou's four railways stations are connected with cities across China through an ever-expanding number of high-speed railway lines.
Take a Line 3 subway train from Guangzhou and get off at Shiqiao Station in Panyu (番禺) then walk to Baiyue Square (百越广场) and take the No. 7 bus to Shawan Town (about 20 minutes).

Shawan is an ancient cultural town on the Pearl River Delta, formed more than 800 years ago. Its name comes from its location on a half-moon-shaped sandy beach near a bay ("sha" means "sand" in Chinese, while "wan" means "bay"). Since it sits near Qingluo Mountain, it was also once called Qingluo Village.

Located at the foot of Aoshan Mountain (鳌山) of the Sanshan Village (三善村) area of Shawan, the well-preserved Aoshan Architectural Complex of the Qing Dynasty comprises a large number of ancient temples and more. Commonly known as Luban Temple (鲁班庙), the Masters' Ancient Temple (先师古庙) used to hold a statue of Luban (a legendary craftsman, engineer, and inventor). With a distinct Lingnan-style layout, the temple was decorated by vivid frescos and paintings of flowers, birds, landscapes, and figures.

Built in the Yuan Dynasty, He Ancestral Hall (何氏祠堂) comprises a front gate and Yi Hall (仪宫), as well as the Fishing Terrace (钓鱼台), Entertainment Hall (享殿), Sleeping Hall (寝殿), and wing-rooms, and the Village Ancestral Hall (村祠). It was constructed with slate, timbers and oysters (in

A view of Liugeng Hall

Lake view of the Treasure Chamber in Treasure Ink Garden

Cantonese, "oyster" is a homophone for "grand", so oyster shells frequently feature along the walls in these Cantonese-speaking regions). The ancestral hall of the He Family in Fanyu District is old, large, and is particularly famous for its surprising number of pillars: there are a total of 112 wood and stone pillars in the hall.

Also known as Blue Water and Green Mountain Chamber (水绿山青文阁), the Kuixing Chamber (魁星楼) — dedicated to Kuixing, the god who determines academic achievements — was built in the Kangxi Period of the Qing Dynasty, and named after the story of "a carp leaping through the Dragon Gate". Chinese legend says a carp that leaps through the Dragon Gate will become a dragon. Kuixing similarly leapt through the gate, turning himself from a near invalid to a deified scholar. Ancestors of the Hes used this name to encourage their descendents to study hard for the laurel of scholars.

The Treasured Ink Garden (宝墨园) was built in the late Ming and early Qing dynasties, but was destroyed in the 1950s. The 1995-2003 reconstruction expanded the garden to cover an area 200 times larger than its predecessor. The garden employs Lingnan garden architecture and water town features, with the many scenic spots and buildings in it.

Another unique story is told in Longtu Hall (龙图馆). Bao Zheng supposedly contributed to the reunion of the emperor Zhao Zhen and his mother. In gratitude, Zhao painted a portrait for Bao. In ancient China, emperors were believed to be dragons, so the painting by Zhao was called a "Dragon Painting", the pronunciation of which is "Longtu". Bao hung the painting in his mansion, which was later called Longtu Hall. Bao himself,

who lived in the hall, was called Bao Longtu.

The renowned "Shawan Flying View" (沙湾飘色) is a local folk performance that has been passed on from the late Ming and early Qing dynasties. The "Flying View" is performed by a travelling team of many three-dimensional stages. Each stage, namely the "View Board", is 150 centimetres long, 77 centimetres wide and 63 centimetres high. The actor sitting or standing on the Board is called the "screen" and the actor in midair is called the "Flying", the two of which are connected by a carefully forged steel branch (called the "view bone") to form a integrated story.

The performance is usually held on the third day of the third month of the lunar calendar (early April to late May), when crowds flood to the 17 places in the villages of Shawan where the tradition is performed.

With a history of rich culture, Shawan is also known as the "the town of music in Guangdong". During the late Qing Dynasty and the early Republic of China Period, Shawan gave birth to many famous Cantonese Opera and popular singers.

Awakening Lion

Shawan is one of the places where the Lion Dance was developed and became popular. Shawan's version, the Shakeng Awakening Lion (沙坑醒狮), is known across China. The darting, flipping, and tumbling in the performance is unbelievably smooth, mimicking swift lions.

Shakeng Awakening Lion

Shilong Town 石龙镇

The Town of Weightlifting

"There is a stone in the shape of a dragon resting on the riverbed in Dongjiang", the legend goes. "When it snaked north and arrived at this place, the stone dragon lifted its head above water to look far into the distance. The place was blessed by the lingering dragon and became a happy land named Shilong ". ("Shi" is Chinese for "stone"; "long" means "dragon".)

Shilong Town, Dongguan City, Guangdong Province
广东省东莞市石龙镇
Nearest city: Shenzhen
Shenzhen Baoan Airport is one of China's busiest airports. The city has also been integrated into China's fast developing high-speed rail network, providing easy access to Guangzhou City and beyond.
Take a high-speed train from Shenzhen Luohu Railway Station (深圳罗湖站) to Shilong Station (石龙站), which takes 40 minutes and costs 45 yuan. Then take a 10-minute taxi ride from the railway station to Shilong Town.

Shilong Town is located in the north of Dongguan City, in an area where the northern stream of the ever-beautiful Dongjiang River meanders down and joins with the southern branch. The town is not far from Hong Kong. Because of its convenient water transportation, Shilong has been an important town since the late Ming and early Qing dynasties, when water transportation was heavily relied upon.

Zhongshan Road (中山路), the town's main street which was built in 1929 and named in memory of Sun Zhongshan (or Sun Yat-sen), the father of modern China, is lined by traditional arcade towers. Their good condition, grand scale and unified style are rarely seen in the Pearl River Delta area.

Sun Yat-sen arrived at the frontline in Shilong to preside over battles with Chen Jiongmin, a warlord in Huizhou. In memory of the feats achieved by Sun, the town renamed Shilong Park, built in 1924, calling it Zhongshan Park.

The park is also home to a podium used multiple times

Zhongshan Park

Ouxian Place

by Zhou Enlai, China's prime minister in the Mao era and a renowned diplomat and statesman. The podium is built with grey bricks and a copper statue of Zhou stands on it.

Shilong Town is also famous for weightlifting: it has been home to several champion Chinese weightlifters.

Ouxian Place (欧仙院) was built in the Qianlong reign of the Qing Dynasty. As a young man, Ouxian went to study with Huang Yeren, a mysterious figure who was said to be a demigod, on Putuo Mountain and returned home as an elder. He bought a boat for fishing on the river, and a ferry those who needed to go across. It was said that a Daoist priest helped him become an immortal the next night. In memory of this kind and generous man, the town raised funds and built a temple for him in a quiet place. The temple is now Mater Ou's Temple (欧公祠).

Located on the southern bank of the Dongjiang River is Jinshawan Park (金沙湾公园), where dragon boat races are held each year. There is a fountain, two small plazas, an artificial sandy beach, and rows of classical-designed benches on the long dam by the river. When night falls, the interplay of glowing lamps and glistening water forms a poetic landscape.

Located by Dongjiang River in the main scenic region of the New District, Jinshawan Plaza (金沙湾广场) is a large space for exhibitions, relaxation, and gatherings. In the middle of the plaza is what is said to be the largest "dragon" character in the world, at 10,000 square metres. The plaza also houses the Picture of Shilong Ancient Town, a 100-meter relief carved on Fujian slates, which reproduce the past glory of this ancient town.

The Azalea Corridor (杜鹃花长廊), is located on the east embankment of the Dongjiang River, which boasts four lanes. Hundreds of thousands of azalea trees are planted on the slope, stretching for 3 kilometres.

Studies say that the town's Bamboo Appliance Street (竹器街) is more than 400 years old. There are more than a dozen kinds of bamboo appliances, including ladders, beds, sleeping mats, bins, baskets, and fishing tools.

The town is also famous for its fireworks. A large fireworks evening party is held annually on the second day of the first month of the lunar calendar (usually January to early March).

Buddha Bathing

"Buddha Bathing Day" (浴佛节) is on the eighth day of the fourth month of the lunar calendar (early May to late June), the birthday of the Supreme Buddha. Ancient Shilong was made up of temples and nunneries. In each temple and nunnery was a small Buddha statue. On Buddha Bathing Day each of these statues would be washed and the water used was made into sweet soup or sesame paste for children. The tradition survives today. On every Buddha Bathing Day, each family makes sweet soups for relatives and friends. The traditional dragon boat race on the tenth day of the fifth month of the lunar calendar (early June to late July) also has a long history. The Dongjiang River in beautiful Jinsha Bay bustles with excited crowds on each race day.

Tangjiawan Town 唐家湾镇

The Prime Minister's Home Town

Located in the east of Tangjiawan Town is Qi'ao Isle, opposite Golden Star Isle, with Tang peninsula to the west, inspiring the visual metaphor "two dragons playing with a pearl".

Tangjiawan Town, Xiangzhou District, Zhuhai City, Guangdong Province
广东省珠海市香洲区唐家湾镇
Nearest city: Shenzhen
Shenzhen Baoan Airport is one of China's busiest airports. The city has also been integrated into China's fast developing high-speed rail network, providing easy access to Guangzhou City and beyond.
Long-distance buses from Shenzhen Luohu Bus Station (深圳罗湖汽车站) to Zhuhai will pass by Tangjiawan Bus Station (唐家湾汽车站) two hours in. From Tangjiawan, take the No. 3, No. 10, or No. 69 bus to the Pearl Paradise Park (珍珠乐园) and walk about eight minutes to Gongleyuan Park (共乐园), which is located in Tangjiawan Town.

In the southern part of Xiangzhou District in Zhuhai City, Tangjiawan Town (Tang's Bay Town) consists of Tang Isle isle, Jinding Isle, and Qi'ao Isle. It has been recorded in the history books since over 700 years ago, and was once called "Fuyongjing" (釜涌境). In the 1300s, the families Tang and Liang moved to south because of wars, and the area was called "Tang's Village" after the former family. Now those with the family name Tang make up half of the town's permanent population.

Qi'ao Isle (淇澳岛) is a famous ecological isle and tourist resort. With its wetland ecology and an area of 5.33 square kilometres, Qi'ao mangrove forest is the largest expanse of mangrove forest in the Pearl River Delta area. It is also the largest cultivated ordered mangrove forest in China.

View of Tang's Bay

Situated at No.99 of Shanfang road in Tang's Bay, the Former Residence of Tang Shaoyi (唐绍仪) (the first Prime Minister of China during the Republic of China period) is a combination of two houses, a front and a back. The rear house was built by Tang Shaoyi's grandfather in the Qing Dynasty, and the front was extended by Tang himself in 1929. Now the residence is watched over by Tang Shaoyi's grandnephew, Tang Hongguang (唐鸿光), and visitors can sample his homemade mint tea.

Three hundred metres from the residence is the Happy Together Garden (共乐园). It was Tang Shaoyi's private garden. Combining both Chinese and western styles, the garden is elegant, refined, and sweet.

The Wangcishan house (望慈山房), at No.12 Shanfang Road, was built in 1929 by the former prime minister, in memory of his mother. His mother's name was inscribed on the upper part of the main door. The protruding watchtower in the main building faces the grave of Tang's mother, so it was called the "watching building". It is said that Tang Shaoyi every morning stood in the tower to watch his mother. Later, the building became the governmental administration building of Zhongshan County.

The town's three main temples are at the intersection of Datong Road and Xindizhi Street. They are the Shrine temple (圣堂庙), Civil and Military Temple (文武庙), and Golden Flower Temple (金花庙), and they stand side-by-side. The layout of the buildings is precise, with tilted and lifting wooden beams, and walls made from grey bricks and oyster shells. The temples are separated by watery alleys, with the doors of the connected corridors decorated with stone, brick, and wood carvings, and colourful pictures. On the ridges are ornaments of cod fish, Buddha's relics, a dragon with horns, flying fish, and cornices. The ceilings have delicate relief sculptures on the eaves. In the inner part of the eaves, there are some traditional Chinese paintings, poems, and frescos with stereoscopic features.

It is said that the Shrine Temple dates back to the early days of the Tang family, and therefore it is also called the Tang's Ancestral Temple. The

Artocarpus heterophyllus on a tree

divine figure in the temple is the Bodhisattva. The Golden Flower Temple was built in the early Qing Dynasty. Within the temple is a series of representations of divine feminine figures. The Civil and Military Temple, meanwhile, built in the early Qing Dynasty, is a Daoist temple.

Tangjiawan Town is home to some famous old-style private schools, such as Pengxuan School (鹏轩学舍), and Polite and Harmonious school (礼和学堂).

Also in the town are relics associated with the various revolutions in China, such as Qi'ao White Stone Street (淇澳白石街), and Qi'ao Ancestral Temple (淇澳祖庙), which witnessed the tragic history of the peasant movement.

Opium War

Introduced by the experts, Golden Star Corner (金星角) on Qi'ao Isle in the town was a postal house used by merchants from the United States and United Kingdom to smuggle opium in the lead-up to the Opium Wars. The merchants were later forced to compensate the locals with 3,000 taels of silver and to build White Stone Street. The villagers thus recorded one of the first anti-western battle successes in Chinese history.

Qiuchang Town 秋长镇

The Red Hakka town

Qiuchang Town faces picturesque Dayawan beach and Huizhou port to the east. Native sons of Long Autumn Town include well-known General in the Communist Northern Expedition, Ye Jianying, and the "King of Kuala Lumpur" Ye Yalai.

Qiuchang Town, Huiyang District, Huizhou City, Guangdong Province
广东省惠州市惠阳区秋长镇
Nearest city: Guangzhou
Guangzhou Baiyun International Airport is the second busiest in China, and Guangzhou's four railways stations are connected with cities across China through an ever-expanding number of high-speed railway lines.
Take a train from Guangzhou East Railway Station (广州东站) to Huizhou Railway Station (惠州站, about 90 minutes). From Huizhou there are regular buses to Qiuchang Town (about one hour).

Qiuchang Town (Long Autumn Town) has a long revolutionary tradition. During the Chinese Civil War, the communist revolutionary Ye Wenkuang (叶文匡) from the town, established the Chinese Communist Huiyang County Committee (中共惠阳县委). In the Sino-Japanese War, Zeng Sheng(曾生) set up the main guerrilla outfit of Huibao to fight against the Japanese (惠宝人民抗日游击总队). The headquarters was in the Yuying Building (育英楼) in the town's Zhoutian Village (周田村).

Qiuchang is home to 48 old revolutionary villages. Since the Xinhua Revolution of 1911, over 130 "martyrs" have come from Qiuchang. Among them, General Ye Ting (叶挺将军) is the most famous. Ye Ting's former residence is 6 kilometres from Zhoutian Village (周田村) in the northeast of the town. It was built by Ye's grandfather, Ye Peilin (叶沛林), and is a small circular Hakka house. For more than 100 years, the whole layout and the display of the house was preserved according to the original construction. On the 10th of September in 2002, then-Chinese president Jiang Zemin (江泽民) inscribed a board for the residence. The more than 150 precious photos, objects, and relics within the residence tell the story of Ye Ting's life.

Qiuchang Town is an important homeland for some prominent overseas Chinese. Among them is the "King of Kuala Lumpur", Ye Yalai (叶亚来). From 1862 to 1885, Ye helped build the Malaysian capital, then a city with less than 1,000 residents. Biyan Building (碧滟楼) in Zhoutian Village (周田村), built in the Qing, is Ye's former residence. It is also a typical traditional Hakka circular house.

The town is home mostly to Hakka people. According to family records, the founder, Ye Yu (叶裕), moved to Long Autumn from Fujian Province in late Southern Song Dynasty. He settled down in Jiangtian (蒋田). Later, his Nanyang residence (南阳世居) was built. After that, people mostly from Meizhou, colourful wooden-carved paintings.

Qiuchang Town now has more than 100 Hakka circular houses of various styles. Among them, over 40 houses are large, well-preserved, and with a high cultural and artistic value. It is one of the densest and most well-maintained circular house areas in eastern Guangdong. The 1,000-year-old circular house — Jiangtian Nanyang residence (蒋田南阳世居) — has an area of more than 3,500 square metres, and has courtyards of different shapes. With a rectangle shape, its architectural space is rich and its original earthen wall can still be seen clearly. According to textual research, it was built in the late Southern Song Dynasty and it is the oldest circular house to be found in Huiyang.

The statue in Ye Ting's former residence in the Long Autumn town

in Guangdong continuously settled here. They've left a great number of Hakka houses. In front of the building is a moon-shaped pool, steles with records of honours and a grain field. At the back is a flower platform and watchtower. The inner layout is symmetrical, individual, strongly private and with three halls and two horizontal bars as its core. The material of the walls is mainly a mixture of lime, clay, and sand, with a little soil. It has delicate and

Long Autumn Culture

Hakka folk songs, dragon dancing, and traditional martial arts have a unique style in Qiuchang. Local cuisine highlights include tofu with meats, Hakka wine, and Long Autumn meat.

Biyan Building

Jieshi Town 碣石镇

The Ancient Ming Wei

Jieshi is a commercial fishing town. As one of the 36 wei (or states) in Ming Dynasty China, Jieshi — the name means "stone" — was once a great town. The place is also a spiritual centre for people who speak the Minnan dialect.

Jieshi Town, Lufeng City, Guangdong Province
广东省陆丰市碣石镇
Nearest city: Guangzhou
Guangzhou Baiyun International Airport is the second busiest in China, and Guangzhou's four railways stations are connected with cities across China through an ever-expanding number of high-speed railway lines.
Buses from the Guangzhou Tianhe Bus Station (广州天河客运站) to Lufeng County (陆丰市) pass by Jieshi Town after about three hours.

Located in the south of Lufeng City (陆丰市) and facing Jieshi Bay to the east, Jieshi Town is beside Jinxiang Town (金厢镇), separated from it by a river. . It is 115 nautical miles from both Hong Kong and Shantou (汕头).

In the Hongwu reign of the Ming Dynasty, the Jieshi state, or "wei", was set up However, the roots of the town are much deeper. Yuanshan Temple (元山寺) was originally built in 1127 during the Yanyan reign of the Southern Song Dynasty. The temple was rebuilt into Xuanwu Temple (玄武庙) in the 27th year of the Ming Hongwu reign, and extended as Yuanshan Temple (元山寺) in the Wanli reign of the Ming. Constructed along the mountain, the temple features a group of courtyards like symmetrical temples. Along the numerous stairs, the temple has three halls directly connecting to the main hall.

Within the temple, the decorations are golden and splendid. The carvings and paintings on the main gate are delicate and depict dragons and phoenixes. The two stone lions aside are vivid, like two dutiful guards watching the temple day and night. Many precious historical relics are displayed inside: the copper statue of the Zhenwu King (北极真武) from the Song Dynasty; the wooden statue of Sakya Muni from the Ming; and a stele inscribed by Qing Tongzhi Emperor.

At the back of Yuanshan Temple is Xuanshan Tower (玄山塔), also known as Lucky Star Tower. It has long been a useful navigation mark for travellers in Jieshi Bay and has been called "Buddhist light". The peak of the tower offers great views of the town and across the sea. Built in the Wanli reign, the octagonal earthen tower has three storeys. The three steles with the inscriptions "three yuan palace" (三元宫), "Wenchuang Palace" (文昌殿 and "Kuiyuan" (魁垣) are

The stele arch of the southern gate in Jieshi

scenery. When the tide ebbs, the colourful and various shapes of marine stacks show themselves to the visitors. Another popular spot is the Ocean Statue park. This includes a stone forest, the Queen's Palace (天后宫), and the old banyan tree in Qian'ao Village (浅澳村) on the foot of Tianwei Mountain (田尾山).

on each storey. They have a group of dragons of various positions with pearls around as decorations. Bells hang on the top and sound with a clear ring when the wind blows. Animal carvings run along its base, including a vivid stone lion in front with a pearl in its mouth. A huge rock sits to the east of the tower. To the west is the "dragon rock" (起龙岩), which factors into the legend of the fish that leapt over a gate to become a dragon (meaning to succeed in civil service examinations). According to geologists, the rock formed 100 million years ago. The Four Beauties Pavilion (四美亭) and Zide Residence (自 得居) surround the west of the tower.

In front of Yuanshan Temple is an old theatrical stage. It was originally built in the Wanli reign of the Ming and rebuilt in the Qianlong reign of the Qing, but destroyed during the mayhem of the Cultural Revolution. It was rebuilt in the 1980s. It has a variety of wooden and stone carvings of different features.

On the foot of Xuanwu Mountian (玄武 山) are various lesser known historical relics. At the foot of Dragon Spring Mountain (龙泉山) is an old garrison city built in the Xuanwu reign. It surrounds Jieshi, and allows guards to easily overlook the sea.

Built in the Qing Dynasty, Qian'ao Old Emplacement (浅澳古炮台) was located in the "remote place" (天涯海角) 5 kilometres from Jieshi. The emplacement is a significant point from which the town was guarded. From the point, you can view the sea, sky, and perfect

Lucky Star Tower

Celebrate Anew

The annual "renewal celebration" was first held in the Qing Guangxu reign at Yuanshan Temple. On the festival day, locals busy themselves with grand activities such as repairing the temple, and renewing the Buddha statues. There are also folk cultural artistic activities including decorating the colourful street, playacting, fireworks, dragon dancing, fish lantern dancing, and stilt-walking. Every family lights their lanterns and decorates their homes. Thousands of people are around the street, which bustles with noise and excitement, making the festival a good time to visit the town.

Hongyang Town 洪阳镇

A Classic Cantonese Town

Hongyang, situated in the plains of the middle portion of Rongjiang River is known as "a pearl in a tray" due to its geographic surroundings — it is embraced on three sides by green hills and the waters of rivers flowing from different directions.

Hongyang Town, Puning City, Guangdong Province
广东省普宁市洪阳镇
Nearest city: Shenzhen
Shenzhen Baoan Airport is one of China's busiest airports. The city has also been integrated into China's fast developing high-speed rail network, providing easy access to Guangzhou City and beyond.
Buses from Shenzhen Luohu Bus Station (深圳罗湖汽车, a five-minute walk from Luohu Railway Station) to Jieyang City (揭阳) and Puning City (普宁市) will pass by Hongyang Town after about three hours.

During the Wanli reign of the Ming Dynasty, the administrative unit of Puning County was founded in Hongyang, and was a county for 374 years from the Ming to the Republic of China Period. In December, 1986, Hongyang officially became a town. It has a long history and is home to an abundance of historic sites, such as Peifeng Pagoda (培风塔); Fangfang Memorial Hall (方方纪念馆); and Chenghuang Temple (城隍庙).

Tieling (铁岭), also known as Iron Mountain (铁山), is situated at the south of Hongyang, and is 480 metres tall. The mountain is mostly famous for the wild chypre that grow between the cliffs. Their fragrance surrounds the mountain when they blossom, and "Iron Mountain chypre" has become a local symbol.

Peifeng Pagoda (培风塔), commonly referred as Wuli Pagoda (乌犁塔) and located in Hongyang's Houkeng Village (后坑村), was built during the Qianlong reign of the Qing Dynasty. It is a seven-storey octagonal fengshui tower made of tibia. The top of the tower houses a small iron gourd weighing over 1,000 kilograms. Climb to the top, and you can see all of Hongyang town to the south, and the flowing Rong River (榕江) to the north.

De'an Li (德安里), located in southeast Hongyang, is the former residence of Fangyao (1834-1891), a naval admiral for Guangdong Province during the Qing. The house, built during the reign of Emperor Tongzhi, consists of four parts: the old stockade (老寨), middle stockade (中寨), New De'an Li (新德安里) and Shao Garden (绍园). The structure of the old stockade is based on a style that features an ancestral hall with several entrances and is surrounded by rooms of different fengshui designs.

Huayan Temple (华严寺) is located at an altitude of 200

metres on Hong Mountain in Shuihou Village (水吼), 5.5 kilometres from north Hongyang. The temple is surrounded by the walls in front. Past the dooryard is the main hall, where three saintly Buddha statues sit in the middle. Outside the temple is an ancient well made of oblong stones. The most handsome aspect of Hong mountain is Huihua Rock (慧花岩). But Hong Temple, with the surroundings of tall trees and the poetic beauty of its remoteness, is still a perfect place to visit.

Linghui Spring (灵汇泉), also known as Linghui Sweetwater (灵汇甘泉), was formed between the time of the Emperor Qianlong of the Qing and the Republic of China period. It is in Yutang Village, northeast of Hongyang Town. It is said that Emperor Qianlong once travelled to the Yangtze River region and happened to come by the well. He tried the spring and was full of praise for it, legend has it." (登灵山逍遥天界，临雨堂普济万方).

Wenchang Pavilion (文昌阁), in northeast Hongyang was first constructed during the Kangxi reign of the Qing, later rebuilt during the time of Emperor Tongzhi. It has three entrances, two dooryards and nine halls. The floor is made of red brick and in the middle hall are four giant prismatic columns. The back entrance is a two-storey attic building where the Wenchang statue sits. During Emperor Daoguang's reign, the imperial envoy Lin Zexu (林则徐) was bypassing Puning on his way to Guangxi from Fujian Province, and he stayed in the town to take a rest. Unfortunately, he died of disease here. The patriotic spirit of Lin Zexu, who is known for battling the opium epidemic, attracts Chinese people from all over the country to come and pay tribute to him.

Chenhuang Temple

Near Wenchang Pavilion is Chenghuang Temple (城隍庙), built during the reign of Emperor Jiajing's during the Ming Dynasty. Therefore the temple has a history of more than 400 years. The building covers an area of about 1,400 square metres. The front hall is a Sanshan door, and to the left and right of the gate are horse shrines (马宫). Within the gate is a statue of a Daoist god. The middle hall is where the statue of the Town's God (城隍爷) is situated. The back hall comprises three parts, and they are dedicated to wife of the Town's God (城隍夫人), the Eighteen Disciples of Buddha (十八罗汉), and the Buddhist deity Guanyin (千手观音). The structure of the temple displays Chinese philosophy through both Confucianism and Buddhism. It houses 108 statues of gods.

Peifeng Pagoda

De'an Li

Wuyang Town 吴阳镇

"Chinese Pattaya"

Wuyang has been the centre of Wuchan County throughout the ages, so its cultural relics and historic sites are abundant. These cultural and historical sites are combined with gardens.

Ancient China: Towns

Wuyang Town, Wuchuan City, Zhanjiang City, Guangdong Province
广东省湛江市吴川市吴阳镇
Nearest city: Guangzhou
Guangzhou Baiyun International Airport is the second busiest in China, and Guangzhou's four railways stations are connected with cities across China through an ever-expanding number of high-speed railway lines.
Buses to Zhanjian from the Guangzhou Tianhe Bus Station (广州天河客运站) will pass by Wuyang Town after about four hours.

Wuyang Town, located to the south of Wuchuan City (吴川) in Guangdong Province, is the eastern shore where the water of the Jian River (鉴江) flows into the sea. But the town is mostly situated on the Jian River Plain (鉴江平原), where the well-irrigated land is flat, the rainfall is rich and goods are plentiful.

Within the town is Jipu Pavilion (极浦亭) of the Southern Song Dynasty; Reading Building (读书楼); Saint Hall (圣殿) and Two-humped Tower (双峰塔), built in the Ming Dynasty; Champion House (状元府), built in the Qing.

Two-humped Tower(双峰塔) is located in Wuyang's Tajiao Village. In the Wanli reign of the Ming, the magistrate of Wuchuan County, Wu Yiao, ordered that a fengshui tower be built by the nearby river. He wished the tower to be "upright, tall, and close to the sky". Since Tesi Mountain (特思山), also known as Jian Mountain (尖山) and Li Mountain (丽山), is situated in front of the tower, it is called Two-humped tower. It is a seven-storey octagon tower that stands 23.15 metres tall. A false terrace is set in each floor. The foot of the tower, about 1 meter high, is decorated with stone carvings. The corners on the edges of the towers are the stone sculptures of "Tower-Holding Strong Men" with simple designs but varied postures.

The reason for building the tower has been recorded in a book called "Records About the Renovation of Jiayang" (重修江阳书院碑记). Jiangyang Academy (江阳书院) was built during the Wanli reign, the book says, when the magistrate of Wuchuan was Zhou Yingao. The water from the mountains of Wuchuan once leaked into a gate of the town. Zhou then

Champion Corner

ordered the construction of the tower in the mountain. Later, below the tower, an academy was built. Since then, the town became more prosperous and generated scholars. Two-humped Tower and Jiangyang Academy were thus built at the same time. Magistrate Zhou, after having taken a poll of public opinion and considered suggestions from engineers, believed that because the water of the Wuchan River was flowing into the county from the west and joining into the sea, the spirit of the local earth had been washed out. With the poor spirit of the earth, it was difficult for people to get rich, so he directed the construction of the tower near the place where the rivers join the sea.

Wuyang Golden Sea Coast (吴阳金海岸), covers an area of 12 square kilometres, and is located on the edge of the South Sea in east Wuyang. The sea is wide and the water is crystal blue. With white sand, green plants, and flowers, the coast features spring-like weather year-round. This has earned it the name "Chinese Pattaya", after the beach resort in Thailand.

Xianmen Fei Xue (限门飞雪), or the "Blowing Snow of Xianmen", is one of the "eight ancient great views" of Wuchuan. It is the only tourist spot to have sustained almost no damage since ancient times. The mouth of the Jian River (鉴江) is located in Shayu Corner (沙鱼角) in the south of Wuyang. The beach shines under the sunlight. Tides from the south and east meet and hit each other here, and form a circle of small waves that are said to resemble blowing snow.

Fishermen Casting Nets (极浦渔归), another of the "eight ancient great views", is a reference to Jipu Pavilion. It was built in the Southern Song Dynasty, and is located near the mouth of the river, where boats sit at anchor or sail. By sunset, the fishermen are back from work and the lights of households light up.

Two-humped Tower

Ancient Sightseeing
Six of the "Eight Ancient Great Views" of Wuchuan" were situated in Wuyang, and they are "Sunrise of East Sea" (东海朝阳), "Yi Lan Ping Gao" (一览凭高), "Fishmen Casting Net"(极浦渔归),"Yan Hua Nong Yue"(延华弄月), "Xian Men Fei Xue"(限门飞雪).

Memorial Hall of the Wuyang Revolution

Dawei Town 大圩镇

Bamboo Groves and Deep Pools

Dawei Town has been described in the poem "Dawei" (大圩), written by Ming Dynasty poet Xiejin. The poem reads: "Near Dawei River is Lutian Temple, embraced by bamboo groves and deep pools. After breakfast in the early morning, firewood is prepared in shops. The Zhuang people go back home with a pack of salt wrapped in lotus leaf."

Dawei Town, Linchuan County, Guanxi Zhuang Autonomous Region
广西壮族自治区灵川县大圩镇
Nearest city: Guilin
You can fly to Guilin Liangjiang International Airport from major Chinese cities or take a bus or train to Guilin Railway Station or Guilin North Station. Guilin Bus Station (桂林汽车, located near Guilin Railway Station) has direct services to Dawei Town (about 15 kilometres and 5 yuan).

Though the poem was written centuries ago, the poet delicately captures the spirit of this simple and beautiful town.

Dawei is located 13 kilometres southeast of the tourist Mecca of Guilin (桂林市). To its east is the Chaotian River (潮田河), which connects to the Fu Lima River (福利马河); to the its west is Lovesick River (相思江）, which leads to Yongfu (永福).The Li River (漓江) flows through Guilin(桂林), to north Dawei, and other river systems connect the town to Guangzhou.

During the Northern Song Dynasty, Dawei had already developed into a prosperous town, known as "Little Chang'an" (长安), after the Song Dynasty capital. By the end of the Southern Song, a tax affairs office and street with many shops were set along the river. The town gets its name from the large fairs held on the 5-kilometre street: "Da" is Chinese for "big", while "wei" means "fair". During the Ming Dynasty the town was the largest of the four biggest fair towns.

The 800-metre Stone Slate Street (石板街), built during the Republic of China period, is a highlight of the town. At the time when the local water shipping trade prospered and merchants gathered here for business, entrepreneurs from across China gave money to build an assembly hall for different provinces. Most of the shops on both sides of the street are two-storey buildings with brick walls and wooden doors, and living quarters to the rear.. The buildings on the street stretch to the edge of the river and are known as "tube houses" (筒子屋).

There are several imposing connected houses with high gates on Jianshe Street (建设街). The most impressive of these is the former house of Liao

Zhongyuan, built during the reign of Emperor Xianfeng of the Qing. Inside the house are many vats that were used to make wine. The doors and windows are carved with poems, calligraphy, paintings, and vivid patterns of beasts.

Longevity Bridge (万寿桥), located in the eastern part of the town, is a rainbow-shaped arched stone bridge with just one lane. Under the bridge is Ma River(马河), also known as Huisha River. The bridge connects Siyin Street (泗瀛街) in the east to Blue Slate Street(青板街) on the opposite side. From a distance, it supposedly looks like a dragon resting on the river. The bridge was built more than 400 years ago, during the reign of Ming emperor Wanli. It was originally an arched wooden structure, but after being destroyed in a flood, it was rebuilt with stone during the Qing emperor Guangxu's reign.

The mosque on Shengchan Street (生产街) was built for the Hui people who came to reside in the town. It was originally erected during Qianlong's reign during the Qing years, and is the only ancient mosque in Dawei. The mosque's yard has the imam's living place to one side, and a reception room opposite. The chapel, covering an area of about 100 square metres, is on the second storey.

Dawei grew prosperous through its water transportation. From the Qing Dynasty to the early time of The Republic of China, 13 ports were built here. Each port had its own function. Drum Building Port (鼓楼码头), for example, was mostly used to load bulk commodities such as ginkgo trees, tung oil, or daily products. The Big Port (大码头), with its wide water surface, was for parking bamboo rafts and was a starting point for shipments. Tang Fang Port (塘坊码头) was an ancient water station where governmental boats parked.

Ancient Waterfall

The Ancient East Waterfall (古东瀑布) in Dawei's Ancient East Village is the only multi-cascaded waterfall in China that is sourced from gushing underground fountains. The waterfall consists of eight connected cascades, all of which have a different shape; some have been likened to mandarin ducks playing water; others to dragons spitting water. Trees grow on both sides of the waterfall, and the surrounding environment has a tranquil remoteness. On the foot of the mountain is a thick subtropical rainforest, where vines grow on vertical cliffs.

Ancient Residence in Dawei

Dawei's 800-metre Stone Slate Street

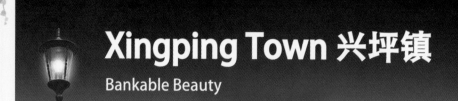

Xingping Town 兴坪镇

Bankable Beauty

Xingping Town is a pastoral fishing village of green bamboo and thick woods set beside the Xingping River. With the bamboo by the end of the islet and smoke fuming from the farmhouse, Xingping offers fine views.

Xingping Town, Yangsu County, Guangxi Zhuang Autonomous Region
广西壮族自治区阳朔县兴坪镇
Nearest city: Guilin
You can fly to Guilin Liangjiang International Airport from major Chinese cities or take a bus or train to Guilin Railway Station or Guilin North Station.
Guilin Bus Station (桂林汽车, located near the Guilin Railway Station) has direct buses to Yangsu Bus Station (阳朔汽车站, about 90 minutes). Transfer to a mini-bus to Xingping Town (30 minutes). If you plan to go to Fishing Village, you can just walk about 20 minutes, which will bring you to Majingdi Port (马颈底渡口).

Xingping Town is located east of Li River in northeast Yangshuo Country, in Guangxi Zhuang Autonomous Region. In the early part of the Three Kingdoms Period it was governed as Xiping County. In the Sui Dynasty, Xiping moved to the foot of Yangjiao Mountain. The name "Xiping"(熙平) was mistakenly extended to "Xingping"(兴坪).

Xingping River meets the Li River here; the surrounding

The picture on the back of the RMB20 note

hills follow a large circle. A famous landscape painting "Shadow of the Yellow Cloth" (黄布倒影) depicts the beautiful scenery of the Li River here. The painting hangs in the Chinese embassy at the United Nations and was the picture used on the back of the RMB20 during the fifth rendition of the currency, published in 1999.

Xingping Old Street is the old country fair. The pattern of the ancient town and the alleys still

Xingping Water Stockade Village

remain: On the sides of the ancient street are the 1-kilometre stone street, the Banyan Pool from the southeast of ancient Xingping Town to the Li River, an ancient wharf, and guild halls. The profile of the city's walls is still clear today,

with the debris of ancient bricks and tiles seen everywhere.

The alleys in the old town are all connected. The town's central street goes straight toward the riverbank, and meets the Banyan Pool and ancient wharf by the Li River. The huge stone bricks here are carved with dragons and phoenixes on the stone base, the site of the ancient turret pavilion used at the ancient wharf. Walk up along the stone steps and you can spot the sites of the ancient three-layer turret pavilion and North Emperor Temple (北帝庙). Climbing up the mountain and looking into the distance, you see a fishing village on the other side of the river. In the distance hills stand by the river and thin fog floats above.

The Lord Guan Temple (关帝庙), built in the Qianlong reign of the Qing Dynasty, is located by the old street of Xingping. The "10,000-year stage" (万年戏台) is the oldest and most well-preserved Qing stage in north Guizhou, and is important for the theatrical history of Guangxi. The two columns by the stage entrance have more than 20 holes made by the fork in the performance, which are still visible. By the edges of the stage are four wooden carvings of vivid figures that have been appraised as four traditional drama pictures.

Under the Old Stockade Village Mountain

The Friendship Pavilion in Old Stockade Village Mountain

you can still sail to President Fishing Village (总统渔村). Written on the village gate are four large Chinese characters that read "Southeast Protection". There were many bandits here in the past, but once the village gate was closed, they could not enter the village. About 100 metres behind the village gate is the 300-year-old Family Zhao Ancestral Hall (赵家祠堂), now an exhibition hall. Several metres beside the hall is the former residence of local progressive literary figure Zhao Wenhui. The stone boards of the front gate carved double kylins — mythical Chinese dragons — that protect the fortune of the family. The two round "heaven and earth" wooden carvings on the gate, together with the kylins, are called "kylins protecting the eight diagrams". In the fishing village are 48 well-preserved traditional residences, most of them in the Qing Dynasty "mountain south" style. The Zhao house is famous for the exquisite carved patterns on its doors and windows.

Steps of Friendship

Beside the Banyan Pool ancient wharf is the Old Stockade Village Mountain, the highest mountain in Xingping. Though the mountain is precipitous, the stone steps are flat. A number of things are written on the steps: some are numbers, some are encouraging words, but most are proclamations of Sino–Japan friendship. They were funded by a Japanese man, Hayashi Katsuyuki, who in 1996, during his studies in Yunnan, was amazed by a painting of the Li River. Hayashi came to the river before the end of his studies and never left. From 1997, he gathered funds and started to build the climbing road, as well as "friendship pavilion" and "peace pavilion", as a contribution to communication and friendship between China and Japan. Later, he became a Xingping resident. His former home is the "assembly house of China–Japan culture communication", which welcomes people from all over the world.

Huangyao Town 黄姚镇

The Stone Fish Village

Huangyao is a 1,000-year-old town that got its start in the Song Dynasty, and was developed in the Ming Dynasty Wanli years, finally reaching its peak in the Qianlong reign of the Qing Dynasty. The town is home to 300 residences from the Ming and Qing dynasties.

Huangyao Town, Shaoping County, Guangxi Zhuang Autonomous Region
广西壮族自治区昭平县黄姚镇
Nearest city: Guilin
You can fly to Guilin Liangjiang International Airport from major Chinese cities or take a bus or train to Guilin Railway Station or Guilin North Station.
Guilin Bus Station (桂林汽车, located near the Guilin Railway Station) has two daily services to Gongqiao County (巩桥乡), at 9:15 and 13:10 (about four hours). From Gongqiao, catch a taxi for the 5-kilometre ride to Huangyao Town.

Huangyao is located in the lower district of the Li River in the Guangxi Zhuang Autonomous Region. Huang and Yao are the two most common surnames in town, giving it its name, Huangyao. The ancient town inhabits a typical karst landscape.

The whole town is built in nine blocks in a structure invoking the eight diagrams of Taoism. The rivers or connecting houses on the outside serve as boundaries. The ancient town has many gates with bridges or pavilions. The streets in the town are connected to a main street and many small alleys. During the Sino-Japanese War years, the Guangxi working communities of the Communist Party were established here due to the ancient town's unique geographic environment that made it easy to defend but challenging to attack.

It is said that there are 99,999 bluestone bricks in Huangyao's ancient streets. The stores that stand along the street are well-preserved and names of the old stores are faintly visible in some cases.

Among the eight bluestone streets of Huangyao is Carp Street (鲤鱼街). When the street was built, one of the natural stones in the middle had a outstanding ridge. The craftsmen cleverly made the ridge into a two-inch stone fish, three-inches high on the surface of the street. This has become one of the most famous sights in Huangyao, known as the "circle stone fish".

Every street in Huangyao was once a residence reserved for those of one surname, and each name has its own ancestral hall. There are roughly 10 such halls in the town. The Wu Family Ancestral Hall (吴家祠) was built in the Ming Dynasty on Jinde Street. It is a brick-wood structure with elaborated glazed elements. The hall's courtyard is occupied

The town is built in nine blocks in an eight diagram structure, without walls

by wall hangings, brush paintings by folk artists. The side rooms by the courtyards are places for the Wu children to study and live, reflecting the intention of the family to encourage studies.

Wenming Pavilion (文明阁), or "Civilisation Pavilion", is located to the west of Tianma Mountain, southeast of the town. The ancient pavilion is hidden in the mountains and forest, and was built during the Wanli reign of the Ming. It originally had 12 buildings, but only eight remain. It houses the carvings of poems by great people from all generations.

The ancient theatre stage (古戏台), built in the Ming Dynasty, stands solemnly beside the rushing Yao River. It is a pavilion-style ancient building built upon a 1-metre high stone, supported by eight angled

Residence interior

eaves. Behind is a long and flat room for applying makeup. The column-base under wooded columns is carved with beautiful pictures. A few steps beside the stage is the Jewellery Temple. Watching inside from the round gate, you can spot a huge banyan standing by the wall. The main hall is now an exhibition hall that displays historic photos and tells the story of the Communist Party's Guangxi Worker Committee.

The double-hole stone Dragon Bridge (龙桥) is built over the Yao River, connecting Xinxing Street on the foot of Zhenwu Mountain and the main streets inside An Gate. The bridge is built with huge stone bricks, connected with iron tendons, forming the bridge as a whole. The beautiful bridge is offset by exuberant forests. Thirty metres behind the bridge, along the stone, is a gate that reads "Xinxing Street" (新兴街), which is associated with the people in the town surnamed Liang. The streets are high and backed by the Zhenwu Mountain. By the gate of the street is a huge blockhouse built with bricks. When you stand inside the blockhouse you will get views of the whole ancient town; this also serves well as a place to stand guard. There is a house on the street said to be the mansion of a Qing Dynasty official surnamed Liang.

There is an ancient well (仙人古井) in the town; the spring churns constantly, regardless of droughts or floods. It is said that the water fetched in the morning on the seventh day of the seventh month of lunar calendar (usually mid to late July) stays fresh for three years, keeping people that drink it safe from diseases. The well is formed with several square wells, used to drink, and wash vegetables and clothes.

Imperial Sauce

Huangyao black-bean sauce was given as a tribute to the emperors of the Qing Dynasty and sold in Southeast Asia in the early 1900s. The sauce is used in special local dishes, and is definitely worth trying out. The best time to visit Huangyao is late September to early November, when the weather is perfect and fruits are ripe.

The ancient banyan and green bamboo cover the ancient town

Yacheng Town 崖城镇

Town of Exiles

Since the Tang and Song dynasties, many famous people who had fallen out of favour were exiled to Yacheng Town. The famous monk Jianzhen left some classic Buddhist works in the town, which he originally planned to bring to Japan.

Yacheng Town, Sanya City, Hainan Province
海南省三亚市崖城镇
Nearest city: Sanya
Flights from all over the country arrive at Sanya Phoenix International Airport, while trains (via a ferry ride) pull into Sanya Railway Station.
From Sanya Airport take a taxi or shuttle bus to downtown Sanya East Bus Station (三亚汽车东站, 30 minutes), then transfer to a shuttle bus to Yacheng Town (50 minutes).

Located in the west of Sanya City, Yacheng Town is 45 kilometres from downtown Sanya and 33 kilometres from Sanya Phoenix International Airport.

Since the Song Dynasty the original city, known as Yazhou, was a major political capital. The first city made from bricks was built during the Southern Song Dynasty. After that it was expanded several times. Much of the original city no longer exists, but remnants include the southern "Civillised Gate"(文明门), 50 metres of city walls west of the North Gate, the 200-metre moat in the northwest, and the brick-arch bridge in the moat.

The South Asia arcade house block (南洋骑楼街区) of Yacheng, built in the early 1900s, is now a 220-metre long street. The architecture on the street features arcade houses in the style seen in South Asia. They are both commercial and residential: shops below and living areas above . In the street are some public buildings such as guilds, most of which are well-preserved.

The ancient residences in four districts of Yacheng Town were mostly built in the Qing Dynasty, and are also well-preserved. Liao Yongyu's ancestral house (廖永瑜祖居) is the biggest and most intact residence in the town. Lin Zantong's (林缵统故居) remaining former residence covers 600 square metres. The Shengde Hall (盛德堂) located in the middle of Water-South Village has a history of more than 800 years, and is the former residence of Pei Wenyi (裴闻义), the tenth grandson of a famous Tang Dynasty prime minister. Pei lived there while guarding Changhua City (昌化) during the Southern Song. The great prime minister Zhao Ding (赵鼎) and official Hu Quan (胡铨) of that dynasty were demoted and exiled here. Shengde Hall is isolated from the residential complex, surrounded by paddy fields to the south and west, and a coconut grove in the east.

Yacheng School (崖城学宫) is the largest and most prestigious ancient governmental school in Hainan Province, and also the southernmost Confucius Temple in China. It was built during the Qingli reign of the Song Dynasty, but has moved several times throughout history. The most recent renovation was during the Tongzhi reign in the Qing. Today the Great Hall, Great Gate, East Room, West Room, Emperor Pavilion, Kunming Pool and other important buildings are well-preserved. The drum mirror lotus stone columns are in the Song Dynasty style, while a portion of the seven-beam wooden structure still has a Ming Dynasty style.

It is worth mentioning that the Baoping village area of the town, has more than 70 old residences. It is the biggest combined Ming and Qing residential complex in Hainan. One of the Qing buildings is a shrine, with exquisite carvings of dragons, phoenixes, cranes, pines, plums, and bamboo.

The ancient Dadan Harbour (大旦港), located in south Dadan village, was an important transportation harbour in ancient Yazhou. All kinds of immigrants moved into the city via the harbour. But it has been out of repair for years and was abandoned in the Qing Dynasty era.

Song and Dance

The folk art of Yacheng is diverse and beautiful. Highlights of local culture include traditional Li, Miao, Mai, and Jun folk songs, the Miao dragon dance, textiles, bamboo and rattan weaving, and gold and silver jewellery techniques. Yazhou folk songs have been passed down for hundreds of years, and originate from the "firewood gathering dance" of the Li people in the town's Langdian Village.

Ya City School is the southernmost Confucius Temple in China, and a classic work of the ancient Yazhou traditional architecture.

Puqian Town 铺前镇

The Prosperous Ancient Fishing Port

Puqian Town lies in the Qiongzhou Strait, adjoining the hinterland of northern Hainan Province. The port has a rich fishing town culture.

Puqian Town, Wenchang City, Hainan Province
海南省文昌市铺前镇
Nearest city: Sanya
Flights from all over the country arrive at Sanya Phoenix International Airport, while trains (via a ferry ride) pull into Sanya Railway Station.
From Sanya Railway Station take a high-speed train to Haikou East Railway Station (海口东火车站, 90 minutes), then continue by taxi to Haikou East Bus Station (about 15 minutes). From the bus station (海口汽车东站), there are shuttle buses heading to Qianpu Town (90 minutes).

Puqian Town, formerly known as Xibei (溪北), is situated 18 nautical miles from Haikou, the capital of Hainan. Puqian Old Street (铺前老街), also known today as Victory Street (胜利街), was first built in 1895. The street covers 180 metres from north to so, and its arcade-style shops connect with one other via corridors, forming an architectural style akin to arcades in Southeast Asia (南洋骑楼). In the town's most prosperous period, a saying circulated among the local people said that it is "better to go to Puqian and Haikou than to travel around the world" (东奔西走，不如到铺前和海口).

The shops have decorations on the roofs and distinctive balconies and flower fences, as well as beams and peaks. The decorations display high artistic and aesthetic values, tactfully using techniques and sensibilities from the west.

Xibei Academy (溪北书院), one of the distinguished academies in Hainan, is perfectly preserved. It was launched in the 19th year of Guangxu Period (1893) by Pan Cun, a famous calligrapher from the late Qing Dynasty, and built with the financial support of local officials and tycoons.

Seven Stars Hills (七星岭), 117.4 metres above sea level, is located in the northeast of Puqian, facing the sea to the north. There are more than 10 peaks, seven of which are relatively tall and together supposedly look like the seven stars of the Big Dipper. With verdant forests covering them, these hills are rich in animal and plant resources. At the foot of the hills stands the classically beautiful Seven Stars Goddess Temple (娘神庙). At the foot of the main peak, about 200 metres to the east, lies a freshwater lake called Dinosaur Pond (恐龙塘) by the locals.

The grand Doubing Tower (斗柄塔) stands on the top of Seven Stars hills' main peak. Built in the Tianqi Period of the Ming Dynasty, it is a seven-storey octagonal tower. The doorway faces west, above which is a stone board inscribed with three

Shops in the style of Southeast Asian arcades

Chinese characters, which read "Doubting Tower". Climbing along the spiral staircase, you can reach to the tower's top, from where you can overlook the Qiongzhou Strait.

Puqian has three fine natural ports: Puqian Port (铺前港), Mulan Port(木兰港), and Xingbu Port(新埠港). The first is a commercial and fishing port first used in the Ming, whose government had once set up a navy here to defend against pirates and Japanese invaders. From the Ming to the early Republic of China period, Puqian was one of the most important ports in north Qiong Island . The bays in the port have clear water and flat and wide beaches, and are great for swimming and sunbathing.

Sea Bed Village

Sea Bed Village (海底村庄) lies on the sea floor of Dongzai Port (东寨港) in Haikou City and Puqian Town (铺前镇). It is buried under the sea due to a huge earthquake that struck during the Wanli reign of the Ming Dynasty. Historical records show that at that time 72 villages sunk 3 to 4 metres into the sea. During each May and June, when the tide is out, visitors can via boat dimly see the outline and ruins of the villages under the sea. These villages are the only ancient cultural site in China that is known to have sunk into the sea because of an earthquake.

Xibei Academy

Mulan Lighthouse

边 疆 古 镇
Borderland Towns
Salt wells and palaces

Heijing Town 黑井镇
The Lost Salt Town

Heijing Town has a dramatic setting beside the Dragon River, with precipitous high mountains filling the sky. This ancient ethnic Dali town was built on the salt industry and was once the richest in Yunnan Province.

Heijing Town, Lufeng County, Chuxiong Yi Autonomous Prefecture, Yunnan Province
云南省楚雄彝族州禄丰县黑井镇
Nearest city: Kunming
There are direct flights between Kunming Wujiaba International Airport and other leading Chinese cities, while the new Kunming Changshui International Airport was due to become operational during 2012. Kunming is the main rail hub of Yunnan Province.
From Kunming Railway Station (昆明火车站, an hour taxi ride from Kunming Changshui International Airport) take a train to Heijing Station (黑井站). From there, it is a 10-minute taxi ride to the town.

Heijing (Black Well) Town is located at the foot of the Northwest side of Jade Mountain (玉璧山).

There is still a major salt well in town, the Black Cow Salt Well (黑牛盐井). The stone well is about 80 metres deep and 1.2 metres wide. The Qing'an Dyke (庆安堤) behind the well shows how the locals had to fight nature to ensure the development of the industry. Between the start of the Yuan Dynasty and today, there have been 17 major floods in the region. The Guangxu Emperor of the Qing Dynasty (1875-1908) allocated funds to build the dyke to prevent flooding and debris from getting into the well.

This former salt capital has left behind its former glory, but still retains the technology to produce high-quality salt. If you like, you can spend some time to learn how salt is made. The town's well is lined with wood barrels, where the salt is first caught. The wet salt is then spread out on dishes and baked at a high temperature to remove impurities. Patterns are often drawn into the salt before the baking process. After about 20 minutes on the fire, the salt is wrapped up and stamped with an official chop to prove its authenticity.

The Wu Family Garden (武家大院), built in the Qing Dynasty during the reign of Emperor Daoguang (1836) is

The old streets of Black Well Town

gorgeous if a bit rundown. It features an elegant stele hanging on the eave inscribed by the Emperor Xianfeng (1850-1861), which used to make people feel as if they were under the emperor's watchful eye. The whole structure is shaped like the Chinese character for "king" (王 , wang). There are courtyards on both the east and west sides of the grounds. The gate faces north and there is a fengshui pagoda in the opposite direction. Standing on the third floor of the compound, you can enjoy a full view of HeijingTown.

Walking northwest from the garden, you will reach Golden Spring Mountain (金泉山). Flying Temple (飞来寺), built in the Ming Dynasty, sits boldly on the cliff. To the east looking of the temple is Jade Mountain (玉碧山), just across the river. There is a small mountain next to Jade Mountain that is home to a nine-storey stone pagoda.

Sky Temple (诸天寺), located at the foot of Jade Mountain and on the east bank of Longchuan River, was built in 1637, during the Ming Dynasty. There is a set of three openwork tile carvings surrounding by Buddha on a platform in the temple's main hall. There are also patterns of a crane holding a fish in its mouth, a horse flying in the sky, and bees swarming around flowers. The Flying Temple was built on a cliff of Golden Spring Mountain, beside Dragon River (龙川江).

The Five Horses Bridge, built in the Yuan Dynasty and located in the north part of town, was rebuilt in 1705 and is now a stone arch bridge with wooden beams.

In the past the Temple of Literature (黑井文庙) was used as a place to worship Confucius,. Today it is a school. There is a sage tablet in the middle of the temple, with the words "become a master with a big achievements" (大成至先

师) on it. The temple also has stone tablets and five animals relief works from the Ming and Qing dynasties and the Republican Period. The painting "Nine Lions Playing with Balls" (九狮戏珠球) is the most famous piece of art in the temple.

In 1901, the Chastity Archway (贞节牌坊) was built with three gates inlaid with marble and four pillars. In total, there are 68 dragon heads and 54 elephant noses on three brackets. There are several works of relief art, including Fairy Tale of a Cowboy and a Weaver (牛郎织女) and Eight Immortals Crossing the Big River (八仙过海). The archway's scale and beauty make it a rarity in Yunnan Province.

Weekends are always bustling times in the town. You can take in a Yunnan opera or a dancing dragon show. Crowds spill in from nearby towns to shop in Heijing Town's extensive market.

Modern technology has eclipsed traditional salt making methods, resulting in the end of Heijing Town's prosperity. The town now serves as a living museum of the ancient methods.

Writing Brush Pagoda

In Dai Village (摆依汉村), which is about 1.5 kilometres away from Heijing Town, there is the nine-storey square Writing Bush Pagoda (文笔塔). The structure is made mainly of stone. Starting on the third floor, each level has its own shrine. According to legend, the Dai ethnic group used to live in the village, and the Han moved in after the village was abandoned.

Fading glory leaves behind a wealth of splendid historical sites.

Shaxi Town 大理沙溪镇

The Tea Horse Road Market Town

Shaxi Town's ancient road, stage, and market have survived for thousands of years despite the battering of history. The ancient market is still prosperous and locals still perform on the old theatre stage.

Shaxi Town, Jianchuan County, Dali Bai Autonomous Prefecture, Yunnan Province
云南省大理白族自治州剑川县沙溪镇
Nearest city: Dali
You can fly to Dali Airport from Kunming or Lijiang. Otherwise, you can take a train to Dali Railway Station. From Dali International Airport (大理国际机场), take an airport taxi to the downtown Xiaguan City Bus Terminal Station (下关汽车客运站站 50 yuan, 30 minutes). Transfer to a bus to Jianchuan Bus Station (剑川汽车站, about three hours). From there, hop on a bus to Shaxi Town (about 50 minutes).

Located in the southwest of Jianchuan County of Dali City, Shaxi is surrounded by green mountains and has a pleasant climate. The town's residents are mainly members of the Bai ethnic group, though there are also Han, Yi and Lisu people.

The stone single-arch Jade Bridge (玉津桥) crosses the Heihui River (黑惠江) and was the first major bridge to connect with Dali City in Shaxi. Built in 1935, the semi-young bridge has a short history but is full of artistic imagination. The most beautiful part of the bridge is on the Sideng Street (寺登街) side. There are four dignified stone lions and a carved dragon lying on the bridge. The dragon's head faces north, looking at the Heihui River.

Shaxi Town is home to the only surviving market on the ancient Tea-Horse Road. The market is located on Sideng Street. Here you can find opera stages, taverns, temples, and beautiful gates. The ancient east gate is made of earth, its width only enough for two horses to walk through. Sideng Street was once a major transportation hub for thousands of horses and merchants cutting back and forth through the town. Most of the buildings on Sideng Street are in typical Bai architectural style. Usually the front doors of the dwellings are vaulted.

The Ouyang Family Mansion, built in the early Republican Period, is a classic Bai folk home. A screen wall, vivid with fish and flowers, is as a stunning piece of art to see when you first walk into the dwelling. The complex contains three wooden houses. The delicate carvings on the windows show the exquisite skills of the area's carpenters. Walking through the compound, you will find a courtyard full of thriving trees and fragrant flowers.

Walking down along the street, you will encounter

Sideng Street

the ancient Square Street (四方街) . There are three gates on the street and old horseshoe prints are still visible in places. The South Gate leads to the long, narrow ancient street. Worn-out shops stand quietly on both sides of the street and some of the shops feature old-style counters, with the table set outside. This made it convenient for passers-by to do business without having to tie up their horses.

The Atuoli Buddha Temple (阿吒力佛教寺院) was built by the Bai people in the Ming Dynasty. Also called Xingjiao Temple (兴教寺), it is the only remaining Bai temple in China and it is located on the west part of Square Street. Worshipers adhere to Buddhist traditions that are unique to the Bai people. One way the traditions differ is that monks are allowed to keep their hair. Nearly every family in town has a small shrine at home, though the religion's heyday was during the Nanzhao Kingdom period (738-902). There are three courtyards on the Xingjiao Temple grounds, which is typical of Tibetan Buddhist temples.

To the east of Square Street is the Star Pavilion Stage (魁星阁戏台). It was established during the Jiaqing period of Qing Dynasty (1796-1820) and was rebuilt in 1878 during the Guangxu period. The Kuixing Cabinet Stage has a stage on its first floor and a pavilion at the top. As the entertainment centre of town, when Chinese New Year rolls around, people gather here to watch traditional opera shows

Every Friday is market day in Shaxi but during traditional Bai festivals, the market is especially lively. People dress up, perform shows. The most famous festival is Prince Day (太子会), on the eighth day of the second month of the lunar calendar (usually mid February). Prince Day commemorates the Shakyamuni Buddha. Locals and visitors from other towns gather at Xingjiao Temple and Huinv Street(回女街) to celebrate, carrying the statue of Shakyamuni Buddha. The whole thing is capped off by a big traditional opera.

Tang Grottoes

Located about 4 kilometres to the north of Shaxi is Shibao Mountain (石宝山). The mountain has 17 unique grottoes that were dug during the Tang and Song dynasties. Each grotto feature meticulous carvings and their special blend of Han, Tibetan, and local culture make them especially interesting.

Kuixing Cabinet Stage — the first floor is a stage and there is a pavilion at the top

Heshun Town 和顺镇

A Cultural Crossroads on the Silk Road

Heshun Town was a cultural crossroads for people from all over the world. Though the Silk Road no longer brings its caravans, swaying ancient camphor trees and ancestral halls all contribute to a quiet and scholarly Confucianism air which infiltrates this beautiful small town on the southern Yangtze River.

Heshun Town, Tengchong County, Baoshan City, Yunnan Province
云南省腾冲县和顺镇
Nearest city: Baoshan
There are direct flights to Baoshan Tengchong Tuofeng Airport from Chengdu and Kunming.
From Baoshan Airport, the simplest way to reach Heshun is to take a taxi (about 50 yuan, 30 minutes). A tourist bus tour of the Heshun Scenic Area costs around 10 yuan per person.

Heshun Town is located to the south of the Tengchong Plain, about 4 kilometres from Tengchong County. The town has strong connections with overseas Chinese communities.

Highlights of the beautiful scenery of Heshun are Daying River (大盈江) and a famous waterfall called "the curtain hanging over the dragon's cave" (龙洞垂帘). The town also has numerous ancient buildings, including ancestral halls, archways, pavilions, stages, and well-preserved stone balustrades.

A small stream flows in front of the village, and two stone bridges cross it like two rainbows, hence their name Two Rainbow Bridge (双虹桥). The bridges were built during the Daoguang period of the Qing Dynasty (1820-1850). The fancy design of the bridges is complemented by adjacent trees, which also offer pleasant shade. With ducks and fish in the river, it is a picture of countryside scenery.

Heshun Library

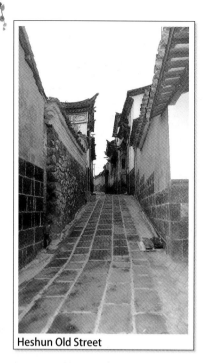

Heshun Old Street

Established in 1928, the Heshun Library (和顺图书馆), located opposite Two Rainbow Bridge, was once the biggest town library in China. Walking through the second gate is a two-storey building that combines western and Chinese architectural styles. The library holds 70,000 books. About 20,000 of them are woodcut books published in the last century. Most were donated by overseas Chinese.

During the Guanxu period of the Qing Dynasty (1830-1850), village traders built six different laundry pavilions along the river for their wives while they were away. These unique public facilities provided shelter for the women from the rain and the hot sun. There are still seven of the laundry pavilions in the town, two of them near the lake.

Literature Palace (文昌宫) was built during the Daoguang period of the Qing Dynasty with funds from overseas Chinese. It was built to show respect for education and the big stone tablet, has a record of Heshun's official candidates from two dynasties, totalling eight Juren and 403 Xiucai (types of successful scholar in the imperial examinations). With its grand hall and exquisitely carved beams and rafters, this imposing and dignified museum is a highlight of a visit to Tengchong.

Walking alongside east from Two Rainbow Bridge along the stone road of the river for about half a kilometres to east you will come to the picturesque Shuidui Village (水碓

View of Heshun Town

Aisiqi Memorial Hall

Old homes of Heshun

村). There is a small spring located beside the village, which is surrounded by mountains. At the south end of the spring is the intersection of Handsome Head Slope (帅头坡) and Phoenix Mountain (来凤山). The Dragon Pavilion (元龙阁), built in 1762, sits at this junction. In front of the pavilion, the spring water ripples with Black Dragon Mountain's (黑龙山) ancient trees as a backdrop. Along with the mountain gate, the Dragon King Temple (龙王殿), Kuanyin Temple (观音殿), and the main building of Kuixing Cabinet (魁星阁) have hexagonal eaves with a beautiful carvings. Looking down from the pavilion, you can take in panoramic views of Shuidui Village.

Aisiqi Memorial Hall (艾思奇纪念馆) sits on the small slope of the north part of the spring, The hall combines western and Chinese architectural styles. The western style balcony is simple but elegant.

Supernatural Horse Art

Tengyue Supernatural Horse Art – woodblocks carved with divine horses – are an influential art of Yunnan Province. This images on the woodblocks are both primitive and fantastic. You can even create your own engravings to decorate your home or to give friends as gifts.

Two Rainbow Bridge

Nayun Town 娜允镇

A Relic of the Dai's Chieftain System

Nayun Town is the central hub for four branches of the Dai ethnic minority in Menglian County. The town faces north, with its back to Golden Mountain, which is full of ancient trees. Nanlei River flows through Golden and Silver mountains and is used by locals for fishing.

Nayun Town, Menglian Dai Nationality, Lahu-Va Autonomous County, Si Mao District, Yunnan Province
云南省思茅地区孟连傣族拉祜族佤族自治县娜允镇
Nearest city: Kunming
There are direct flights between Kunming Wujiaba International Airport and other leading Chinese cities, while the new Kunming Changshui International Airport was due to become operational during 2012. Kunming is the main rail hub of Yunnan Province.
From Kunming West Bus Station (昆明西部汽车站, a one hour taxi ride from Kunming Changshui Airport), take a direct bus to Nayun Town (about eight hours, 180 yuan).

Nayun is a homophone for "inner-city" in the Dai language. The town is located in the Menglian Dai-Lahu-Va Autonomous County. In 1289, the king of the Dai people, Hanbafa (罕罢法), set up Nayun Town in Menglian County (孟连县). The Yuan Dynasty also set up an army post in the area. The area was under the rule of the chieftain for 700 years until it ended with the Communist victory in 1949.

The homes in Nayun are a combination of Han and Dai styles. Nayun Town has three smaller "inner-cities" and two townships (Mangfang Hillock 芒方岗 and Mangfang House 芒方冒). In the chieftain era, the upper side of town was for the leader and his family, the middle for officials and the lower for low-ranking officers. Mangfang Hillock and Mangfang House were the living quarters for forestry officers and hunters.

Rebuilt from 1878-1919, the office for Menglian County's top official is located on the upper side of town

The Meeting House

and covers 10,000 square metres. The building is called Hehan (贺罕) in the Dai language, which means "golden palace" and it is best-preserved ancient example of Han-Dai architecture. The classic front building has a three open archways and beautiful brackets below the eaves. When you walk down the 13 steps of the building, the view of Nayun is magnificent. The grand meeting house has triple eaves and two floors. According to Dai custom, you need to take off your shoes when you go to the second floor. The second floor houses a small museum of rare treasures and historical paintings of the town. You will also find official robes, flags presented by the royal court, and official letters written in both Han and Dai scripts. One highlight is an embroidered robe presented by a Qing emperor. The gorgeous designs include clouds, birds, and dragons.

The Shangcheng Buddha Temple (上城佛寺), established in 1869, faces west and covers about 5,000 square metres. The building comprises a gate, a Buddha hall, monk rooms, an octagonal pavilion, and two Burmese-style pagodas. The Shangcheng Buddha Temple was only used by the chieftain's family in ancient times — others were not allowed in. However, it later became a worship space for all Dai Buddhists in Nayun.

Facing west and built in 1910, the gate, sub-gate, Buddha hall and monk rooms comprise the Middle Buddha Temple (中城佛寺). This served as the temple for mid-ranking officers in the past, but is now open to tourists and religious devotees alike.

Hinayana Buddhism is the most popular Dai religion and the Golden Pagoda is the symbol of Hinayana culture. The eighth generation of chieftain officers sent four people to Burma to help develop Hinayana in Menglian County. Since then, Buddhism has been the main religion of the Dai. The local Dai clan culture boasts unique art, music and dancing, and architecture.

The Dai have preserved many traditional customs. When boys reach their seventh or eighth birthdays, they are sent to a temple to study Buddhism, while male adults must be tattooed. A needle is used to etch a tiger, elephant or other animal or plant patterns on the body, along with Buddhist scriptural passages. It is said that men with tattoos can avoid evil spirits and prevent disaster. Meanwhile, many Dai women are skilled at traditional weaving, especially the older generation, who spend a great deal of time with a braiding machine everyday.

The Open-Door Festival (also called the Thousands Lamps Festival 千盏灯节) is a traditional Dai festival marking the end of the three-month rainy season and the last day of the rice harvest. Usually held on the 25th day of the 12th month of the lunar calendar (usually in late January), during the festival restrictions on interactions between young men and women are relaxed and boys and girls can date and marriage ceremonies are held. People also dress up and bring food, flowers, and money to the temple to worship Buddha.

The Middle Buddha Temple

All Good Fun

Other famous traditional festivals include the "Water-Sprinkling Festival"(泼水节, usually held in early May), the festival "Calabash Festival"(葫芦节, late April or early May), the "God Fish Day" (神鱼节, late May or early June, and "Rice Day"(新米节), in January). Local people will get together, celebrate and have fun during the festivals.

Sa'gya Town 萨迦镇

A Second Dunhuang

The small mysterious town of Sa'gya is hidden away in Tibet, its remoteness only making it more impressive. The main attraction here is the Sa'gya Temple - the meaning of Sa'gya in Tibetan is "grey soil".

Ancient China: Towns

Sajia Town, Sajia County, Shigatse City, Tibet Autonomous Region
西藏自治区萨迦县萨迦镇
Nearest city: Lhasa
You can fly direct to Lhasa Gongga International Airport from Beijing, although the return flight currently requires a stopover in Chengdu. The more adventurous can take the 47-hour train journey from Beijing across the Qinghai Plateau to Lhasa Railway Station.
From Lhasa West Bus Station (拉萨西郊汽车站), take a bus to Shigatse City (日喀则市 about three hours and 50 yuan), then transfer to a direct route to Sajia Town (three hours, 27 yuan).

Sa'gya is situated beside the Zhongqu River (仲曲河) in Tibet, about 150 kilometres from Shigatse City. During the reign of the Sa'gya Emperor, state and religious authorities were combined, which explains why the town has so many temples and monasteries, as well as government buildings. (日喀则市).

Sa'gya Temple (萨迦寺) was once actually made up of two temples, but now only the south temple remains. It was built in 1268. The temple is located on the plain of the south bank of the Zhongqu River and there is a moat surrounding the grounds. The city gate is shaped like the Chinese character "工" (gong , meaning "work"), and the whole layout is of a small "回" (hui, meaning "return") character surrounded by a bigger "回". The colour of the walls is amaranth, with some black and white. The colours have symbolic meaning in Tibetan Buddhism. The amaranth stands for Manjuist Bodhisattva (文殊菩萨), black for Golden Dharma Protector (金刚护法神), and white for the Guanyin Bodhisattva (观音菩萨). The colours are combined into a flower. The temple combines Han and Tibetan architectural styles, and is also representative of the Pingchuan style (平川式) of Tibetan buildings.

The main building of the Sa'gya Temple is the 5,700 square metre Assembly Hall (大经堂), located in the middle of the temple. The main hall is supported by 40 big stakes in the roof. The main hall is about 10 metres high and could hold 10,000 lamas chanting sutras. The Buddha of Three Periods (三世佛), Sakya Pandita (萨迦班智达) and Phags-pa Lama are worshipped here. On the north side of the hall is the palace for the King of Sa'gya, while

A lama of Sa'gya Temple

South Sa'gya Temple

the south and back sides are living quarters for monks.

The most important construction on the second floor of the south temple is Pingcuo's Palace Pagoda (平措颇章灵塔), which is used for keeping scriptures and books. Walking out from the temple, you will reach the front courtyard from the corridors, then walk along the stairs to the top of the main hall. There are spacious galleries on the west and south sides of the platform, with rare paintings on the walls. The south wall's painting is of Sa'gya's founder. The west painting is of Mandala.

Most of the temple's books and reference materials are kept in the Wuze (乌责室) and Gurong (古绒室) rooms on the north side of Sa'gya Temple — a total of about 24,000 copies. The temple houses perhaps the most famous Tibet scripture, the "Eight Thousands Songs Tie Huan Book" (八千颂铁环本), which has a length of 1.31 metres and a width of 1.12 metres. This classic scripture is an extremely valuable cultural relic. Owing to its extensive library and excellent mural paintings, scholars have compared Sa'gya Temple with the famous Buddhist grottos of Dunhuang.

There is also the interesting Oudonglakang Temple (欧东拉康) in town, which houses 11 pagodas for the Sakya King. On the wall of the back hall there are mural paintings of significant events such as the meeting of the Saban Lama and the Kuden General. The Pukang Temple (菩康寺) on the south side of Oudonglakang Temple is the home of the Esoteric Buddhist.

In 1265, during the reign of Phags-pa Lama, the lama built a house for himself to hold his possessions. As time went by, it was separated into four smaller houses, collectively called La Rang. The four houses are individually called Xituo House (细脱喇让), Lakang House (拉康喇让), Renqingang House (仁钦岗喇让), and Duque House (都却喇让).

Dharma Events

The most important Dharma events held at Sa'gya Temple are the annual Summer God Dance Festival (夏季神舞节) and Winter Buddha's God Dance Festival (冬季金刚神舞节). Dancers wear masks of guardian deities of Sa'gya or other spirits and beasts and the dances tell stories of how the Golden Dharma Protector fought against demons and monsters. Every year during these two festivals, thousands of monks come from near and far to participate.

The Sa'gya Temple combines Han and Tibetan architectural styles

Changzhu Town 昌珠镇

The Changzhu Temple

Changzhu Town gets its name from the Changzhu Temple, which was built under the command of Songtsen Gampo more than 1,300 years ago. The temple is one of the oldest in Tibet, as well as the first temple in Tibet built during the Tubo period.

Changzhu Town, Naidong County, Shannan District, Tibet Autonomous Region
西藏自治区山南地区乃东县昌珠镇
Near city: Lhasa
You can fly direct to Lhasa Gongga International Airport from Beijing, although the return flight currently requires a stopover in Chengdu. The more adventurous can take the 47-hour train journey from Beijing across the Qinghai Plateau to Lhasa Railway Station. From Lhasa West Bus Station (拉萨西郊汽车站) there are direct buses to Zedang Town (泽当, about 2.5 hours). From Zedang, take a motor rickshaw to Changzhu Town (15 minutes, 10 yuan). Admission to the Changzhu Temple is 30 yuan. Yongbulakang Palace costs 60 yuan to get in.

Changzhu Town is located south of Gongri Mountain (贡日山), 2 kilometres south of Zedang Town (泽当镇). The Like other ancient Tibetan towns, the highest spot of Changzhu Town is occupied by a temple, which is also the most magnificent construction in town.

The word Changzhu means eagle and dragon in Tibetan. Legend says that when Princess Wencheng came to Tibet for the first time, she studied the area's geography and discovered that it was shaped like a supine ogre Raksasi. This was a very unlucky omen for the future of Tubo Kingdom, so temples had to be built on the Raksasi's heart and limbs to suppress it. Changzhu Temple was built on Raksasi's left arm.

Consisting of the main hall, sutra-chanting corridor and yard, Changzhu Temple has two floors, and is a masonry-timber structure. In its main building, Cuoqin Hall (措钦大殿), the statues of Songtsen Gampo, Sakyamuni (释迦牟尼), and Avalokitesvara (观世音) are all located on the first floor. The hall on the second floor is called Naidingxue (乃定学), and is believed to be the oldest hall in the temple. It is dedicated mainly to the worship of Padmasambhava (莲花生). In the main hall rests the greatest treasure of the whole temple – a pearl thangka that once belonged to Naidongzecuoba (乃东泽措巴). Funded by the wife of Lord Naidong (乃东王) during the Pamozhuba period (帕莫竹巴), which was in the late Yuan and early Ming dynasties, the thangka is called Resting Avalokitesvara, or Portrait of Jianqimuersong. Its lines are made of pearl strings, making it a rare treasure.

There is a clay stove in Tuoqielakang Hall (托且拉康殿), with a pot on it. It is believed that Princess Wencheng used the bowl. The word "Tuoqie" means "thank" or "grate" in Tibetan, which has given rise to much speculation about the origins of the name.

The relics in Changzhu Temple also include some delicate sorcery-dancing masks and the Tubo-age murals that stand in charming contrast to the exquisite modern wall paintings. It is believed that many Buddhist masters, including Padmasambhava and Milariba (米拉日巴), were affiliated with Changzhu Temple and the area still remains a shrine for many Buddhists.

Yongbulakang (雍布拉康) is on Zhaxiciren Mountain (扎西次仁山) to the east of Yalong River (雅砻河), 7 kilometres south of Changzhu Town. As a shaman temple, it is said to have been built by the first Lord of Tibet, Niechizanpu, and is considered to be the earliest construction in Tibet. The word "yongbu" means "doe", "la" means "hind leg", and "kang" means "palace". This temple was named as such because Zhaxiciren Moutai supposedly looked like a crouching doe, with Yongbulakang on its hind leg.

There are two kinds of constructions in Yongbulakang: watchtowers and halls. The former may be remnants of palaces of a later period, while the halls were built by Songtsen Gampo. The halls enshrine Songtsen Gampo, Princess Wencheng, Princess Chizun (赤尊公主), Ludongzan (禄东赞), and Sangbuzha (桑布扎).

Harvest Festival

When you walk out of Changzhu Temple, you will find Changzhu Plaza (昌珠广场) and the Folk Culture Village (民俗文化村) right across the street. During the Harvest Festival (望锅节) in August or September, villagers gather here to hold a grand ceremony. To the sound of Buddhist horns and amid the smoke of incense, people hold up the portraits of Padmasambhava, Bodhisattva, Panchen, and Princess Wencheng, recite sutras, celebrate the harvest and express their gratitude.

Changzhu Temple

Cuoqin Hall, Changzhu Temple

Lukeqin Town 鲁克沁镇

The Birthplace of Twelve Muqam Art

A town on the ancient Silk Road, located about 45 kilometres west of Shanshan County in Turpan, Lukeqin Town is the birthplace of Twelve Muqam art and the historical site of the Turpan Palace. In the Qing Dynasty, it was the political, economic, and cultural centre of the Turpan region.

Lukeqin Town, Shanshan County, Xinjiang Uygur Autonomous Region
新疆维吾尔自治区鄯善县鲁克沁镇
Nearest city: Urumchi
Urumchi Diwobao International Airport is one of China's top airports while Urumchi is Xinjiang's major rail hub.
From Urumchi Bus Station (乌鲁木齐汽车站), there is a daily scheduled bus to Shanshan County (鄯善县). It is about 50 kilometres from Shanshan County to Lukuqin Town. You can take the minibus from Shanshan Bus Station (鄯善客运站) into town. On the trip you can enjoy the beautiful Flaming Mountains.

Twelve Muqam art, an Uyghur combination of music dance and singing, was born in Lukeqin. Similar to the birth of the art forms feng (风, ballads), ya (雅, festival odes) and song (颂, sacrificial songs), twelve Muqam also derived from worship rituals. Later, because of social unrest, it nearly became extinct. In the early 17th century, Muqam artist Eliniyaz Cheyi started to restore the art. After generations of performance and study, it continues to enjoy great popularity among local people.

The first heritage centre of Muqam in Xingjiang was established in September 2006, and covers an area of 1,500 square metres. The building's 44 tall and smooth-lined pillars are exquisitely curved and colourfully painted. The grand pergola in the front is made of eleven 8.5-metre-high white pillars lined up in four rows. The back hall, which is designed

Lukeqin — the birthplace of Twelve Muqam

Lukeqin sits at the foot of Flaming Mountain | Shuantai Mosque in Liuzhongcheng (柳中城)

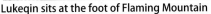

to be half sunk into the ground, covers a floor area of 900 square metres.

Lukeqin was a stronghold for the Han Dynasty. Because of the great number of willows planted in this area, it was called Liushu (willow) or Liuzhongcheng (city in the willow woods) during in the Han era. In the Qianlong period of the Qing Dynasty, the Turpan King Eein Hoja built his palace here.

Today there are still many historical sites in and around Turpan Palace. The king's palace is located in the west of the inner city. Originally built in 1758, one part of it is called King's Terrace (王爷台) by locals and is completely made from rammed yellow clay. On the terrace, there is a magnificent three-storey palace. The palace is in a traditional Chinese style, with overhanging eaves, huge pillars, carved beams, painted walls, sumptuous pearl-studded curtains, and embroidered damask portieres. Climbing onto the top level of the building, you get a panoramic view of Lukeqin. If you look far into the distance, you can even see Shengjingkou (胜金口), a group of ancient tombs. To spot them, look northeast out into the Gobi Desert.

At Amanshia Nantan (阿曼夏南滩) in the east of the city, there are also some ancient tombs. Many relics including saddles, knives, swords, carpenter tools, pottery, and wooden

wares have been unearthed from these tombs in recent years. Located on the outskirts of town is the King's Garden (郡王花园), decorated with gorgeous ponds, pavilions, flowers, and trees. The garden used to be a private retreat for the king. About 5 kilometres northeast of the city is the Sirkep Mountain Pass — an ancient Buddhist site. There was once a square tower here, more than 10 metres high and filled with Buddhist statues with different postures and expressions. Only after the 15th century did the Buddhist buildings here start to be gradually abandoned.

Taste of Honeydew

The clean snow waters of the Kaner wells, fertile soil, and unique geographic location have bred honeydew melons, grapes, and unparalleled sweet pomegranates and jujubes, earning Lukeqin the title of "the hometown of honeydew melons in China". The honeydew melons from are not only popular in China but in Hong Kong, Macao, Taiwan, and Southeast Asia as well.

Duolunnaoer Town 多伦淖尔镇

Town of Seven Lakes

Duolunnaoer means "seven lakes". The town sits on the Mongolian Plateau and has been famous for its beautiful mountains and lakes since ancient times. It is a charming place with great scenery. The town also has many temples.

Duolunzhuoer Town, Duolun County, Xilin Gol League, Inner Mongolia Autonomous Region
内蒙古自治区锡林郭勒盟多伦县多伦淖尔镇
Nearest city: Hohhot
There are flights from major Chinese cities to Hohhot Baita International Airport, or you can just take a train from Beijing West Station to Hohhot Railway Station. The journey takes about nine hours.
From Hohhot Bus Station (呼和浩特长途汽车站located at the Hohhot Railway Station呼和浩特站 and a 30-minute drive from the Hohhot Baita International Airport 呼和浩特白塔国际机场) there is a direct bus to Duolun County (多伦县) everyday at 7:00am. The ride takes about 5.5 hours.(Tel:0471-6965969)

Located on the southeast of the Xilinguole Steppe where the Yinshan Mountains, the Greater Khingan Range, and Hunshandak Desert come together, Duolunnaoer Town was once a major commercial centre in the Mongolian Grasslands.

Embodying this commercial legacy, the Shanxi Association (山西会馆) is in the southwest of Duolunnaoer was built by wealthy Shanxi businesspeople in the 10th year of the Qianlong reign (1745). Its big stage, carved wooden doors and corridors are replicas of the imperial city The building has four courtyards in a row, five archways, a front gate, and Zhengda Hall. The theatrical stage is the most characteristic building of the association, and is a classic embodiment of Yellow River architecture. The stage faces north and has a gold-plated rectangle tablet with "water mirror terrace" written on it. The main hall enshrines Lord Guan (a warlord of the Three Kingdoms Period) and the wing

Duolunnaoer Town is a city of water in Xilinguole

The front gate of Huizong Temple

rooms on both sides have paintings of the stories of the Three Kingdoms legends.

Alliance Monument (会盟纪念碑) and Huizong Temple (汇宗寺), built in the 30th year of the Kangxi reign (1691) are in the old northern areas of Duolunnaoe. The temple covers an area of 181,400 square metres with lots of beautiful thangkas and delicate paintings on its beams. The Kangxi Emperor ordered the temple be built on the location where the Duolunnaoer alliance between the emperor and Mongolian lords took place in memory of the event. He also assigned the first Zhangjia Living Buddha to expound the texts of Buddhism here from Youning Temple in Qinghai. Hundreds of temples and folk houses were built in the area and Duolunnaoer became a Tibetan Buddhist holy lands for the Mongolians.

Xishan Bay Sandy Island (西山湾沙岛) in Duolunnaoer is 30 kilometres away from downtown Duolunnaoer, right beside Xishan Bay Huanku Luyou Road (西山湾环库旅游路). The "island" is surrounded by water on three sides with a 50-metre natural sand road connecting it to land. When Xishan Bay Reservoir is full, the road is covered by water and Xishan becomes a true island. Tourists can wade along the sand road to get to the island.

Girl Lake (姑娘湖) is associated with a tragic legend. After the port of Duolunnaoer was opened, Hong Changshun, a young businessman from the capital Heshengkui, visited the town of business. Heavy snow blocked the roads when he reached Duolunnaoer, so he had to lodge at a herdsman's house. Wulantuoya, the daughter of the herdsman, fell in love with Hong Changshun, and they were secretly engaged. When the local patrol officer, who had courted the beautiful girl for a long time, learned of the engagement, he sentenced Hong to death on the grounds of forbidden marriage between a Mongolian and a Han Chinese. Wulantuoya was so sad that she committed suicide by jumping into Moon Lake. After Hong Changshun was bailed out of jail, he wandered around the lake every day, hoping she would return to him. One day, the delirious young man saw Wulantuoya rising up from the center of the lake, so he ran to her, shouting her name, and drowned. After that, Moon Lake's name was changed to Girl Lake.

Duolunnaoer's folk traditions blend Mongolian and Han culture. The town's main cultural activities are folk songs and dance, making sacrifices to the Lord Guan Temple (关帝庙祭祀活动), and Chahaer wedding shows (察哈尔婚礼演出). There is a big temple fair on the 15th day of the sixth month of the lunar calendar (around July). There is wrestling (博克), horse racing, and archery at the Nadam Fair (那达慕大会).

There are many people from the Hui ethnic group living in Duolunnaoer, so it also has a long history of Muslim food culture. Finger mutton (手扒肉) is a traditional Mongolian food, and is called "finger mutton" because people use their fingers to eat it instead of chopsticks. Toasting guests and serving finger mutton is a traditional way of showing respect.

Craters

According to geologists, the location of Duolunnaoer Town is in one of the largest circular meteorite craters remaining in the world. There are more than 100 craters in the area. The volcanic cone is more than 20,000 years old, forming a complex and unique geologic environment. The steppe under the blue sky, the beautiful sandy lands, lakes, rivers, primitive forests, and pleasant weather make Duolunnaoer the perfect place for summer sightseeing, and hunting.

Wangyefu Town 王爷府镇
The Mongolian Prince's Mansion

Wangyefu was the political and cultural centre of the Harqin Banner region from the Qing Dynasty to the Republican Period. The town has the oldest, biggest, and most intact Qing-era Mongolian prince's mansion in Inner Mongolia.

Wangyefu Town, Harqin Banner County, Chifeng City, Inner Mongolia Autonomous Region
内蒙古自治区赤峰市喀喇沁旗王爷府镇
Nearest city: Chifeng
Flights from Beijing and Huhhot serve Chifeng Yulong Airport and there are two rail stations, Chifeng Station and Chifeng East Station.
From Chifeng Bus Station (赤峰汽车站, adjacent to the Chifeng Railway Station), there are regular buses to Wangyefu Town (about 90 minutes).

Twenty kilometers to the southwest of Harqin Banner (喀喇沁旗), Wangyefu was built in 1757, during the Qianlong reign of the Qing Dynasty. Because it was the location of Prince Zhasake's mansion during the Qing Dynasty, the town was named Wangyefu (meaning "prince's mansion").

The mansion belonged to Prince Gong in the Qing Dynasty. It was built in the 18th year of the Kangxi reign of the Qing (1679) and is located 70 kilometres southwest of Chifeng City. Covering about 100,000 square meters, the mansion (王爷府) has two courtyards. Its main buildings include an audience hall, second hall, inner gate, main hall and Chengqing Building (承庆楼).

Twelve generations of Mongolian princes governed from this mansion. The last, Kung Sang No Erh Pu, was a famous thinker, politician, and reformer. His courtesy

There are old pine and cypress trees, splendid buildings and halls in the yards of the Harqin Prince's Mansion

Harqin Banner Prince's Mansion Museum

Harqin. First built in the early Qing Dynasty, it is a typical Tibetan Buddhist temple. It has a rectangular shape, covers an area of about 10,000 square metres, and is divided into two yards. The outer yard was built with red bricks and the main temple in the inner yard has five halls. On the platform of the main temple stand three Heavenly Kings Halls (天王殿) with four statues of the Four Heavenly Kings (四大天王像) inside. The second-level hall (二层殿) has five rooms, enshrining the Buddha of Longevity (长寿佛) with all kinds of Buddha figures in a mural. The third-level hall has two floors, 49 rooms, cornices, bucket arches, and enshrines the statue of Tsongkhapa (宗喀巴像). The fourth-level hall has three main halls and enshrines the statue of Gautama Buddha (释迦牟尼像). The fifth-level hall has two floors and three main halls. Fuhui Temple holds its temple fair on every 15th day of the seventh month of the lunar calendar (usually in September).

name was Leting, and he was a descendant of the meritorious minister Wulianghaijilama of Genghis Khan. He was reportedly a quiet and easygoing person who mastered Mongolian, Manchu, Chinese, Tibetan, calligraphy, and painting. Kung Sang No Erh Pu was an important figure in modern Mongolian history, and he pioneered Mongolian education by establishing Chongzheng School, the Yuzheng Girls' School, and Shouzheng Martial Arts School. His reforms set an example for other Mongol tribes.

It is just a 10-minute walk from Prince Harqin's Mansion (喀喇沁亲王府) to Fuhui Temple. (福会寺). Known as the "big temple" among locals, Fuhui was the family temple of the Prince

Wangyefu Town is also home to Shantong Temple (善通寺), Longxing Temple (隆兴寺), and lots of other temples and ancient folk houses.

Mansion Museum

Opened in 2002, the Harqin Banner Prince's Mansion Museum (喀喇沁旗王府博物馆) used to be the prince's residence. It is the biggest Mongolian prince's mansion museum in China. The building combines the mighty, solemn Qing architectural style with older palace characteristics like axial symmetry and structures reflecting hierarchy. There are 17 exhibition rooms, including rooms dedicated to calligraphy and painting, mansion restoration, and education history.

Exploring the past

Ancient World is a new series of travel books with a unique focus on the legacy of the past. Every ancient village, town and city covered by our Ancient World guides bears the mark of an ancient way of life. Ancient World guides make this heritage accessible with detailed directions and information about culture and history.

Make-Do Publishing,
Hong Kong.
All rights reserved.

© Make-Do Publishing, 2012.
© Chinese content, China Rail Publishing, 2012

English edition first published 2012.
Editors: Nikhil Sonad and Meggan McCann
Series Editor: Claire Liu
Art Editor: Gia Kei

ISBN 978-988-18419-9-5

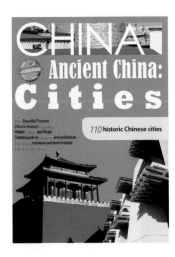

Ancient China: Cities

110 Ancient Chinese Cities.

Ancient China: Cities has sections on ancient capitals, walled cities, and cities with a special significance in Chinese history. Ancient Chinese cities are differentiated from towns by their greater emphasis on political and military functions. Over 5,000 years of Chinese history, China has had numerous capitals, with one giving way to another as dynasties rose and fell.

·Ancient Chinese capitals.
·Centres of the ancient Chinese world.
·Unique urban architecture.
·Cities associated with China's revolutions.
·From opera to temple fairs.
·Full directions.
·Cultural treasures.

Chinese

Dynasty	Dates
Xia 夏朝	B.C. 2070—B.C 1600
Shang 商朝	B.C. 1600—B.C 1046
Zhou 周	
Western Zhou 西周	B.C. 1046—B.C 771
Eastern Zhou 东周	B.C. 770— B.C 256
Spring and Autumn 春秋	B.C. 770— B.C 476
Warring States 战国	B.C. 475—B.C 221
Qin 秦朝	B.C. 221—B.C 207
Han 汉	
Western Han 西汉	B.C. 206— A.D 8
Xin Chao 新朝	A.D. 9 — 23
East Han 东汉	25 — 220
Three Kingdoms 三国	
Wei 魏	A.D. 220— 265
Shu Han 蜀汉	221—263
Wu 吴	222—280
Jin 晋	
Western Jin 西晋	265—316
Eastern Jin 东晋	317—420
Sixteen Kingdoms 十六国	304—439
South 南朝	
Song 宋	420 — 479
Qi 齐	479 —502
Liang 梁	502 —557
Chen 陈	557 — 589

Dynasties

Dynasty	Dates
North 北朝	
Northern Wei北魏	386 — 534
WesternWei西魏	534 — 550
Eastern Wei东魏	534 — 550
Northern Qi 北齐	550 — 577
Northern Zhou 北周	557 — 581
Sui 隋	581 — 618
Tang 唐	618 — 907
Five Dynasties and Ten Kingdoms 五代十国	907 — 960
Song 宋	
Northern Song 北宋	960 — 1127
Southern Song 南宋	1127 — 1279
Liao 辽	907 — 1125
Da Li 大理	937 — 1254
Western Xia 西夏	1032 — 1227
Jin 金	1115 — 1234
Yuan 元	1206 — 1368
Ming 明	1368 — 1644
Qing 清	1616 — 1911
Republic of China 中华民国	1912 — 1949
People's Republic of China	1949 — Now

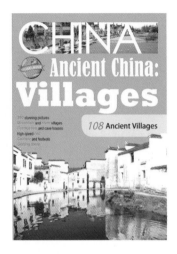

Ancient China: Villages
108 Ancient Chinese Villages.

Ancient China: Villages is a guide to a lost world of Chinese villages that have remained largely unchanged for generations. Most ancient villages were situated near rivers and were designed according to traditional feng shui principles. Ancient Chinese village architecture includes courtyard residences, temples, colleges, wells, bridges, theatre stages, memorial arches, towers, shrines and tombs. Many of the beautiful villages in Ancient China: Villages look like details from Chinese ink paintings.

·River and mountain villages.
·Fortresses and cave houses.
·Villages with good fengshui.
·Fascinating rural culture and customs.
·Directions for nearest tourist hubs.
·Festivals.
·A unique ecology.